BIBLICAL GREEK SYNTAX GUIDE

BY

NELSON NOEL NG'UONO WERE

Copyright © April 2015 by Far Eastern Bible College

All Rights Reserved
Printed in the United States of America
ISBN 978-0-9962591-1-8
Far Eastern Bible College Address:
9A Gilstead Road
Singapore 309063

Telephone: (65) 6256-9256; (65) 6254-9188
Facsimile: (65) 6251-3891
Website: http://www.febc.edu.sg
Email: febc@pacific.net.sg

All Scripture is from the Greek *Textus Receptus* that lies behind the King James Version.

No part of this work may be reproduced without the expressed consent of the holder of the copyright © or publisher, except for brief quotes, whether by electronic , photocopying, recording, or information storage and retrieval systems.

Published by:
THE OLD PATHS PUBLICATIONS, Inc.
142 Gold Flume Way
Cleveland, Georgia, U.S.A. 30528
Web: www.theoldpathspublications.com
Email: TOP@theoldpathspublications.com

ABSTRACT

BIBLICAL GREEK SYNTAX

The New Testament was written in the Greek Language a language which is considered to be the most literary of all the ancient languages. A. T. Robertson wrote, "The most perfect vehicle of human speech thus far devised by man is the Greek. English comes next, but Greek language is a language of precision and a knowledge of the original language of the New Testament is decidedly helpful and informative." Thus for ministers of the Word who handle the very Words of the Most High God (inspired and preserved) to be able to read, understand and exegete the Word in the original language is necessary. To assist the minister in this task of correctly dividing the Word of truth, there are many materials written to explain the syntax and grammar of New Testament Greek.

Koine or biblical Greek is the language that the Holy Spirit chose to use to express and preserve the final revelation from God to man. Thus it is necessary for one who approaches the study of this language and the understanding of the Word of God to do so in faith. The necessity of understanding well this language is testified of by the many heresies and false teachings which have arisen because one has failed to understand or apply the Greek grammar correctly. The Bible is unlike any other writings in that its author is divine. God is the author and holy men of God wrote as they were moved by the Holy Spirit and as such, though the student is to apply principles and practices of interpretation, but unlike human writings, understanding is granted by the Holy Spirit (1 Cor 2:9-15).

This material presents the basics of Greek grammar and syntax to enable the student to be able by the help of the Holy Spirit to be able to understand the different parts of a Greek sentence and how they relate to one another and by this be able to enrich his understanding of God's Word and through it God's will.

CONTENTS

ABSTRACT 3
BIBLICAL GREEK SYNTAX 3
CONTENTS 5
DEDICATIONS 11
INTRODUCTION TO BIBLICAL GREEK SYNTAX 13
SYNTAX 15
ESSENTIALS OF BIBLICAL INTERPRETATION 15
    Presuppositions 15
    Rules of Interpretation 16
Important Doctrines Concerning the Bible 17
CHAPTER I: TERMS, DEFINITIONS AND REVIEW OF ELEMENTARY GREEK GRAMMAR 23
TERMS AND DEFINITIONS 23
    Terms Related to Sentences in General 23
    SUBJECT 23
    PREDICATE 23
    SENTENCE 23
    Terms Related to Verbs 23
    VERB 23
    Finite Verb 24
    Non-Finite Verb 24
    Parsing a Verb 24
    Terms Related to Nouns 25
    NOUN 25
    SUBSTANTIVE 25
    Object 25
    Other Related Terms 26
    INFLECTION 26
    DECLENSION 26
    CONJUGATION 26
    ELEMENTARY GREEK GRAMMAR 26
    Nouns 26
    NOUN CASES 26
    Verbs 27
    VOICE OF VERBS 28
    MOODS OF VERBS 28
    TENSES OF VERBS 29
    NON-FINITE VERB FORMS 30
    Participles 30
    Infinitives 31
CHAPTER II: NOUN CLASSIFICATIONS 33
    Parsing Guide for Nouns 33
    NOMINATIVE CASE SYNTACTICAL CLASSIFICATION 33
    Subject Nominative 34
    Predicate Nominative 34
    Nominative of Apposition 35
    Nominative of Appellation 36
    Independent Nominative 37
    GENITIVE CASE SYNTACTICAL CLASSIFICATION 39
    1. Adjectival Genitive 39
    a. Genitive of Description 40
    b. Possessive Genitive 40
    c. Genitive of Relationship 41
    2. Adverbial Genitive 41
    a. Adverbial Genitive of Time 42
    b. Adverbial Genitive of Place 43
    c. Adverbial Genitive of Reference 43
    d. Adverbial Genitive of Measure 44
    3. Genitives with Nouns of Action 44

a. Subjective Genitive	45
b. Objective Genitive	45
4. Genitive of Apposition	46
a. Simple Apposition	46
b. Epexigetical Genitive	46
5. Genitive Absolute	47
6. Genitive of Advantage	48
7. Genitive of Association	48
8. Genitive of Attendant Circumstances	49
9. Genitive of Oaths	49
10. Genitive of Root idea (Direct Object)	49
Ablative Case Syntactical Classification	50
Ablative of Separation	51
Ablative of Source	52
Ablative of Agency	52
Ablative of Means	53
Ablative of Comparison	53
Ablative of Cause	54
Ablative of Rank	55
Ablative of Opposition	55
Ablative of Purpose	55
Ablative of Exchange	56
Partitive Ablative	56
DATIVE CASE SYNTACTICAL CLASSIFICATION	57
a. Dative of Indirect Object	58
b. Dative of Advantage and Disadvantage	58
c. Dative of Possession	59
d. Dative of Reference or Dative of Respect	60
e. Dative of Root Idea or Dative of Direct Object	61
LOCATIVE CASE SYNTACTICAL CLASSIFICATION	61
a. Locative of Place	61
b. Locative of Time	62
c. Locative of Sphere	63
INSTRUMENTAL CASE SYNTACTICAL CLASSIFICATION	63
a. Instrumental of Means	64
b. Instrumental of Cause	65
c. Instrumental of Manner	65
d. Instrumental of Measure	66
e. Instrumental of Association	67
f. Instrumental of Agency	67
ACCUSATIVE CASE SYNTACTICAL CLASSIFICATION	67
a. Accusative of Direct Object	68
b. Cognate Accusative	69
c. Double Accusative	69
i. A personal and impersonal object	70
d. Adverbial Accusative	70
i. Adverbial Accusative of Measure	**71**
ii. Adverbial Accusative of Manner	71
iii. Adverbial Accusative of Reference or Adverbial Accusative of Respect	72
e. Accusative with Oaths	72
f. Accusative Absolute	73
g. Accusative of Purpose	73
h. Accusative of Result	74
i. Accusative of Cause	74
j. Accusative of Possession	74
k. Accusative of Comparison	75
l. Accusative of Relationship	75
m. Predicate Accusative	76
CHAPTER III: THE SYNTAX OF THE ARTICLE	**77**
a. Identification	78

CONTENTS

    b. Monadic Article 78
    c. Anaphoric Article 79
    d. Article with Abstract Nouns 79
    e. Article with Proper Names 80
    f. To Show a Generic Class 80
    g. Bracket Use 81
    h. In Place of a Noun 81
    i. Article with Nouns Connected by the Conjunction "kai" (Granville Sharp Rule 82
    j. As a Pronoun 83
    k. The Definite Article used with Nouns 84

CHAPTER IV: THE SYNTAX OF ADJECTIVES AND PRONOUNS 87
THE ADJECTIVE 87
The Function of the Adjective 87
Attributively 88
Predicatively 88
Substantivally 89
Adverbially 90
THE PRONOUN 90

CHAPTER V: THE SYNTAX OF THE VERB 93
VERB TENSES 94
The Present Tense 96
1. Descriptive Present 97
2. Durative Present 98
Simple "Point" Present (Aoristic Present) 98
3. Iterative Present 99
4. Gnomic Present (Present of General Truth) 99
5. Conative Present (Tendential Present) 99
6. Futuristic Present (Present of Anticipation) 100
7. Historical Present 100
8. Perfective Present 101
The Imperfect Tense 101
1. Descriptive Imperfect 102
2. Durative Imperfect 102
3. Imperfect of Repeated Action 103
4. Tendential Imperfect 103
5. Voluntative Imperfect 104
6. Inceptive Imperfect 104
The Future Tense 105
1. Predictive Future 105
2. Progressive Future 106
3. Imperative Future 106
4. Deliberative Future 107
5. Gnomic Future 107
The Aorist Tense 107
1. Constantive Aorist 109
2. Ingressive Aorist 110
3. Culminative Aorist 110
5. Gnomic Aorist 111
6. Epistolary Aorist 111
7. Dramatic Aorist 112
8. Futuristic Aorist 112
The Perfect Tense 112
1. Intensive Perfect 114
2. Consummative Perfect 114
3. Iterative Perfect 114
4. Dramatic Perfect 115
4. Gnomic Perfect 115
5. Aoristic Perfect 116
The pluperfect tense 116
1. Intensive Pluperfect 117

2. Consummative Pluperfect	117
VOICE	118
A. Active Voice	118
1. Simple Active	118
2. Causative Active	119
B. Middle Voice	119
2. Indirect (Indirect Reflexive, Intensive, Dynamic) Middle	120
3. Permissive or Causative Middle	120
C. Passive Voice	121
1. Regular (Simple) Passive	121
2. Deponent Passive	122
VERB MOODS	122
The Indicative Mood	123
1. The Declarative Indicative	123
2. The Interrogative Indicative	124
3. The Potential Indicative	124
The Imperative Mood	126
1. The Imperative of Command	127
2. The Imperative of Prohibition	127
3. The Imperative of Entreaty	128
4. The Imperative of Permission	128
5. Imperatives with Conjunction kai'	129
The Subjunctive Mood	130
(a) Subjunctive in Independent (Main) Clauses	131
1. The Hortatory Subjunctive	131
2. The Prohibitory Subjunctive	132
3. The Deliberative Subjunctive	132
4. The Subjunctive of Emphatic Negation	133
(b) Subjunctive in Dependent (Subordinate) Clauses	133
1. Purpose (Final) Clause	134
2. Conditional Clause	134
3. Result Clause	134
4. Relative Clause	134
5. Comparative Clause	134
6. Indefinite Local Clause	135
7. Temporal Clause	135
8. Concessive Clause	135
9. Substantival Clause	135
10. Imperatival Clause	135
The Optative Mood	136
1. The Voluntative Optative	136
2. The Potential Optative	137
3. Deliberative Optative	137
Conditional Sentences	138
1. First Class – Condition of Reality	139
2. Second Class – Condition of Unreality	140
3. Third Class – Condition of Assumed Probability	141
4. Fourth Class Condition – Condition of Assumed Possibility	141
CHAPTER VI: THE SYNTAX OF VERBAL FORMS: INFINITIVES AND PARTICIPLES	**143**
The infinitive	**143**
1. The Verbal Infinitive	144
1. Purpose	144
2. Result	145
3. Temporal	146
4. Cause	146
1. Infinitive of Command	147
2. Infinitive Absolute	147
3. The Substantival Infinitive	147
1. Subject	147
2. Object	148

CONTENTS

1. Modifier 149
THE PARTICIPLE 150
1. Attributively 151
2. Substantively 152
3. Predicatively 153
4. Adverbially 155
1. Temporal Participle 156
2. The Telic (Purpose/Final) Participle 157
3. The Causal Participle 158
4. The Conditional Participle 158
5. Participle of Concession 158
1. Instrumental Participle (Participle of Means) 159
2. The Modal Participle (Participle of Manner) 159
3. The Complementary Participle 160
4. Participle of Attendant Circumstances 160
5. Imperatival Participle 161
CHAPTER VII: CONCLUSION 163
INDEX OF WORDS AND PHRASES 165
BIBLIOGRAPHY 169
ABOUT THE AUTHOR 173

DEDICATIONS

To
The Far Eastern Bible College,
Bomet Bible Institute
and
Faith College of the Bible
Institutions raised of God for the preparing of laborors for the Lord's Vineyard holding forth the Word of Life and holding fast the faithful Word.

Nelson Were
October, 2015

INTRODUCTION TO BIBLICAL GREEK SYNTAX

Of the original biblical languages, perhaps Greek is the most written, as there are many aids to learning the Greek language and grammar and syntax works available in the market. But sadly they almost altogether fail at one point: they are based on the critical texts[1] and adopt Textual Criticism[2]. There are many Greek grammar books for the beginning student and of these some of the widely used and highly recommended are listed below and a glimpse on their approach is seen in what they say in their prefaces and introductions. For example:

Daniel B. Wallace in his book **Greek Grammar Beyond the Basics - An Exegetical Syntax of the New Testament** published by Zondervan rejects the longer ending of Mark and when he cites Mark 16:16 states, *"This is a part of the longer ending of Mark, a text most likely not original (but still valuable for illustrative purposes)."*[3] And concerning the Greek text he writes,

> For statistical purposes, the Nestle/Aland$^{26/27}$/UBS$^{3/4}$ text is used. Usually, this text will also be used for the illustrations (with variants relevant to thee grammatical point at hand discussed). Whenever the illustration involves a reading not found in this text, it will be noted.[4]

Moulton who has his **Grammar of New Testament Greek** in four volumes in his volume three writes, *"I have designed volume III specially for three classes of readers: first, the teacher with an interest in exegesis; ... then the textual critic whom characteristic differences in the author's style may help to decide between variants; and also the student of comparative philology..."*[5] and in favour of Markan priori, he adds, *"What C H Turner once commenced to do for Markan syntax needs completing and carrying out for other authors too. Light has been thrown on the infancy narrative and even on the elusive Q from a careful study of Luke's characteristic style."*[6] And in His volume 4 (Style) which provides comparison of the Greek writing style of the different

---

[1] Examples of critical texts include: (1) The Westcort and Hort Text published in 1881 (under the title *The New Testament in the Original Greek;* an *Introduction [and] Appendix,* authored by Hort, appeared in 1882 (revised edition by F. C. Burkitt in 1892). (2) *The Greek New Testament According to the Majority Text* edited by Zane C. Hodges and Arthur L. Farstad. The first edition appeared in 1982 with a slightly revised second edition appearing in 1985. (3) The United Bible Society Greek New Testament which was originally compiled by Kurt Aland, Matthew Black, Bruce M. Metzger, and Allen Wikgren; Carlo M. Martini joined the committee for the second and third editions; the fourth edition was prepared by Barbara Aland, Kurt Aland, Johannes Karavidopoulos, Martini, and Metzger. ["*Critical Editions of the New Testament*" URL: http://www.skypoint.com/~waltzmn/CriticalEds.html 07/01/04.]

[2] Textual criticism is the so-called science that claims to trace the history of a given biblical reading, passage or book by analysing manuscripts and ancient translations (or versions) to ascertain the most likely original readings. The assumption being that it requires man's judgements about the earliest forms of the texts in the original languages to ascertain which words belong to and which words are not part of Scripture because over the years, words have been lost and God has not preserved the words He perfectly inspired. Thus Textual Criticism goes astray right from its presuppositions and exalts man above the Word of God making him judge of what is or is not the Word of God.

[3] Daniel B. Wallace, *Greek Grammar Beyond the Basics: An Exegetical Syntax of the New Testament* (Grand Rapids Michigan: Zondervan Publishing House, 1996), 688.

[4] Ibid., xii.

[5] J. H. Moulton and Nigel Turner, *Grammar of New Testament Greek, vol. iii,* (Edinburgh: T. & T. Clark, 1908), 1.

[6] Ibid., 2.

New Testament authors, he writes, *"it is widely granted that the first evangelists used sources, certainly Mark and probably also Q and other documents."*[7]

Ernest De Witt Burton in his **Syntax of the Moods and Tenses in New Testament Greek** also adopts the critical text of Westcott and Hort saying, *"In quoting examples from the New Testament I have followed the Greek text of Westcott and Hort as that which perhaps most nearly represents the original text, but have intended to note any important variations of Tischendorf's eighth edition or of Tregelles in a matter affecting the point under discussion."*[8]

Dana and Mantey in their **A Manual Grammar of the Greek New Testament** published by Macmillan Company write,

> The illustrations have in the main been taken from the actual text of the Greek New Testament, but have in some cases slightly altered for purpose of brevity and greater clearness. The discussion throughout has been based on the WH text and kept free from technical problems of textual criticism, with which the student at the stage of training contemplated by this book is rarely acquainted.[9]

Even the voluminous work of A. T. Robertson **A Grammar of the Greek New Testament in the light of Historical Research** is not exempt from this trend as he also writes,

> of these, only 3 (Mk 13:31; Mt. 12:32; Luke 22:68, —| |—) add to the examples of οὐ μή. The remaining 4 are only variants of the existing examples. Readings —| |— (ἠ ἀπολύσητε) are in the judgement of W. H. (introduction §385) 'outside the pale of probability as regards the original text so that only Mk. 13:31, Mt. 12:32 can claim any right to be counted as additional examples of οὐ μή.'[10]

From this overview of Greek syntax texts it is clear to see how far the leaven of textual criticism has leavened the study of the Greek language. And is it any wonder that even fundamentalists so-called are questioning the authenticity of the Scriptures? The attempt to deconstruct the Textus Receptus of the Reformation which underlies the King James Version of the Holy Bible has been aided by the many Greek syntax and grammar texts which have imbibed Textual Criticism and have thus passed it on to students through the years. And as the battle of these times is on the Verbal and Plenary Preservation of the inspired words in the original languages, the time has come to revisit and revise the Greek syntax and grammar books and rid them of this leaven. The purpose of the material presented here is to better equip people with the ability to discover many of the hidden riches in the Word of God with the presupposition of a present, perfect, tangible, inspired and preserved text in the original languages.

---

[7] J. H. Moulton and Nigel Turner, *Grammar of New Testament Greek, vol. iv. Style*, (Edinburgh: T. & T. Clark, 1908), 31.

[8] Ernest DeWitt Burton, *Syntax of the Moods and Tenses in New Testament Greek*, (Edinburgh: T. & T. Clark, 1908), preface.

[9] H. E. Dana and Mantey, *A Manual Grammar of the Greek New Testament*, (New York: Macmillan, 1950), ix.

[10] A. T. Robertson, *A Grammar of the Greek New Testament in the light of Historical Research*, (Nashville: Broadman press. 1923), 1405.

Many words, phrases, and paragraphs in the New Testament cannot adequately be known without some knowledge of Koine (biblical) Greek and the ability to use some of the many study aids available today. This work is to offer a syntax syllabus for teaching intermediate Greek (Greek Reading I and II) and attempts to use Greek grammar and syntax to give insight into New Testament passages. Today there are more study aids available for the Greek NT than ever before. We have study aids and helps available to us that were virtually non-existent ten years ago and which are accessible and usable even by those with little or no prior knowledge of the Greek. Thus with a little knowledge and the right books, one can get at many of the riches only previously available to people that have studied Greek for years.

But the focus of this work is on learning enough of the basics of Greek grammar and syntax to be able to use the Greek study helps available and to begin applying what we are learning and to enrich our understanding of God's Word and correctly interpret the inspired and preserved Word of God. Thus we plan to use many NT examples that will be able to assist us in understanding many aspects and functions of the parts of speech of Greek language of the NT such as: (1) Greek verb tenses. (2) Greek participles and the understanding of the actions of the NT Greek. (3) How to find the emphasis of the writer in any particular sentence. (4) How light is shed on hard-to-understand passages by the understanding Greek syntax.

SYNTAX

Syntax is simply the study of the structure of grammatical sentences in a language. Syntax involves the pattern or structure of the word order in a sentence.[11] The study of syntax Involves the reading and translating Greek sentences and deciphering the different parts of speech and their roles in the sentence. This includes, finding the subject of the sentence, finding the main verb, looking for any direct object (usually the accusative case, as you have studied in elementary Greek) and/or any indirect object (dative case endings). It also involves searching for the phrases or clauses that add meaning to the sentence, noticing verb forms (present tense, etc.), and noticing the main words as used by the author within the considered sentence and immediate context.

ESSENTIALS OF BIBLICAL INTERPRETATION

"All scripture is given by inspiration of God, and is profitable for doctrine, for reproof, for correction, for instruction in righteousness: That the man of God may be perfect, throughly furnished unto all good works" (2Tim 3:16-17).

Presuppositions

The Bible is the inerrant and infallible Word of God.
1. God cannot make mistakes or lie (Num. 23:19; Rom. 3:4).

---

[11] According to the Webster's 1828 Dictionary, Syntax is defined as: "1. In grammar, the construction of sentences; the due arrangement of words in sentences, according to established usage. Syntax includes concord and regimen, or the agreement and government of words. Words, in every language, have certain connections and relations, as verbs and adjectives with nouns, which relations must be observed in the formation of sentences. A gross violation of the rules of syntax is a solecism. 2. Connected system or order; union of things. [Not in use.]"

2. The Bible is the revealed, inspired and preserved Word of God (2 Timothy 3:16-17; 2 Peter 1:20-2; Psalm 12:6-7; Matthew 5:18).
3. Therefore, the Bible is absolutely without error and all confusion, misunderstanding, and apparent contradictions in the Bible are the result of human misunderstanding or inaccurate interpretation.

From these three presuppositions, and more especially number 3, we need to consider what rules and principles of interpretation make for a Biblical and more accurate intepretation of Scripture.

Rules of Interpretation

<u>The Rule of Grammatical Interpretation</u> – this rule focuses on the grammar of the text and to interpret grammatically means to study the text giving due regard to the

- Meaning of words,
- Form of sentences,
- Peculiarities of idioms, and
- Grammatical style (historical narrative, poetical, etc.) in the original language employed by the writer.

<u>The Rule of Literal interpretation</u> – this rule emphasises the natural usage and understanding of words and their meaning in interpretation. Scripture is revelation and was written in human language for understanding, thus the true sense of Scripture is determined by the words being taken and understood according to their normal and customary usage. The words of Scripture must be taken in their common meaning unless such meaning is shown to be inconsistent with:

- Other words in the sentence,
- The argument being presented,
- The context of the passage under consideration, or
- The rest of what Scripture has to say about the matter being considered.

"If the literal sense makes good sense, then to try to make any other sense is nonsense."

<u>The Rule of Historical Interpretation</u> – this rule addresses the context of Scripture. To who was the passage originally addressed? And why?

<u>The Rule of Contextual Interpretation</u> – this rule provides the boundaries within which the text being read it so be understood. "A text out of context becomes pretext." Since Scripture can be taken out of context and twisted to say anything one desires and since it is easy to distort the Scripture to make it conform to one's prejudices or preconceived notions, there is a need of being governed and restricted.Context provides the boundaries for reading and understanding. God has condemned the ignoring of context and abuse of context and Paul calls it "handling the word of God deceitfully" (2 Corinthians 4:2). Thus we need to:

- Carefully examine the context of the immediate passage.

- Be aware that Chapter and verse indications were added as in index to the Scriptures centuries after the Bible was completed. They are not inspired, nor are they part of the original text.
- Interpret each passage within the context of the distinct message and characteristics of the book in which it appears.
- Consider the message and purpose of the Bible as a whole.
- Compare Scripture with Scripture. Remember that the Bible cannot contradict itself. Consider everything the Bible teaches about a given theme before developing any conclusions.
- Use the proper reasoning process.

Important Doctrines Concerning the Bible

1. Inspiration[12]

The Bible was "breathed out" by God, who directed specially prepared men to write down what they heard from Him. It is a divine revelation, God-breathed through the person of the Holy Spirit, and absolutely inerrant and infallible in relation to any subject with which it deals (1 Corinthians 2:1-16).

While allowing the human authors to bring their own distinctive personalities and experiences with them to the task of writing His word, God the Holy Ghost so directed the effort that those men recorded the exact message that God intended to be recorded, down to the very spelling of every word they recorded.

The original autographs (hand-written documents produced by the original writer) were verbally inspired (in every word, every letter, and every part of every letter) by the Holy Spirit (Isaiah 30:8; 2 Timothy 3:16; Exodus 4:10-12). That verbal inspiration is extended equally and completely to every part of Scripture (plenary inspiration), and was delivered to faithful men who were specifically prepared by God to receive His revelation (2 Samuel 23:2; 2 Peter 1:20, 21) the Holy Spirit superintending the human authors such that, through their individual personalities and different styles of writing, they composed and recorded God's word to man (2 Peter 1:20, 21), without error in the whole or in the part (Isaiah 30:8; 40:8; Matthew 5:18; 2 Timothy 3:16).

The doctrine of verbal plenary inspiration is clearly and sufficiently attested of in the whole of Scripture. Apart from the classic proof texts for inspiration (namely 2 Tim. 3:16, and 2 Pet. 1:20-21), in reading through the Scripture, one finds that (a) the Old Testament writers claimed inspiration (Deut. 4:2; Isa. 51:16; Jer. 1:7-9; 5:14; Ezek. 1:3; 3:17; Mic 3:8), (b) the New Testament corroborated the claims of the Old Testament writers and also claimed inspiration (Acts. 1:16; 28:25; Heb. 1:1; 1 Pet. 1:10-11;

---

[12] This key doctrine means that the Holy Spirit gave the very exact words of Scripture that the inspired writers penned down and that the inspired writers were not left to themselves to write what they wanted to write. Commenting on verbal inspiration, Herbert Lockyer writes this excellent statement: *"Some say, 'The thoughts, not the words, are inspired,' but we think in words. Words give precision, definiteness of form and color to thought. We are not sure of the thought until it is spoken or put into exact written words."* [Herbert Lockyer, *All the Doctrines of the Bible*, (Grand Rapids: Zondervan, 1964), p. 9.]

2 Pet. 3:15-16; 1 Thess. 2:13; Rev. 14:13), and (c) Scripture testifies of its own inspiration and that God put His words in the mouth of men (Ex. 31:18; 32:16; 34:27-28; Jer. 13:12). Thus inspiration can be described in Wuest's words as, "Inspiration, is the act of God the Holy Spirit enabling the Bible writers to write down in God-chosen words, infallibly, the Truth revealed"[13]

2. **Preservation**

Just like the doctrine of inspiration, the doctrine of verbal plenary preservation is equally attested of in the whole of Scripture. The Bible teaches the attributes of God which include omniscience, omnipotence and omnipresence and thus all "evangelicals" believe that God is able to do anything (Jer. 32:17, 27; Matt. 19:26; Mark 14:36; Luke 1:37; Job 42:2; Isa. 43:13; Hab. 3:6). Thus if He therefore chooses to preserve the Scriptures, no angel, spirit, man or human effort can thwart Him or destroy them. The question of preservation, many "evangelicals" would say is not a question of God's ability but rather, is whether or not He has chosen to preserve the Scriptures.

What answer does Scripture provide to this question? Scripture is clear on this doctrine, classic proof texts for this doctrine would include Psa. 12:6-7; 119:89, 152; Isa. 40:8; Matt. 5:18; 24:35; Mark 13:31; Luke 21:33. Apart from these, as one reads through Scripture, one finds that (a) Scripture emphasises the importance of the very words, warning man against adding or subtracting (Deut. 4:2; 12:32; Prov. 30:6; Rev. 22:18-19) (b) the purpose for which Scripture is given demands the preservation of the words (Ex. 24:3-4, 7-8; Deut. 28:58-59; 30:9-10; John 12:48; 20:31; Rom. 15:4; 1 Cor. 10:11; 1 John 5:13 Rev. 1:3) (c) Scripture emphasises and presents the word of God as sure and unfailing (Luke 21:33 cf. 1 Kings 8:56; Rev. 17:17). (d) Scripture testifies of preservation of the Words of God (Ex. 31:18, 32:15-16, 19 cf. 34:1-4, 28; Jer. 36:1-4, 23 cf. 28-32). (e) none of God's people in Scripture questioned the written words of Scripture but accepted it as the same words as the words God inspired and continued to use it as such (Joshua 1:7-8; 8:34-35; 23:6; 1 Kings 2:3; 1 Chron. 16:40; 2 Chron. 23:18; 35:12; Ezra 3:2; Neh. 8:14-15).

The same Holy Spirit who inspired and directed the writing of the original autographs (the hand-written original documents) has also preserved His word in such a manner that we can be sure that the Bible we have today is of the same inerrancy and authority as the actual parchments that the prophets originally wrote (Psa. 12:6-7 cf. Mt. 5:17-18; 24:35; Mk. 13:31; Lk. 16:17; 21:33). And God who promised to preserve His words is not a man that He should lie (Num. 23:19) and as Joshua testifies, of all what He has spoken none has ever failed (Josh. 23:14) and indeed non can or will ever fail for *"I know that, whatsoever God doeth, it shall be for ever: nothing can be put to it, nor any thing taken from it: and God doeth it, that men should fear before him"* (Ecc 3:14).

The Word of God is not a human product but God spake and revealed His Word through holy men (2 Pet. 1:20-21) and every word of the Bible was God-breathed (2 Tim 3:16-17) and written perfectly in the autographs. Although we do not have the

---

[13] Kenneth Wuest, *Untranslatable Riches*, (Grand Rapids Michigan: Wm. B. Eerdmans Publishers, 1942), 15.

autographs presently, we have God's promises to preserve His Word throughout all generations and thus His singular providential care and protection according to His promise ensures that the inspired words are not lost. The Westminster Confession of Faith, is properly clear on this matter and rightly distinguishes between the *autographs* and the *apographs*. For the autograph, it states that they were "immediately inspired by God" pointing to verbal plenary inspiration and with regard to the apographs it states that these were "by his singular care and providence kept pure in all ages, and are therefore authentical" pointing to the verbal plenary preservation. Paragraph eight on the Holy Scriptures reads,

> The Old Testament in Hebrew (which was the native language of the people of God of old), and the New Testament in Greek (which at the time of the writing of it was most generally known to the nations), being immediately inspired by God, and by his singular care and providence kept pure in all ages, are therefore authentical (Matt. 5:18); son as in all controversies of religion and church, the church is finally to appeal unto them (Isa. 8:20; Acts 15:15; John 5:39, 46). But because these original tongues are not known to all the people of God, who have right unto and interest in the scriptures, and are commanded, in the fear of God, to read and search them (John 5:39), therefore they are to be translated into the vulgar language of every nation unto which they come (1 Cor. 14:6, 9, 11, 12, 24, 27, 28), that the word of God dwelling plentifully in all, they may worship him in an acceptable manner (Col. 3:16), and, through patience and comfort of the scriptures may have hope (Rom. 15:4).[14]

From this well-framed and comprehensive statement on the Holy Scriptures, it is clear that the inspired words of the autographs have been "kept pure in all ages" and preserved in spite of and despite whatever variations found in the copies in the transmission process. Owing to God's singular and special providential care over the transmission of his Word, the words have been preserved in the copies. This is also affirmed by the Helvetic Consensus Formula of 1675, in which we read in the First Canon:

> God, the Supreme Judge, not only took care to have His Word, which is the power of God unto salvation to every one that believeth. (Rom : 16), committed to writing by Moses, the Prophets, and the Apostles, but has also watched and cherished it with paternal care ever since it was written up to the present time, so that it could not be corrupted by craft of Satan or fraud of man. Therefore the Church justly ascribes it to His singular grace and goodness that she has, and will have, to the end of the world, a "sure word of prophecy" and "Holy Scriptures" (2 Tim. 3 :15), from which, though heaven and earth perish, "one jot or one tittle shall in no wise pass" (Matt. 5 : 18).[15]

---

[14] *The Subordinate Standards and other Authoritative Documents of the Free Church of Scotland*, (Edinburgh Scotland: William Blackwood and Sons LTD., 1973), 5-6.

[15] J. Gaberel, Histoire de l'Église de Genève depuis le commencement de la Réformation jusqu'à̂ nos jours, Cherbuliez, Genève, 1862, Tome III, p, 496. Une traduction anglaise du Consensus Helveticus se trouve dans John H. Leith (Editor), *Creeds of the Churches*, (Atlanta: John Knox Press, 1977), 308-323.

Thus the content and transmission of Holy Scripture to us has been controlled and protected by God and has been preserved in all ages and is present in this age in the Textus Receptus underlying the King James Version. They are to be accepted as the full and final authority over Christian faith and conduct (Deuteronomy 18:15, 18, 19; Matthew 5:17-19; 24:34, 35; John 17:17; 1 Corinthians 2:12, 13; Hebrews 4:12).

3. <u>Interpretation</u>

Being assured of an inspired and divinely preserved text, the exegete can engage confidently and boldly in the process of exegesis with the intent of drawing out from the text and proclaiming the word of everlasting life. As such, there are a number of steps which provide guiding principles to the achieving of the goal of exegesis. Chamberlain summarizes them thus

> The interpreter should ask first, what does the author say; second, what does he mean by this statement. In Greek, the student will find many words of which he does not know the meaning, but in spite of that fact he should go over the passage to be interpreted, keeping these two questions in mind, and get all of the meaning possible out of it. This should be done before a lexicon, commentary or grammar is consulted. The next step should be to consult the best lexicons for the meaning of unfamiliar words. Great care should be exercised to get the meaning which suits that particular passage. After one has used a lexicon, then one or more good grammars should be used in order to understand the syntactical constructions accurately. In the verb, the voice-, mode-, and tense-signs should be watched for the total idea. The same care should be exercised in dealing with the noun, participle, infinitive, etc. After these three steps have been taken, the interpreter should have a good idea of the meaning of the passage. Then commentaries should be consulted to check one's conclusions and to note thoughts overlooked in the previous steps. The exegete will need now and again to go back and re-examine the various processes as he advances in interpreting a passage.[16]

Chamberlain outlines five steps to assist the exegete in examining the two types of questions an exegesis requires. Generally these steps can be broadly classified under three basic headings Observation, Interpretation and Application.

- Observation: What does the Passage say? – i.e. Observe the text
- Interpretation: What does the Passage mean? – i.e. Interpret the text in respect to the original setting and audience
- Application: How is the Passage relevant today? – i.e. Apply the text to the contemporary issues

In addressing and answering these questions, the exegete will have had (1) Gone over the passage and through this step, established the context of the passage in the biblical book as a whole. (2) Consulted the best lexicons and through this step analysed the content of the text as well as its context and in the process also established the

---

[16] William Douglas Chamberlain, *An Exegetical Grammar of the Greek New Testament*, (Grand Rapids Michigan: Baker Book House, 1941), 5.

meanings of unfamiliar words. (3) Consulted good grammar books to help in analysing and understanding the syntactical construction of the text and the theology of the text, drawing out application for the present days. (4) Consulted commentaries to check his conclusions and findings and established the message of the text in its historical setting and context for the passage.

In the progress of this process the student would write out thoughts and inferences drawn out from the text. It is to be noted that through the study of the passage of text and the interpretation process, valid hermeneutic principles are called for, i.e., the interpretation must be: 1) In agreement with the rules of communication and grammar or as Chamberlain observes – "Lexically and syntactically." 2) In agreement with the context, both immediate and remote or as Chamberlain observes – "contextually." 3) In line with the historical situation and occasion depicted by the text and in line with the purpose of Scripture and recognizing its supreme authority of faith and practice or as Chamberlain observes – "historically." 4) Neither contradicting the Analogy of Scripture, nor the Analogy of Faith or as Chamberlain observes – "analogy of Scripture."

The Bible can be properly interpreted only through the enlightenment of the Holy Spirit (1 Cor. 2:9-14) and is to be understood in its natural, historical, grammatical, theological, canonical and intended sense. It is to be accepted as the full and final authority over Christian faith and conduct.

CHAPTER I

TERMS, DEFINITIONS AND REVIEW OF ELEMENTARY GREEK GRAMMAR

TERMS AND DEFINITIONS
Terms Related to Sentences in General
SUBJECT

The subject of a sentence is a word or a group of words about which something can be said or asserted. It must be a noun or a group of words functioning as a substantive.

PREDICATE

The predicate of a sentence is the part of the sentence that makes the assertion about the subject. The main part of the predicate is a finite verb (which must be present). The predicate can be a verb alone, or a verb and other words related to it. Any part of the sentence that is not a part of the subject is part of the predicate.

SENTENCE

A sentence is a group of words expressing a complete thought. A sentence can either be complete or incomplete. A complete simple sentence must include both a subject and a predicate (which is comprised of or includes a verb). Smyth writes,

> Complete sentences are simple, compound or complex. In simple sentences, the subject and predicate occur only once. A compound sentence consists of two or more simple sentences co-ordinated .... A complex sentence a main sentence and one or more subordinate sentences.[17]

Incomplete sentences on the other hand does not include both subject and predicate but one part only. Smyth says,

> Incomplete sentences consist of a single member only. Such sentences stand outside the structure of the sentences. The chief classes of incomplete sentences are: (a) Interjections ... (b) Asseverations which serve as a predicate to another sentence spoken by another. ... (c) Headings, titles ... (d) Vocatives and nominatives used in exclamations ... (e) Exclamations without a verb.[18]

Terms Related to Verbs
VERB

A verb is a word expressing action, occurrence, existence, or state of being. It is used to tell or assert something about a noun (or substantive). In the broadest sense, a verb shows 'action'. "In grammar, a part of speech that expresses action, motion, being, suffering, or a request or command to do or forbear any thing. The verb affirms, declares, asks or commands."[19]

---

[17] Herbert Weir Smyth, *Greek Grammar for Colleges*, digital book obtained at URL: http://www.textkit.com
[18] Ibid.
[19] Webster's 1828 Dictionary, s.v. "verb"

Finite Verb

A finite verb is one whose form changes in order to match the form of the subject. It can be the main verb in the predicate part of a sentence (whose form is governed by the subject of the sentence).

Non-Finite Verb

A verb whose form does not change based upon any noun in the sentence and thus cannot function as the main verb in the predicate of a sentence.

Parsing a Verb

There are five basic parts that are clearly defined by every Greek verb form. Parsing a verb means to identify or describe these five "parts" that make up that verb. These five parts are Person, Number, Tense, Voice, and Mood. There are two main categories of verbs:

1. Transitive Verbs

"When the action expressed by a verb is exerted on an object, or terminates upon it, the act is considered as passing to that object, and the verb is called transitive"[20] Thus a transitive verb is a verb that 'transfers' the action to and affects a noun (substantive). This noun that it transfers motion to is called the 'direct object'. Therefore by the very nature of a transitive verb, it is a verb that requires a direct object. Thus, if there is a verb that has a direct object, it must be a transitive verb.

2. Intransitive Verbs

"In grammar, an intransitive verb is one which expresses an action or state that is limited to the agent, or in other words, an action that does not pass over to, or operate upon an object."[21] Thus as an intransitive verb is one that does not transfer action to a noun (direct object), therefore it is a verb that, by nature, does not have a direct object. In essence, the action begins and ends with the subject of the sentence.

3. Linking (Copulative) Verb

"In grammar, the copulative conjunction connects two or more subjects or predicates, in an affirmative or negative proposition"[22] A linking verb (sometimes referred to as a copulative verb by grammarians) is a special class of intransitive verbs. It is used to equate, identify, or join together one interchangeable substantive with another. It connects the subject of the sentence with a coordinating (or complementary) predicate. As with other intransitive verbs, there is no direct object since there is no action transferred. Examples of linking verbs in the Greek would be εἰμι, γίνομαι and ὑπάρχω.

---

[20] Webster's 1828 Dictionary, s.v. "transitive"
[21] ibid., s.v. "intransive"
[22] ibid., s.v. "copulative"

Terms Related to Nouns
NOUN

"In grammar, a name; that sound or combination of sounds by which a thing is called, whether material or immaterial."[23] Thus a noun is a word that denotes a person, place, thing, or idea.

SUBSTANTIVE

"In grammar, a noun or name; the part of speech which expresses something that exists, either material or immaterial. Thus man, horse, city, goodness, excellence, are substantives. [Better called name, L. *nomen*, or even noun, a corruption of *nomen*.]."[24] Smyth writes,

> The function of the substantive may be assumed by a pronoun, adjective (in masculine and feminine more frequently with the article), numeral, participle, relative clause; … by the article with an adverb, or with the genitive; by a prepositional phrase, a preposition with a numeral; by an infinitive with or without the article; or by any word or phrase viewed merely as a thing.[25]

Thus a substantive is a noun, pronoun, or any word functioning like a noun. This could include such items like an adjective, participle, or infinitive used as the subject or a direct object of the sentence. A substantive may be one word or a group of words.

Object

"In grammar, that which is produced, influenced or acted on by something else; that which follows a transitive verb. When we say, "God created the world," world denotes the thing produced, and is the object after the verb created. When we say, "the light affects the eye," eye denotes that which is affected or acted on. When we say, "instruction directs the mind and opinions," mind and opinions are the objects influenced."[26] In grammar, there are two categories:

1. **Direct Object**

    The direct object in a sentence is the substantive that receives the action of a transitive verb.

2. **Indirect Object**

    An indirect object is the person or thing that is indirectly affected by the action of the verb. It is often translated in English by the phrase "to somebody" or "for somebody (or something)."

---

[23] ibid., s.v. "noun"
[24] ibid.
[25] Herbert Weir Smyth, *Greek Grammar for Colleges*, digital book obtained at URL: http://www.textkit.com
[26] Webster's 1828 Dictionary, s.v. "object"

Other Related Terms
INFLECTION

"In grammar, the variation of nouns, &c., by declension, and verbs by conjugation."[27] Thus inflection is the variation (changing) of the form of words to indicate the role each word plays in the sentence.

DECLENSION

"In grammar, inflection of nouns, adjectives and pronouns; the declining, deviation or leaning of the termination of a word from the termination of the nominative case; change of termination to form the oblique cases."[28] In Greek, the stem of the noun contains the basic meaning of the noun, but a suffix is added to indicate the noun's role in the sentence. The endings are changed according to certain patterns, or 'declensions', that indicate what is the number, case, and gender of the noun form. To "decline" a noun means to analyse it and break it down into its basic parts according to **number**, **gender**, and **case**

CONJUGATION

"In grammar, the distribution of the several inflections or variations of a verb, in their different voices, modes, tenses, numbers and persons; a connected scheme of all the derivative forms of a verb."[29]

ELEMENTARY GREEK GRAMMAR
Nouns

A noun in the Greek language is viewed just like the English noun. Greek nouns are grouped into three categories, called declensions. The concept of declension in nouns is basically the same as conjugation involving verbs. Both conjugation and declension involve the inflection of the words.

NOUN CASES

The term "case" relates to substantives and adjectives classifying their relationship to other elements in the sentence. Noun cases are formed by putting the 'stem' of the noun with an 'ending'. The case form is shown by the ending of the word. There are four different case forms in Greek. The four cases are Nominative, Genitive, Dative, and Accusative. (There is another case not included in the four main noun cases because it is so closely related to the nominative: the Vocative.)

1. **The nominative case** is the case of the subject of the sentence.

---

[27] Webster's 1828 Dictionary, s.v. "inflection"
[28] ibid., s.v. "declension"
[29] ibid., s.v. "conjugation"

"Pertaining to the name which precedes a verb, or to the first case of nouns; as the nominative case or nominative word."[30] A noun or pronoun that is the subject of the sentence is always in the nominative case. Likewise a noun that is in the predicate part of a sentence containing a linking verb should also be in the nominative case.

2. **The accusative case** is the case of the direct object.

"A term given to a case of nouns, in Grammars, on which the action of a verb terminates or falls; called in English Grammar the objective case."[31] The accusative case as the case of the direct object, receives the action of the verb. Its main function is that as the direct object but this is not the only function for the accusative has a wide variety of uses but the direct object will most often be in the accusative case.

3. **The genitive case** roughly corresponds to our English possessive case.

"In grammar, an epithet given to a case in the declension of nouns, expressing primarily the thing from which something else proceeds."[32] For the most part, the genitive is often viewed as the case of possession. In more technical terms one noun in the genitive case helps to qualify another noun by showing its "class" or "kind." The genitive case has more uses than most other cases, but in general a noun in the genitive case helps to limit the scope of another noun by indicating its "kind" or "class."

4. **The dative case** is the case of the indirect object.

"In grammar, the epithet of the case of nouns, which usually follows verbs that express giving, or some act directed to an object."[33] The dative is the case of the indirect object, or may also indicate the *means* by which something is done. The dative case also has a wide variety of uses, with the root idea being that of "personal interest" or "reference."

5. **The vocative case** is the case of direct address.

"In grammar, the fifth case or state of nouns in the Latin language; or the case in any language, in which a word is placed when the person is addressed."[34] The vocative is the case of direct address. It is used when one person is speaking to another, calling out or saying their name, or generally addressing them.

Verbs

Just like Greek nouns, the Greek verb also changes form (inflection). The form changes based upon the subject of the verb and the kind of action indicated. The stem of the verb shows the basic meaning or action of the word, but the ending (suffix) changes to show various details. Not only the ending of the verb may change, but also the verb form may have a (prefix) added to the beginning of the verbal stem. Sometimes the actual stem of the verb may change to indicate certain other details. The Greek verb form has five basic parts (or aspects when declining) that are clearly defined or indicated by every Greek verb form. These five parts are: Person (1st, 2nd or 3rd), Number (singular

---

[30] Webster's 1828 Dictionary, s.v. "nominative"
[31] Webster's 1828 Dictionary, s.v. "accusative"
[32] ibid., s.v. "genitive"
[33] ibid., s.v. "dative"
[34] ibid., s.v. "vocative"

or plural), Tense (present, aorist, imperfect, perfect, pluperfect, and future), Voice (active, middle or passive), and Mood (indicative, imperative, subjunctive and optative).

VOICE OF VERBS

Grammatical voice brings out the relationship between the subject and the action. Voice indicates whether the subject is the performer of the action of the verb (active voice), or the subject is the recipient of the action (passive voice) or a participant in the action of the verb (middle voice).

Active Voice – If the subject of the sentence is executing the action, then the verb is referred to as being in the active voice.

Passive Voice – If the subject of the sentence is being acted upon, then the verb is referred to as being in the passive voice.

Middle Voice – The Greek middle voice shows the subject acting in his own interest or on his own behalf, or participating in the results of the verbal action. Sometimes the middle form of the verb could be translated as (reflexive action) i.e. "the subject as acting in some way upon or concerning himself."[35]

MOODS OF VERBS

Grammatical 'mood' of a verb brings out the mind with which the sentence is to be viewed. Mood has to do with the statement's relationship to reality, whether the asserted statement is actual or if there is only the possibility of its actual occurrence. There are four moods in the Greek:

Indicative Mood – The indicative mood is a statement of fact or an actual occurrence from the writer's or speaker's perspective. The indicative mood is "generally used in making statements of asking questions."[36] It may be action occurring in past, present, or future time and "is used with all the six Greek tenses. It is the only mood in which distinctions can regularly be made about the time when the action occurs." "This mood is used in two ways. It may be used to express a wish: … It can also introduce an indirect question."[37]

Imperative Mood – The imperative mood is a command or instruction given to the hearer, charging the hearer to carry out or perform a certain action. "The imperative mood is used to express commands, exhortations and entreaties."[38]

Subjunctive Mood – The subjunctive mood indicates probability or objective possibility. The action of the verb will possibly happen, depending on certain objective factors or circumstances. It is often times used in conditional statements (i.e. 'If ... then ...' clauses) or in purpose clauses. However if the subjunctive mood is used in a purpose or result clause, then the action should not be thought of as a possible result, but should be viewed as a definite outcome that will happen as a result of another stated action.

---

[35] Spiros Zodhiates, *The Complete Word Study New Testament*, (Chattanooga Tennessee: AMG Publishers, 1992), 865.
[36] J. W. Wenham, *Elements of New Testament Greek*, (Edinburgh: Cambridge University Press, 1965), 73.
[37] Spiros Zodhiates, *The Complete Word Study New Testament*, 865.
[38] Wenham, *Elements of New Testament Greek*, 73.

Optative Mood – The optative is the mood of possibility, removed even further than the subjunctive from something conceived of as actual. "The optative mood, though considerably used in classical times is rare in the New Testament. It can be described roughly as the *mood of more doubtful assertion*."[39] Often it is used to convey a wish or hope for a certain action to occur. "This mood is used in two ways. It may be used to express a wish: ... It can also introduce an indirect question."[40]

TENSES OF VERBS

In English, and in most other languages, the tense of the verb mainly refers to the 'time' of the action of the verb (present, past, or future time). In Greek, however, although time does bear upon the meaning of tense, the primary consideration of the tense of the verb is not time, but rather the 'kind of action' that the verb portrays. The most important element in Greek tense is kind of action; time is regarded as a secondary element. The kind of action of a Greek verb will generally fall into one of three categories:

1. **Linear tense** – presents a Continuous (or 'Progressive') kind of action.
2. **Perfective tense** – presents a Completed (or 'Accomplished) kind of action, with continuing results.
3. **Punctiliar tense** – presents a Simple or aoristic occurrence, without reference to the question of progress.

Present Tense – The present tense usually denotes continuous or repetitive kind of action. When used in the indicative mood, the present tense denotes action taking place or going on in the present time. Thus "the present tense in the indicative mood represents contemporaneous action... In moods other than in the indicative mood, it refers only to continuous or repeated action."[41]

Aorist Tense – The aorist is said to be a simple or summary statement of occurrence, without regard for the amount of time taken to accomplish the action, that is "the action of the verb is thought of as simply happening without any regard to its continuance or frequency"[42] this kind of action is commonly called 'Punctiliar'. This sense views the action as a single, collective whole, or one-point-in-time action, although it may actually take place over a period of time emphasis being on the fact of the action's occurrence.

> The Aorist tense is used for simple, undefined action. In the indicative mood, the aorist tense can indicate punctiliar action (action that happens at a specific point in time) in the past. ... With few exceptions, whenever the aorist tense is used in any mood other than indicative, the verb does not have any temporal significance. In

---

[39] Wenham, *Elements of New Testament Greek*, 168.
[40] Zodhiates, *Word Study New Testament*, 865.
[41] Zodhiates, *Word Study New Testament*, 867.
[42] Wenham, *The Elements of New Testament Greek*, 96.

other words, it refers only to the reality of an event, not to the time when it took place.[43]

The aorist tense is the most basic tense of the Greek and it is normally used in narratives as Chamberlain observes, "The historian uses it, unless he wants to picture some act recorded."[44]

Imperfect Tense – The imperfect tense shows continuous or linear type of action just like the present tense. It always indicates an action continually or repeatedly happening in past time. The "the imperfect tense is only used in the indicative mood and refers to continuous or linear action in past time."[45]

Perfect Tense – The basic thought of the perfect tense is that the progress of an action has been completed but the results of the action are continuing on, in full effect. According to Zodhiates, "The perfect tense describes an action, or more correctly a process, that took place in the past, the results of which have continued to the present. It has no exact equivalent in English, but is usually translated by using the auxiliary verb 'has' or 'have'."[46] Unlike the English perfect, which indicates a completed past action, the Greek perfect tense indicates the continuation and present state of a completed past action that is "the perfect represents a present state resulting from a past action".[47]

Future Tense – Just like the English future tense, the Greek future tells about an anticipated action or a certain happening that will occur at some time in the future. "Though on occasion the future tense may refer to linear action, it is almost always refers to punctiliar action. However, the emphasis is always on the fact that the action will take place in the future, not what kind of action is represented."[48]

Pluperfect Tense – The pluperfect (past perfect) shows action that is complete and existed at some time in the past, (the past time being indicated by the context). It "is like the perfect tense, except that the result of the action is also in the past."[49] This tense is defined by Wenham as "The action was done in the past, its results lasted some time, but at the time of narration the whole completed action lay in the past."[50]

NON-FINITE VERB FORMS
Participles

A participle is considered a 'verbal adjective' and being such, "participles share the characteristics of both verbs and adjectives. As a verb a participle has tense and voice and may have an object. As an adjective it agrees with a noun or pronoun

---

[43] Zodhiates, *Word Study New Testament*, 862.
[44] Chamberlain, *An Exegetical Grammar of the Greek New Testament*,, 77.
[45] Zodhiates, *Word Study New Testament*, 865.
[46] Zodhiates, *Word Study New Testament*, 866.
[47] Wenham, *The Elements of New Testament Greek*, 139.
[48] Zodhiates, *Word Study New Testament*, 864.
[49] Zodhiates, *Word Study New Testament*, 867.
[50] Wenham, *Elements of New Testament Greek*, 141.

which it qualifies in number, gender and case."[51] "As such, the participle may function as a verb, noun, or adjective in the sentence."[52] It is often a word that ends with an '-ing' in English.

Infinitives

The Greek infinitive is the form of the verb that is usually translated into English with the word 'to' attached to it, often used to complement another verb. It can be used to function as a noun and is therefore referred to as a 'verbal noun'.

---

[51] Wenham, *Elements of New Testament Greek*, 147-48.
[52] Zodhiates, *Word Study New Testament*, 865.

CHAPTER II

NOUN CLASSIFICATIONS

In elementary Greek, the five Greek noun cases were distinguished according to their functions with the role of each in the sentence identified and primarily defined by the change of form each takes as seen in their endings. Though generally nouns function as naming cases, these five cases were identified generally as expressed by Wenham

(1) Nominative: (a) The *subject* of the verb is in the nominative case. (b) The *complement* to an intransitive verb is in the nominative case. ... (2) Vocative: is the case of *address* ... (3) Accusative is the case of the *direct object* of a transitive verb. (4) Genitive is the case of *possession*, ... (5) Dative is the case of *indirect object*.[53]

The basic role of the substantive in a sentence is thus seen in its ending and as Wenham describes above, and the roles and relationships of the cases in a sentence is to be determined by identifying and classifying the usage or function of the substantive within the case. This implies that within each case there are variations, which amplify and further specify the role of the word within the basic idea as described by Wenham. This section will look at the different variations within the substantive cases, defining and identifying their functions. To "decline" a noun i.e. to analyse it and break it down into its basic parts according to **number, gender,** and **case** can be done as shown below.

Parsing Guide for Nouns

Form	Case	Gender	Number	Root	Syntax
Παῦλος	Nominative	Masculine	Singular	Παῦλος	

NOMINATIVE CASE SYNTACTICAL CLASSIFICATION

Generally the nominative is the case for specific identification and is used to point to a thing or person. William Chamberlain in his *Exegetical Grammar of the New Testament* writes, "The nominative is primarily the 'naming' case. Its commonest use is as the 'subject' of the sentence."[54] Although the Greek verb ending carries in it the subject, the nominative case identifies and specifies this subject. Smyth notes that the Nominative is "the case of the subject of a finite verb and of a predicate noun in agreement with the subject."[55] The nominative is thus the case of specific designation and is thus most commonly used as the subject. The nominative case has the following uses:

---

[53] Wenham, *The Elements of New Testament Greek*, 9.
[54] Chamberlain, *An Exegetical Grammar of the New Testament*, 27.
[55] Herbert Weir Smyth, *Greek Grammar for Colleges*, (New York: American Book Company, 1920), digital book obtained at URL: http://www.textkit.com

Subject Nominative

When a word is used as the subject of a finite verb, it is usually in the Nominative case. When the word in the Nominative "functions as the subject of a finite verb;"[56] answering the question who or what is producing the action of the verb (for active verb), who is receiving the action of the verb (for passive verb) or who is involved with the verb's state of being (for linking verbs) i.e. who or what forms the subject of the verb is a *Subject Nominative.*

Subject Nominative with active verb

John 3:35: ὁ πατὴρ ἀγαπᾷ τὸν Υἱόν καὶ πάντα δέδωκεν ἐν τῇ χειρὶ αὐτοῦ. – "The Father loves the Son and all things He (the father) has given into His (the Son's) hand."

John 1:5: καὶ τὸ φῶς ἐν τῇ σκοτίᾳ φαίνει καὶ ἡ σκοτία αὐτὸ οὐ κατέλαβεν – "And the light is shining in the darkness and the darkness did not apprehend it."

Subject Nominative with passive verb

Romans 6:4: ..., ἵνα ὥσπερ ἠγέρθη Χριστὸς ἐκ νεκρῶν διὰ τῆς δόξης τοῦ πατρός, ... – "So that just as Christ was raised from the dead by the glory of the Father, ..."

Romans 11:7: τί οὖν ὃ ἐπιζητεῖ Ἰσραήλ τούτου οὐκ ἐπέτυχεν ἡ δὲ ἐκλογὴ ἐπέτυχεν· οἱ δὲ λοιποὶ ἐπωρώθησαν – "What then? That which Israel is seeking out of this thing it has not obtained, but the chosen have obtained it: but the remaining ones were hardened."

Subject Nominative with linking verb

John 1:14: Καὶ ὁ Λόγος σὰρξ ἐγένετο καὶ ἐσκήνωσεν ἐν ἡμῖν, – "And The Word became flesh and dwelled with us."

The nominative article as subject of the verb

Matthew 2:5: οἱ δὲ εἶπον αὐτῷ, Ἐν Βηθλεὲμ τῆς Ἰουδαίας. οὕτω γὰρ γέγραπται διὰ τοῦ προφήτου, – "and they said to him, in Bethlehem of Judah. For thus it stands written by the prophet."

Matthew 24:16: τότε οἱ ἐν τῇ Ἰουδαίᾳ φευγέτωσαν ἐπὶ τὰ ὄρη – "then those in Judah flee to the mountains."

Predicate Nominative

The object of a linking or copulative verb when it is in the nominative case, rather than in the accusative it is referred to as a predicate nominative. Thus a predicate nominative is a noun or pronoun in the nominative case, which further identifies, explains or categorises the subject and is sometimes called the "subject complement."

---

[56] James A. Brooks and Carlton L. Winbery, *Syntax of New Testament Greek*, (Lanham Madison: University Press of America, 1979), 3.

CHAPTER 2: NOUN CLASIFICATIONS

Wallace states that "The predicate nominative (PN) is *approximately* the same as the subject (S) and is joined to it by an equative verb, whether stated or implied."[57]

When a liking verb is accompanied by two substantives in the nominative case then the following rules are to be used in determining the subject:

- If one of the substantives is a Pronoun, then it is always the subject
- If one of the substantives is a proper noun and the other is a common noun, then the proper noun is always the subject
- If both are nouns but one has an article and the other does not have, then the noun with the article is the subject.
- If both the nouns are the same (e.g. either both are proper nouns or both are nouns with articles, then the first one in word order is the subject.

These rules are hierarchy rules which means the higher rule is always be observed first and to be given priority.

Predicate Nominative – linking verb accompanied by pronoun and noun

Luke 1:18: … ἐγὼ γάρ εἰμι πρεσβύτης καὶ ἡ γυνή μου προβεβηκυῖα ἐν ταῖς ἡμέραις αὐτῆς. – "I am <u>an old man</u> and my wife is advanced in her days."

Mark 3:11: … καὶ ἔκραζον λέγοντα ὅτι σὺ εἶ <u>ὁ Υἱὸς</u> τοῦ Θεοῦ. – "And they cried saying "You are <u>the Son</u> of God."

Predicate Nominative – linking verb accompanied by proper noun and noun

James 5:17: Ἠλίας <u>ἄνθρωπος</u> ἦν ὁμοιοπαθὴς ἡμῖν, – "Elijah was <u>a man</u> of like passion to us."

Predicate Nominative – linking verb accompanied by two nouns one having an article but the other not having

John 1:1: καὶ <u>Θεὸς</u> ἦν ὁ Λόγος. – "And the Word was <u>God</u>."

1John 4:8: ὁ Θεὸς <u>ἀγάπη</u> ἐστίν. – "God is <u>love</u>."

John 1:14: Καὶ ὁ Λόγος <u>σὰρξ</u> ἐγένετο – "And the Word became <u>flesh</u>"

Predicate Nominative – linking verb accompanied by two nouns that are same

John 15:1: Ἐγώ εἰμι ἡ ἄμπελος ἡ ἀληθινή, καὶ ὁ πατήρ μου <u>ὁ γεωργός</u> ἐστι. – "I am the true vine, and my Father is the <u>husbandman</u>."

Nominative of Apposition

The nominative case (as well as the other cases) can be an appositive to another substantive in the same case. "An appositional construction involves (1) two adjacent substantives (2) in the same case (3) which refer to the same person or thing (4) and have the same syntactical relation to the rest of the clause."[58] Wallace further states "The

---

[57] Daniel B. Wallace, *Greek Grammar Beyond the Basics*, 40.
[58] Wallace, *Greek Grammar Beyond the Basics*, 48

appositive functions very much like a PN in a convertible proposition – that is, it refers to the same thing as the first noun. The difference, however, is that a PN makes and *assertion* about the S (an equative verb is either stated or implied); with appositives there is assumption, not assertion (no verb is in mind)."[59] Thus the noun in apposition is a noun or clause which is placed beside or after a certain word in order to rename or explain it.[60]

Matthew 3:1: Ἐν δὲ ταῖς ἡμέραις ἐκείναις παραγίνεται Ἰωάννης <u>ὁ βαπτιστὴς</u> κηρύσσων ἐν τῇ ἐρήμῳ τῆς Ἰουδαίας – "Now in those days John <u>the Baptist</u> came along preaching in the deserts of Judea."

John 16:13 ὅταν δὲ ἔλθῃ ἐκεῖνος, <u>τὸ Πνεῦμα τῆς ἀληθείας</u>, ὁδηγήσει ὑμᾶς εἰς πᾶσαν τὴν ἀλήθειαν· – "but when he <u>the Spirit of truth</u> shall come, he will guide you to all truth."

1 Peter 1:1: Πέτρος <u>ἀπόστολος Ἰησοῦ Χριστοῦ</u> ἐκλεκτοῖς παρεπιδήμοις διασπορᾶς Πόντου Γαλατίας Καππαδοκίας Ἀσίας καὶ Βιθυνίας – "Peter <u>an apostle of Jesus Christ</u> to the called out pilgrims dispersed throughout Pontus, Galatia, Cappadocia, Asia and Bythinia."

Matthew 16:17: καὶ ἀποκριθεὶς ὁ Ἰησοῦς εἶπεν αὐτῷ Μακάριος εἶ Σίμων <u>Βαρ Ἰωνᾶ</u>, ὅτι σὰρξ καὶ αἷμα οὐκ ἀπεκάλυψέν σοι ἀλλ᾽ ὁ πατήρ μου ὁ ἐν τοῖς οὐρανοῖς – "And Jesus answering said to him blessed are you Simon <u>Barjona</u>, for flesh and blood has not revealed it to you but my father which is in heaven."

Nominative of Appellation

When a proper noun is used in the nominative case, regardless of what role it plays in the sentence, it is regarded as nominative of appellation. The noun used as a title appears in the nominative and functions as a proper name although another case would normally be more appropriate. The nominative is used because of the special character of the individual described. The key is that the nominative is *treated* as a proper name, which is expected to be in another case. That is to say that nominative of appellation is used substantively to describe, clarify or identify another substantive which it stands in apposition to and in English grammar can be put in quotation marks. Care should be taken especially with indeclinable proper nouns. "Indeclinable proper nouns should not be treated as nominatives of appellation but should be given whatever case is required by their use in the sentence."[61]

Matthew 1:23: Ἰδοὺ ἡ παρθένος ἐν γαστρὶ ἕξει, καὶ τέξεται υἱόν, καὶ καλέσουσι τὸ ὄνομα αὐτοῦ <u>Ἐμμανουὴλ</u>, ὅ ἐστι μεθερμηνευόμενον, μεθ᾽ ἡμῶν ὁ Θεός.

---

[59] Ibid.
[60] Wallace states that "the first substantive can belong to any category (e.g., subject, predicate nom, etc.) and the second is merely a clarification description or identification of who or what is mentioned." [Wallace, *Greek Grammar Beyond the Basics*, 48]
[61] Brooks and Winbery, *Syntax of the New Testament Greek*, 5.

– "behold the virgin shall be with child and shall bear a son, and they shall call his name <u>Emanuel</u>, which is being interpreted God with us."

John 13:13: ὑμεῖς φωνεῖτέ με <u>ὁ Διδάσκαλος</u> καὶ <u>ὁ Κύριος</u>, καὶ καλῶς λέγετε· εἰμὶ γάρ. – "You call me <u>"Teacher"</u> and <u>"Lord"</u>, and you say well for I am."

Luke 2:21 Καὶ ὅτε ἐπλήσθησαν ἡμέραι ὀκτὼ τοῦ περιτεμεῖν τὸ παιδίον, καὶ ἐκλήθη τὸ ὄνομα αὐτοῦ <u>Ἰησοῦς</u>, τὸ κληθὲν ὑπὸ τοῦ ἀγγέλου πρὸ τοῦ συλληφθῆναι αὐτὸν ἐν τῇ κοιλίᾳ. – "And when eight days were accomplished to circumcise the child, and his name was called <u>Jesus</u>, the *name* which was called by the angel before he was conceived in the womb."

Independent Nominative

Often times the nominative case will be used in expressions where there is no finite verb exists, such as in Exclamations, Salutations, Titles of Books, and in Parenthetic, Absolute, and Proverbial Expressions. When this is the case, then the nominative is called nominative absolute, hanging nominative or independent nominative. "All independent nominatives follow this general rule: *The substantive in the nominative case is grammatically unrelated to the rest of the sentence.*"[62] Thus the independent nominative is used independently in citing names of persons or things.

Independent nominatives in Exclamations:

Mark 3:34 καὶ περιβλεψάμενος κύκλῳ τοὺς περὶ αὐτὸν καθημένους λέγει· ἴδε <u>ἡ μήτηρ</u> μου καὶ <u>οἱ ἀδελφοί</u> μου· – "and looking around round about on them who were sitting he said: behold my mother and my brother."

John 1:29: Τῇ ἐπαύριον βλέπει ὁ Ἰωάννης τὸν Ἰησοῦν ἐρχόμενον πρὸς αὐτόν καὶ λέγει Ἴδε <u>ὁ ἀμνὸς</u> τοῦ θεοῦ <u>ὁ αἴρων</u> τὴν ἁμαρτίαν τοῦ κόσμου – "on the morrow, John sees Jesus coming to him and says behold <u>the Lamb</u> of God <u>who takes away</u> the sin of the world."

Romans 11:33: Ὦ <u>βάθος</u> πλούτου καὶ σοφίας καὶ γνώσεως Θεοῦ· ὡς ἀνεξερεύνητα τὰ κρίματα αὐτοῦ καὶ ἀνεξιχνίαστοι αἱ ὁδοὶ αὐτοῦ – "O the depth of the riches and wisdom and knowledge of God: how unsearchable *are* His judgements and *how* unsearchable are his ways."

Independent nominatives in Salutations[63]:

Romans 1:1: <u>Παῦλος</u>, δοῦλος Χριστοῦ Ἰησοῦ, κλητὸς ἀπόστολος, ἀφωρισμένος εἰς εὐαγγέλιον Θεοῦ – "<u>Paul</u>, a slave of Jesus Christ called *to be* an apostle separated unto the gospel of God."

---

[62] Wallace, *Greek Grammar Beyond the Basics*, 49.
[63] Smyth writes "In referring to himself in letters a man may use his own name in the nominative either in apposition to the first person contained verb (976) or as the subject of a verb in the third person." [Herbert Weir Smyth, *Greek Grammar for Colleges*, at URL: http://www.textkit.com]

Independent nominative in Titles of Books:

Revelation 1:1: <u>Ἀποκάλυψις</u> Ἰησοῦ Χριστοῦ, ἣν ἔδωκεν αὐτῷ ὁ Θεός, δεῖξαι τοῖς δούλοις αὐτοῦ ἃ δεῖ γενέσθαι ἐν τάχει, καὶ ἐσήμανεν ἀποστείλας διὰ τοῦ ἀγγέλου αὐτοῦ τῷ δούλῳ αὐτοῦ Ἰωάννῃ, – "<u>Revelation</u> of Jesus Christ which God gave to him to give to his servant what is necessary to come to pass shortly and he signified *it* sending by his angel to his servant John."

Independent nominative in Parenthetic:

A parenthetic nominative is the subject of a clause within another clause primarily for explanatory purposes. The sentence, which contains a clause whose subject is a parenthetic nominative, may or may not have a different subject. Wallace notes,

*A parenthetic nominative is the subject of an explanatory clause **within** another clause. … if such a clause seems so unnatural in translation that mere commas do not seem to set it enough apart, then it is probably a parenthesis and its subject is a parenthetic nominative.*[64]

John 1:6: Ἐγένετο ἄνθρωπος ἀπεσταλμένος παρὰ Θεοῦ, ὄνομα αὐτῷ <u>Ἰωάννης</u>· – "There came a man who was sent from God his name was <u>John</u>."

Independent nominative as nominative absolute:

The nominative absolute use of the independent nominative is the use of a participle in the nominative such that it stands out of grammatical connection with the rest of the sentence (similar to the Genitive absolute construction but with the participle in the nominative case).

Revelation 3:12: <u>Ὁ νικῶν</u>, ποιήσω αὐτὸν στῦλον ἐν τῷ ναῷ τοῦ Θεοῦ μου, καὶ ἔξω οὐ μὴ ἐξέλθῃ ἔτι, καὶ γράψω ἐπ' αὐτὸν τὸ ὄνομα τοῦ Θεοῦ μου, καὶ τὸ ὄνομα τῆς πόλεως τοῦ Θεοῦ μου, τῆς καινῆς Ἰερουσαλήμ, <u>ἣ καταβαίνει</u> ἐκ τοῦ οὐρανοῦ ἀπὸ τοῦ Θεοῦ μου, καὶ τὸ ὄνομά μου τὸ καινόν. – "<u>The one who overcomes</u>, I will make him a pillar in the temple of my God and he shall never means go out again and I will write upon him the name of my God, and the name of the city of my God, the new Jerusalem, <u>which is coming down</u> out of heaven from my God, and my new name."

Independent nominatives in Proverbial Expressions and quotations

2 Peter 2:22: συμβέβηκε δὲ αὐτοῖς τὸ τῆς ἀληθοῦς παροιμίας, <u>κύων</u> ἐπιστρέψας ἐπὶ τὸ ἴδιον ἐξέραμα, καί, <u>ὗς</u> λουσαμένη εἰς κυλισμὸν βορβόρου. – "but it has happened to them the true proverb, <u>the dog</u> returning upon his own vomit, and <u>the sow</u> being bathed to her mire wallowing."

---

[64] Wallace, *Greek Grammar Beyond the Basics*, 53.

Matthew 10:16 Ἰδοὺ ἐγὼ ἀποστέλλω ὑμᾶς ὡς <u>πρόβατα</u> ἐν μέσῳ λύκων· γίνεσθε οὖν <u>φρόνιμοι ὡς οἱ ὄφεις καὶ ἀκέραιοι ὡς αἱ περιστεραί</u>. – "behold I am sending you as sheep in the midst of wolves: therefore be <u>wise as the serpents and harmless as the doves</u>."

Matthew 24:28: ὅπου γὰρ ἐὰν ᾖ <u>τὸ πτῶμα</u>, ἐκεῖ συναχθήσονται <u>οἱ ἀετοί</u>. – "for wherever <u>the carcass</u> may be, there <u>the eagles</u> will be gathered together."

GENITIVE CASE SYNTACTICAL CLASSIFICATION

Generally the Genitive is the case of possession and is used to describe or define. Nunn says of the genitive case that

> The Genitive case is an adjectival or descriptive case; a noun in the genitive case is generally connected with another noun which it qualifies very much in the same way as an adjective. The genitive case is generally expressed in the English by the use of the preposition of or by the possessive case.[65]

The genitive case is thus the case of quality, characteristics, attribute, description or kind. Smyth says that the genitive limits "the scope of the substantive on which it depends by referring it to a particular class or description or by regarding it as a part of a whole."[66] The genitive case serves to limit the meaning of the substantives, adjectives and adverbs.[67] The genitive mainly answers the question "What kind?"[68] specifying the genus or class to which the substantive belongs and supplying a conception or understanding of which part they form by narrowing the its reference. Though generally the genitive is usually related to the noun, there are certain verbs, which require that their direct object be in the genitive case. In identifying the genitives in their construction Smyth notes,

> The genitive with substantives denotes in general a connection or dependence between two words. This connection must often be determined (1) by the meaning of the words (2) by the context (3) by the facts presupposed as known.[69]

The Genitive case may be classified under the classes mentioned below:

1. Adjectival Genitive

This broad category really touches the heart of the genitive. If the genitive is primarily descriptive, then it is largely similar to the adjective in functions. "The chief

---

[65] H. P. V. Nunn, *A Short Syntax of New Testament Greek,* (London: Cambridge University Press, 1913), 42.
[66] Herbert Weir Smyth, *Greek Grammar for Colleges,* at URL: http://www.textkit.com
[67] Wallace distinguishes the genitive thus "The genitive and the accusative are similar in that both are cases expressing some kind of limitation … the difference between these two is generally twofold: (1) the genitive limits as to kind while the accusative limits as to extent. Another way to put this is that the genitive limits as to quality while the accusative limits as to quantity. (2) The genitive is usually related to a noun while the accusative is usually related to a verb. [Wallace, *Greek Grammar Beyond the Basics*, 76.]
[68] Brooks and Winbery observe that the genitive defines and describes by "attributing a quality or relationship to a substantive. It does so by answering the question, What kind? Therefore the genitive functions very much like an adjective." [Brooks and Winbery, *Syntax of New Testament Greek*, 8.]
[69] Herbert Weir Smyth, *Greek Grammar for Colleges,* at URL: http://www.textkit.com

thing to remember is that the Genitive often practically does the duty of an adjective, distinguishing two otherwise similar things" However, although the genitive is primarily adjectival in force, it is more emphatic than a simple adjective would be.[70]

a. Genitive of Description

The genitive by and large is descriptive and thus "all genitives are to a greater or lesser degree descriptive"[71] but sometimes the word in the genitive is used as an adjective to describe, give an attribute or quality to the head noun, which it modifies. In this case, "the genitive describes the head noun in a loose manner" thus acting as an adjective but there is a stronger force and emphasis on the quality of the description. This category employs the use of the substantive without a preposition"[72] and is "the 'catch-all' genitive, the 'drip pan' genitive, the 'black hole' of genitive categories that tries to such many a genitive into its grasp!"[73] It is the most common use of the genitive and if the genitive can be turned into or explained as an attributive adjective then it is probably a descriptive genitive.

1 Thessalonians 2:13 διὰ τοῦτο Καὶ ἡμεῖς εὐχαριστοῦμεν τῷ θεῷ ἀδιαλείπτως ὅτι παραλαβόντες λόγον ἀκοῆς παρ' ἡμῶν <u>τοῦ θεοῦ</u> ἐδέξασθε οὐ λόγον ἀνθρώπων ἀλλὰ καθώς ἐστιν ἀληθῶς λόγον <u>θεοῦ</u> ὃς καὶ ἐνεργεῖται ἐν ὑμῖν τοῖς πιστεύουσιν. – "and for this cause we *continually* give thanks to God without ceasing, because having received the word <u>of God</u> hearing from us you received it not as the word of men, but just as it is truly, the word <u>of God</u> which also is working effectually in you who believe."

Matthew 1:1: Βίβλος <u>γενέσεως</u> Ἰησοῦ Χριστοῦ, υἱοῦ Δαβὶδ, υἱοῦ Ἀβραάμ. – "Book <u>of the generations</u> of Jesus Christ, son of David, son of Abraham."

Mark 1:4: ἐγένετο Ἰωάννης βαπτίζων ἐν τῇ ἐρήμῳ καὶ κηρύσσων βάπτισμα μετανοίας εἰς ἄφεσιν <u>ἁμαρτιῶν</u> – "John was baptising in the desert and proclaiming baptism of repentance for remission <u>of sins</u>."

b. Possessive Genitive

This use of the genitive shows the idea of ownership or possession with "the substantive in the genitive possesses the thing to which it stands related. That is, in some sense the head noun is owned by the genitive noun. Such ownership at times can be broadly defined and need not imply the literal (and sometimes harsh) idea of possession of physical property."[74] This class of genitive may be used together with a possessive pronoun. To determine whether a given genitive falls under this class, instead of the word *of* replace it with *belonging to* or *possessed by*.[75]

Matthew 26:51 καὶ ἰδοὺ εἷς τῶν μετὰ Ἰησοῦ ἐκτείνας τὴν χεῖρα ἀπέσπασε τὴν μάχαιραν αὐτοῦ, καὶ πατάξας τὸν δοῦλον <u>τοῦ ἀρχιερέως</u> ἀφεῖλεν αὐτοῦ τὸ ὠτίον. –

---

[70] Wallace, *Greek Beyond the Basics*, 78.
[71] Brooks and Winbery, *Syntax of New Testament Greek*, 8.
[72] Ibid.
[73] Wallace, *Greek Beyond the Basics*, 79
[74] *Ibid*, 81.
[75] Ibid.

"and behold one of those with Jesus stretching the hand drew out his sword and smote the slave of the High Priest cut off his ear."

1 John 1:1 ὃ ἦν ἀπ' ἀρχῆς, ὃ ἀκηκόαμεν, ὃ ἑωράκαμεν τοῖς ὀφθαλμοῖς ἡμῶν, ὃ ἐθεασάμεθα, καὶ αἱ χεῖρες ἡμῶν ἐψηλάφησαν περὶ τοῦ λόγου τῆς ζωῆς, – "that which was from the beginning, which we have heard, which our eyes have looked upon, and our hands have handled concerning the word of life."

c. Genitive of Relationship

This is similar to the genitive of possession with the substantive in the genitive indicating a familial relationship with the person named by the head noun. Thus "this genitive is really a specialized use of the genitive of possession. It indicates some aspect of marital or genital or even social relationship."[76] It should be noted that the article modifying the word in the genitive case is usually present, but not always. The actual word showing the relationship may be omitted (except for the definite article) when it is clearly known by context or by general knowledge.[77] Robertson says, "The substantive is not used because the context makes it clear"[78] The genitive noun is often a proper noun. The substantive employed is without a preposition.

Matthew 20:20 Τότε προσῆλθεν αὐτῷ ἡ μήτηρ τῶν υἱῶν Ζεβεδαίου μετὰ τῶν υἱῶν αὐτῆς προσκυνοῦσα καὶ αἰτοῦσά τι παρ' αὐτοῦ – "Then the mother of the sons of Zebedee came to him with her sons worshipping and asking a certain thing of him."

John 2:1: Καὶ τῇ ἡμέρᾳ τῇ τρίτῃ γάμος ἐγένετο ἐν Κανὰ τῆς Γαλιλαίας καὶ ἦν ἡ μήτηρ τοῦ Ἰησοῦ ἐκεῖ· – "and on the third day there was a wedding in Cana of Galilee and the mother of Jesus was there."

John 21:15: Ὅτε οὖν ἠρίστησαν λέγει τῷ Σίμωνι Πέτρῳ ὁ Ἰησοῦς Σίμων Ἰωνᾶ, ἀγαπᾷς με πλεῖόν τούτων λέγει αὐτῷ Ναί κύριε σὺ οἶδας ὅτι φιλῶ σε λέγει αὐτῷ Βόσκε τὰ ἀρνία μου – "When therefore they had dined, Jesus said to Simon Peter, Simon *son* of Jonas do you love me above all these things? He said to him yea Lord you know that I love you; he said to him feed my sheep."

2. Adverbial Genitive

Dana and Mantey state that "The genitive is sometimes used to define a verbal idea by attributing local or temporal relations, or as qualifying an adjective. Here its attributive function is clearly present, for it is kind of action which is being emphasized."[79] When the genitive is used to modify a verb rather than a substantive, it functions as an adverb and is classified as an adverbial genitive. Goodwin observes "As the chief use of the accusative is to limit the meaning of a verb, so the chief use of the genitive is to limit the meaning of a noun. When the genitive is used as the object of a

---

[76] Brooks and Winbery, *Syntax of New Testament Greek*, 9.

[77] Dana and Mantey write that "The usual construction simply presents the article in the proper gender with the genitive of the person related, omitting the noun which indicates the relationship. It is assumed that the relationship is known or has been made sufficiently clear by the context" [Dana and Mantey, *A Manual Grammar of the Greek New Testament*, 76.]

[78] Robertson, *A Grammar of the Greek New Testament in the light of Historical Research*, 501.

[79] Dana and Mantey, *A Manual Grammar of the Greek New Testament*, 77.

verb, it seems to depend on the nominal idea which belongs to the verb."[80] When used as an adverb, the genitive defines the verb in three ways. It either indicates (a) the kind of time – "the significance here is distinction of time rather than point of time (locative) or duration of time (accusative)."[81] (b) the kind of place – "in this use, the sense of contact is prominent. But attribution is still the emphatic."[82] (c) with an adjective to indicate with reference to – "is sometimes used with adjectives to refer to their qualifying force to certain definite limits."[83]

a. Adverbial Genitive of Time

Hewett writes, "The noun in the genitive may indicate the type of time within which an activity occurs. This is distinct from the dative, which expresses a particular point of time, or the accusative, which expresses the extent of time that an activity occurs."[84] This means that the genitive answers the question "what kind of time?" and indicating "kind of time, time within which, or one time as opposed to another time."[85] This means that in this usage, the genitive answers the question "what time?" and the English preposition normally inserted for the genitive "of", could instead be translated '*during*', '*at*', or '*within*'.

John 3:2: οὗτος ἦλθεν πρὸς τὸν Ἰησοῦν <u>νυκτὸς</u> καὶ εἶπεν αὐτῷ Ραββί οἴδαμεν ὅτι ἀπὸ θεοῦ ἐλήλυθας διδάσκαλος· οὐδεὶς γὰρ ταῦτα τὰ σημεῖα δύναται ποιεῖν ἃ σὺ ποιεῖς ἐὰν μὴ ᾖ ὁ θεὸς μετ' αὐτοῦ – "the same *man* came to Jesus <u>at night</u> and said to him Rabbi we know that you are a teacher come from God: for no one is able to do these signs which you do except God is with him."

Matthew 24:20: προσεύχεσθε δὲ ἵνα μὴ γένηται ἡ φυγὴ ὑμῶν <u>χειμῶνος</u> μηδὲ ἐν σαββάτῳ – "but pray that your flight may not be <u>during winter</u> nor on the Sabbath"

Luke 4:27: καὶ πολλοὶ λεπροὶ ἦσαν <u>ἐπὶ ἐλισσαίου τοῦ προφήτου</u> ἐν τῷ Ἰσραὴλ καὶ οὐδεὶς αὐτῶν ἐκαθαρίσθη εἰ μὴ Νεεμὰν ὁ Σύρος – "and there were many lepers in Israel <u>during the time of Elisha the prophet</u> but none of them was cleansed except Naaman the Syrian."

Luke 11:5: Καὶ εἶπεν πρὸς αὐτούς Τίς ἐξ ὑμῶν ἕξει φίλον καὶ πορεύσεται πρὸς αὐτὸν <u>μεσονυκτίου</u> καὶ εἴπῃ αὐτῷ Φίλε χρῆσόν μοι τρεῖς ἄρτους – "and he said to them which one of you having a friend and going to him <u>at midnight</u> and shall say to him friend lend me three loaves."

Luke 5:5: καὶ ἀποκριθεὶς ὁ Σίμων εἶπεν αὐτῷ, Ἐπιστάτα <u>δι' ὅλης τῆς νυκτὸς</u> κοπιάσαντες οὐδὲν ἐλάβομεν· ἐπὶ δὲ τῷ ῥήματί σου χαλάσω τὸ δίκτυον – "and Simon answering said to him, Master we have labored <u>through the whole night</u> and have taken nothing: but at your word I will let down the net."

---

[80] William W. Goodwin, *A Greek Grammar*, (Boston: Ginn and Company, 1892), 229.
[81] Dana and Mantey, *A Manual Grammar of the Greek New Testament*, 77.
[82] ibid.
[83] ibid. 78.
[84] James Allen Hewett, *New Testament Greek a beginning and intermediate grammar*, (Peabody Massachusetts: Hendrickson Publishers, 1986), 199.
[85] Brooks and Winbery, *Syntax of New Testament Greek*, 11.

b. Adverbial Genitive of Place

According to Brooks and Winbery, "Place is most often expressed by the locative case. When a genitive is used to denote place, the emphasis is usually upon kind of place, one place as opposed to another place, here and not there."[86] In this, the genitive answers the question "what kind of place?" making prominent the sense of contact indicating the place within which the verb it is related to and which it modifies occurs. The English preposition for the genitive may be replaced by '*in*' '*at*' or '*through*'.

Luke 16:24: καὶ αὐτὸς φωνήσας εἶπεν Πάτερ Ἀβραάμ ἐλέησόν με καὶ πέμψον Λάζαρον ἵνα βάψῃ τὸ ἄκρον τοῦ δακτύλου αὐτοῦ <u>ὕδατος</u> καὶ καταψύξῃ τὴν γλῶσσάν μου ὅτι ὀδυνῶμαι ἐν τῇ φλογὶ ταύτῃ – "and he calling said, father Abraham have mercy on me and send Lazarus so that he may dip the tip of his finger <u>in water</u> and cool my tongue for I am tormented in this flame."

1 Peter 1:1: Πέτρος ἀπόστολος Ἰησοῦ Χριστοῦ ἐκλεκτοῖς παρεπιδήμοις διασπορᾶς <u>Πόντου Γαλατίας Καππαδοκίας Ἀσίας καὶ Βιθυνίας</u> – "Peter an apostle of Jesus Christ to the called out pilgrims dispersed <u>throughout Pontus, Galatia, Cappadocia, Asia and Bythinia</u>."

Acts 8:1: Σαῦλος δὲ ἦν συνευδοκῶν τῇ ἀναιρέσει αὐτοῦ Ἐγένετο δὲ ἐν ἐκείνῃ τῇ ἡμέρᾳ διωγμὸς μέγας ἐπὶ τὴν ἐκκλησίαν τὴν ἐν Ἱεροσολύμοις πάντες τε διεσπάρησαν <u>κατὰ τὰς χώρας τῆς Ἰουδαίας καὶ Σαμαρείας</u> πλὴν τῶν ἀποστόλων – "And Saul was consenting to his killing and in those days there came a great persecution upon the church that *was* in Jerusalem and all were dispersed <u>throughout the region of Judaea and Samaria</u> except the apostles."

c. Adverbial Genitive of Reference

Dana and Mantey write that, "the genitive is sometimes used with adjectives to refer to their qualifying force to certain definite limits."[87] Thus in this use, the genitive qualifies and restricts the adjective by completing the meaning of the adjective. Wallace states that "the genitive substantive indicates that in reference to which the noun or adjective to which it stands related is true."[88]

John 11:19: καὶ πολλοὶ ἐκ τῶν Ἰουδαίων ἐληλύθεισαν πρὸς τὰς περὶ Μάρθαν καὶ Μαρίαν, ἵνα παραμυθήσωνται αὐτὰς <u>περὶ τοῦ ἀδελφοῦ αὐτῶν</u> – "and many of the Jews came to them around Mary and Martha in order that they may comfort them <u>concerning their brother</u>."

Acts 24:24: Μετὰ δὲ ἡμέρας τινὰς παραγενόμενος ὁ Φῆλιξ σὺν Δρουσίλλῃ τῇ γυναικὶ αὐτοῦ οὔσῃ Ἰουδαίᾳ μετεπέμψατο τὸν Παῦλον καὶ ἤκουσεν αὐτοῦ <u>περὶ τῆς εἰς Χριστὸν πίστεως</u> – "and after certain days, when Felix came together with Drusilla his wife she being a Jewess he called for Paul and heard him <u>concerning the faith that *is* in Christ</u>."

---

[86] Brooks and Winbery, *Syntax of New Testament Greek*, 12.
[87] Dana and Mantey, *A Manual Grammar of the Greek New Testament*, 78.
[88] Wallace, *Greek Grammar Beyond the Basics*, 127.

Romans 1:3: περὶ τοῦ υἱοῦ αὐτοῦ τοῦ γενομένου ἐκ σπέρματος Δαβὶδ κατὰ σάρκα – "concerning his son who came of the seed of David according to the flesh."

Hebrews 5:13: πᾶς γὰρ ὁ μετέχων γάλακτος ἄπειρος λόγου δικαιοσύνης νήπιος γάρ ἐστιν· – "for everyone who is using milk *is* unskilful with respect to the word of truth for he is a child."

d. Adverbial Genitive of Measure

"This use of the genitive indicates how much and how far. It includes what some grammarians call the genitive of price or genitive of value or genitive of quantity. It also includes what some grammarians call the genitive of penalty."[89] In Greek, the genitive can be used to indicate the price at which something is sold e.g. Matthew 10:29 Wallace observes that "for the word *of* supply the word *for* (in answer to the question "how much?"). Also remember that the noun in the genitive is a monetary/material word, and is related to the verb"[90]

Matthew 10:29: οὐχὶ δύο στρουθία ἀσσαρίου πωλεῖται καὶ ἓν ἐξ αὐτῶν οὐ πεσεῖται ἐπὶ τὴν γῆν ἄνευ τοῦ πατρὸς ὑμῶν – "two sparrows are sold for a farthing. Aren't they? But one of them shall not fall upon the ground without your father."

Matthew 26:9: ἠδύνατο γὰρ τοῦτο τὸ μύρον πραθῆναι πολλοῦ καὶ δοθῆναι πτωχοῖς – "for was not this perfumed oil able to be sold for much and to be given to the poor."

Acts 7:16: καὶ μετετέθησαν εἰς Συχὲμ καὶ ἐτέθησαν ἐν τῷ μνήματι ὃ ὠνήσατο Ἀβραὰμ τιμῆς ἀργυρίου παρὰ τῶν υἱῶν Ἐμμὸρ τοῦ Συχέμ – "and were carried over to Sychem and laid down in the tomb which Abraham bought for a price of silver from the sons of Emmor of Sychem."

1 Corinthians 7:23: τιμῆς ἠγοράσθητε· μὴ γίνεσθε δοῦλοι ἀνθρώπων – "you were bought for a price: do not be slaves of men."

3. Genitives with Nouns of Action

Brooks and Winbery define a noun of action as "a noun the definition of which contains a verbal idea. Often there will be a cognate verb which has the same root."[91] These nouns may be identified either by their form or the context in which they are used. Brooks and Winbery note that "Most nouns which end in -sij or -moj are nouns of action, but there are many others which must be recognized by their meaning."[92] When a word in the genitive is used with a noun of action to modify it, then it can either be a subjective genitive or an objective genitive. Dana and Mantey explain, "Sometimes the noun defined by the genitive signifies action. In this construction the noun in the genitive indicates the thing to which the action is referred, either as subject or object of the verbal idea."[93]

---

[89] Brooks and Winbery, *Syntax of New Testament Greek*, 11.
[90] Wallace, *Greek Grammar Beyond the Basics*, 122.
[91] Brooks and Winbery, *Syntax of New Testament Greek*, 15.
[92] ibid.
[93] Dana and Mantey, *A Manual Grammar of the Greek New Testament*, 78.

a. Subjective Genitive

Nunn states, "The Genitive case is described as subjective when the noun in the genitive is the name of the subject of the action denoted by the word on which it depends."[94] This means that the noun in the genitive functions as the subject of the noun of action and is considered as the source of the action implied in the noun of action. Wallace writes, "The genitive substantive functions semantically as the *subject* of the verbal idea implicit in the head noun."[95] Thus if the noun in the genitive produces the action implied in the noun of action, then it is a subjective genitive.

Acts 1:4: καὶ συναλιζόμενος παρήγγειλεν αὐτοῖς ἀπὸ Ἱεροσολύμων μὴ χωρίζεσθαι ἀλλὰ περιμένειν <u>τὴν ἐπαγγελίαν</u> <u>τοῦ πατρὸς</u> ἣν ἠκούσατέ μου – "and being assembled together with them he commanded them not to depart from Jerusalem but to wait for the promise <u>of the father</u> which you heard from me."

Romans 8:35: τίς ἡμᾶς χωρίσει ἀπὸ <u>τῆς ἀγάπης</u> <u>τοῦ Χριστοῦ</u> θλῖψις ἢ στενοχωρία ἢ διωγμὸς ἢ λιμὸς ἢ γυμνότης ἢ κίνδυνος ἢ μάχαιρα – "who shall separate us from the love <u>of Christ</u> tribulation or distress or persecution or famine or nakedness or peril or sword?"

2 Corinthians 5:14: ἡ γὰρ ἀγάπη <u>τοῦ Χριστοῦ</u> συνέχει ἡμᾶς κρίναντας τοῦτο ὅτι εἰ εἷς ὑπὲρ πάντων ἀπέθανεν ἄρα οἱ πάντες ἀπέθανον· – "for the love <u>of Christ</u> constrains us having judged this that if one died on behalf of all then all these men died."

b. Objective Genitive

Nunn writes, "The Genitive case is described as objective when the noun in the genitive is the name of the object of the action denoted by the word on which it depends" this means that the noun in the genitive is the object that receives the action or as Wallace states, "The genitive substantive functions semantically as the *direct object* of the verbal idea implicit in the head noun."[96] Dana and Mantey state that in this case, "the noun in the genitive receives the action, being thus related as object to the verbal idea contained in the noun modified."[97]

Matt 12:31: Διὰ τοῦτο λέγω ὑμῖν πᾶσα ἁμαρτία καὶ βλασφημία ἀφεθήσεται τοῖς ἀνθρώποις ἡ δὲ <u>τοῦ πνεύματος</u> <u>βλασφημία</u> οὐκ ἀφεθήσεται τοῖς ἀνθρώποις· – "for this cause I say to you all sin and blasphemy shall be remitted to men but <u>the blasphemy of the Spirit</u> shall not be remitted to men."

John 2:17: Ἐμνήσθησαν δὲ οἱ μαθηταὶ αὐτοῦ ὅτι γεγραμμένον ἐστίν <u>Ὁ ζῆλος</u> <u>τοῦ οἴκου σου</u> κατέφαγεν με – "and his disciples remembered that it has been *and* is written <u>the zeal</u> <u>of your house</u> has consumed me."

Mark 11:22: καὶ ἀποκριθεὶς Ἰησοῦς λέγει αὐτοῖς Ἔχετε πίστιν <u>θεοῦ</u> – "and Jesus answering said to them have faith in <u>God</u>."

---

[94] H. P. V. Nunn, *A Short Syntax of New Testament Greek*, 42.
[95] Wallace, *Greek Beyond the Basics*, 113.
[96] Wallace, *Greek Beyond the Basics*, 116.
[97] Dana and Mantey, *A Manual Grammar of the Greek New Testament*, 79.

4. Genitive of Apposition

The substantive in the genitive case is used to refer to the same thing as the substantive to which it is related but the relation is not one of exact equivalent but rather a general sense. Dana and Mantey say, "In this construction a thing denoted as a representative of a class is more specifically defined by attributing to it in the genitive a particular designation. Here the genitive stands in exact apposition with the noun it modifies."[98]

Thus the word in genitive can be substituted for the substantive it modifies and as such serves as a genitive of "definition" or of "identity" Vaughan and Gideon explain, "It stands in exact apposition with the noun it modifies and describes that noun to the extent of identifying it in a specific way. Thus, the two words – the noun in the genitive and the word which it modifies – denote the same person or thing."[99] Thus it is possible to insert *which is*, *namely*, or *who* is between the head noun and the genitive noun without changing or affecting the meaning of the sentence. Brooks and Winbery caution that "one should carefully note that the word which the genitive is in apposition may or may not be in the genitive case. At this point, the genitive of apposition differs from ordinary apposition where the words involved must be in the same case."[100] Wallace on the other hand classifies the genitive of apposition in two namely:

a. Simple Apposition

This is when both the substantive and its modifier are in the genitive case. Thus if the head noun is in the genitive case (due to grammatical and syntactical requirements of the sentence) and the noun in apposition is also required to be in the genitive case. A distinguishing feature of this case is that in this case, the word 'of' could not be used in translation to show the relationship between the two nouns. One of the words (phrases) showing equality must be used.

Colossians 1:18: καὶ αὐτός ἐστιν ἡ κεφαλὴ τοῦ σώματος <u>τῆς ἐκκλησίας</u>· ὅς ἐστιν ἀρχή πρωτότοκος ἐκ τῶν νεκρῶν ἵνα γένηται ἐν πᾶσιν αὐτὸς πρωτεύων – "and the same is the head of the body, <u>the church</u>: who is the beginning, the first-born from the dead in order that in all things he may have pre-eminence."

Titus 2:13: προσδεχόμενοι τὴν μακαρίαν ἐλπίδα καὶ ἐπιφάνειαν τῆς δόξης τοῦ μεγάλου θεοῦ καὶ σωτῆρος ἡμῶν <u>Ἰησοῦ Χριστου</u> – "looking for the blessed hope and the glorious appearing of the great God even our savior <u>Jesus Christ</u>."

Ephesians 1:2: χάρις ὑμῖν καὶ εἰρήνη ἀπὸ θεοῦ <u>πατρὸς ἡμῶν</u> καὶ κυρίου Ἰησοῦ Χριστοῦ – "grace to you and peace from God <u>our father</u> and from the lord Jesus Christ."

b. Epexigetical Genitive

This is also called "genitive of definition" and in this, the genitive is used to help define a substantive or give to it a specific example of the larger category named

---

[98] Dana and Mantey, *A Manual Grammar of the Greek New Testament*, 79.
[99] Curtis Vaughan and Virtus E Gideon, *A Greek Grammar of the New Testament*, (Nashville Tennessee: Broadman Press, 1979), 32.
[100] Brooks and Winbery, *Syntax of New Testament Greek*, 16.

noun. It also requires the words of equality for proper understanding, but the word 'of' can be used (unlike the case with Simple Apposition).

2 Corinthians 5:5: ὁ δὲ κατεργασάμενος ἡμᾶς εἰς αὐτὸ τοῦτο θεός ὁ καὶ δοὺς ἡμῖν τὸν ἀρραβῶνα <u>τοῦ πνεύματος</u> – "now the one who has fashioned us for this same thing *is* God also he has given to us the earnest <u>of the Spirit</u>."

Romans 4:11: καὶ σημεῖον ἔλαβεν <u>περιτομῆς</u> σφραγῖδα τῆς δικαιοσύνης τῆς πίστεως τῆς ἐν τῇ ἀκροβυστίᾳ εἰς τὸ εἶναι αὐτὸν πατέρα πάντων τῶν πιστευόντων δι' ἀκροβυστίας εἰς τὸ λογισθῆναι καὶ αὐτοῖς τὴν δικαιοσύνην – "and he received the sign <u>of circumcision</u> a seal of the righteousness of the faith of which while in uncircumcision so that he may be father of all those who believe through uncircumcision so that righteousness may be imputed to them."

Hebrews 12:11: πᾶσα δὲ παιδεία πρὸς μὲν τὸ παρὸν οὐ δοκεῖ χαρᾶς εἶναι ἀλλὰ λύπης ὕστερον δὲ καρπὸν εἰρηνικὸν τοῖς δι' αὐτῆς γεγυμνασμένοις ἀποδίδωσιν <u>δικαιοσύνης</u> – "now indeed no chastisement whatsoever for the present seems to be joyous but grievous but at the last it yields the peaceable fruit <u>of righteousness</u> to those who are exercised through it."

John 2:21: ἐκεῖνος δὲ ἔλεγεν περὶ τοῦ ναοῦ <u>τοῦ σώματος αὐτοῦ</u> – "but this he said concerning the temple of <u>his body</u>."

5. Genitive Absolute

The genitive absolute construction is a clause that is formed with the following components. (a) A participle without an article in the genitive case (b) an accompanying substantive (noun or pronoun) in the genitive case. "The genitive absolute is so called because it does not have a grammatical connection with the rest of the sentence. It does, however, sustain a thought connection."[101] This means that the noun or pronoun does not denote the same person or thing denoted by the subject or object of the sentence and is loosed from the construction but represents two actions happening concurrently. It is rendered by the English adverbial clause introduced by '*when*', '*since*', '*although*'. Machen observes, "It should be noted that the genitive absolute is normally used only when the noun or pronoun going with the participle is different from the subject of the finite verb."[102] Thus, the genitive absolute clause has only a loose syntactical connection to the rest of the sentence.

Matthew 9:33: καὶ <u>ἐκβληθέντος τοῦ δαιμονίου</u> ἐλάλησεν ὁ κωφός, καὶ ἐθαύμασαν οἱ ὄχλοι λέγοντες ὅτι Οὐδέποτε ἐφάνη οὕτως ἐν τῷ Ἰσραήλ – "<u>and when the demon had been cast out</u>, the mute spoke and the crowds marvelled saying 'not at any time was seen thus in Israel'."

Matthew 18:25: <u>μὴ ἔχοντος δὲ αὐτοῦ ἀποδοῦναι</u> ἐκέλευσεν αὐτὸν ὁ κύριος αὐτοῦ πραθῆναι καὶ τὴν γυναῖκα αὐτοῦ καὶ τὰ τέκνα καὶ πάντα ὅσα εἶχεν, καὶ ἀποδοθῆναι – "<u>and since he not having to pay</u>, his lord commanded him to be sold and his wife and the children and all as much as he had and payment to be made."

---

[101] Vaughan and Gideon, *A Greek Grammar of the New Testament*, 38.
[102] J. Gresham Machen, *New Testament Greek for Beginners*, (Tennessee: The Trinity Foundation, 2000ed), 125.

Matthew 25:5: χρονίζοντος δὲ τοῦ νυμφίου ἐνύσταξαν πᾶσαι καὶ ἐκάθευδον – "And when the bridegroom delayed, they all slumbered and slept."

6. Genitive of Advantage

"This use of the genitive indicates the person or thing on behalf of which something is done."[103]

Colossians 4:3: προσευχόμενοι ἅμα καὶ περὶ ἡμῶν ἵνα ὁ θεὸς ἀνοίξῃ ἡμῖν θύραν τοῦ λόγου λαλῆσαι τὸ μυστήριον τοῦ Χριστοῦ δι' ὃ καὶ δέδεμαι – "withal praying also for us in order that God may open for us a door for the word to speak the mystery of Christ because of which also I am being bound."

Acts 4:9: εἰ ἡμεῖς σήμερον ἀνακρινόμεθα ἐπὶ εὐεργεσίᾳ ἀνθρώπου ἀσθενοῦς ἐν τίνι οὗτος σέσωσται – "if we this day are being judged concerning a good work for a man who is sick by what he has been made whole."

2 Timothy 1:3: Χάριν ἔχω τῷ θεῷ ᾧ λατρεύω ἀπὸ προγόνων ἐν καθαρᾷ συνειδήσει ὡς ἀδιάλειπτον ἔχω τὴν περὶ σοῦ μνείαν ἐν ταῖς δεήσεσίν μου νυκτὸς καὶ ἡμέρας – "I give thanks to God whom I worship from my fathers in pure conscience how without ceasing I have remembrance of you in my prayers night and day."

Ephesians 6:18-19: διὰ πάσης προσευχῆς καὶ δεήσεως προσευχόμενοι ἐν παντὶ καιρῷ ἐν πνεύματι καὶ εἰς αὐτὸ τοῦτο ἀγρυπνοῦντες ἐν πάσῃ προσκαρτερήσει καὶ δεήσει περὶ πάντων τῶν ἁγίων 19 καὶ ὑπὲρ ἐμοῦ ἵνα μοι δοθείη λόγος ἐν ἀνοίξει τοῦ στόματός μου ἐν παρρησίᾳ γνωρίσαι τὸ μυστήριον τοῦ εὐαγγελίου – "through all prayers and supplication praying in all seasons in the Spirit and watching to this thing with all perseverance and supplication for all the saints and for me in order that word may be given to me in opening of my mouth, in boldness to declare the mystery of the gospel."

7. Genitive of Association

In the Greek, the idea of association is usually expressed by the instrumental employing the preposition su/n but it can also be expressed by the genitive case only when it employs the preposition meta/. In this case, "the genitive substantive indicates the one with whom the noun to which it stands related is associated."[104]

Mark 1:13: καὶ ἦν ἐκεῖ ἐν τῇ ἐρήμῳ ἡμέρας τεσσαράκοντα πειραζόμενος ὑπὸ τοῦ Σατανᾶ καὶ ἦν μετὰ τῶν θηρίων καὶ οἱ ἄγγελοι διηκόνουν αὐτῷ – "and he was there in the desert forty days being tempted by Satan and was with the wild beasts and the angels ministered to him."

Mark 1:20: καὶ εὐθέως ἐκάλεσεν αὐτούς καὶ ἀφέντες τὸν πατέρα αὐτῶν Ζεβεδαῖον ἐν τῷ πλοίῳ μετὰ τῶν μισθωτῶν ἀπῆλθον ὀπίσω αὐτοῦ – "and immediately he called them and leaving their father Zebedee in the boat with the hired servants they came after him."

Mark 1:29: Καὶ εὐθέως ἐκ τῆς συναγωγῆς ἐξελθόντες ἦλθον εἰς τὴν οἰκίαν Σίμωνος καὶ Ἀνδρέου μετὰ Ἰακώβου καὶ Ἰωάννου – "and immediately after they came

---

[103] Brooks and Winbery, *Syntax of New Testament Greek*, 18
[104] Wallace, *Greek Grammar Beyond the Basics*, 128.

out of the synagogue they went to the house of Simon and Andrew <u>with James and John</u>."

Mark 1:36: καὶ κατεδίωξάν αὐτὸν ὁ Σίμων καὶ <u>οἱ μετ' αὐτοῦ</u> – "and Simon and <u>those with him</u> followed after him."

8. Genitive of Attendant Circumstances

A substantive in the genitive may be used with **meta/** to indicate emotional reactions or emotional experience, which accompany the occurrence of the verb.

Mark 3:5: καὶ περιβλεψάμενος αὐτοὺς <u>μετ' ὀργῆς</u> συλλυπούμενος ἐπὶ τῇ πωρώσει τῆς καρδίας αὐτῶν λέγει τῷ ἀνθρώπῳ Ἔκτεινον τὴν χεῖρά σου καὶ ἐξέτεινεν καὶ ἀποκατεστάθη ἡ χεὶρ αὐτοῦ ὑγιὴς ὡς ἡ ἄλλη – "and when he had looked around on them <u>with anger</u> while being grieved by the blindness of their hearts he said to the man, stretch forth your hand and he stretched and his hand was restored whole again as the other."

Mark 4:16: καὶ οὗτοί εἰσιν ὁμοίως οἱ ἐπὶ τὰ πετρώδη σπειρόμενοι οἳ ὅταν ἀκούσωσιν τὸν λόγον εὐθέως <u>μετὰ χαρᾶς</u> λαμβάνουσιν αὐτόν – "and these likewise are they which are sown upon the rocks who when they have heard the word immediately <u>with joy</u> they receive it."

Mark 9:24: καὶ εὐθέως κράξας ὁ πατὴρ τοῦ παιδίου <u>μετὰ δακρύων</u> ἔλεγεν Πιστεύω· κύριε βοήθει μου τῇ ἀπιστίᾳ – "and immediately the father of the child cried out <u>with tears</u> he said I believe lord help my unbelief."

Mark 13:26: καὶ τότε ὄψονται τὸν υἱὸν τοῦ ἀνθρώπου ἐρχόμενον ἐν νεφέλαις <u>μετὰ δυνάμεως πολλῆς καὶ δόξης</u> – "and then they shall see the Son of man coming in the clouds <u>with great power and glory</u>."

9. Genitive of Oaths

When used with a verb of swearing, the genitive with the preposition **kata/** indicates the person by whom one swears.

Matthew 26:63: ὁ δὲ Ἰησοῦς ἐσιώπα καὶ ἀποκριθεὶς ὁ ἀρχιερεὺς εἶπεν αὐτῷ Ἐξορκίζω σε <u>κατὰ τοῦ θεοῦ τοῦ ζῶντος</u> ἵνα ἡμῖν εἴπῃς εἰ σὺ εἶ ὁ Χριστὸς ὁ υἱὸς τοῦ θεοῦ – "but Jesus was holding his peace and the high-priest answering said to him I adjure you <u>by the living God</u> that you say to us if you are the Christ the Son of God."

Hebrews 6:13: Τῷ γὰρ Ἀβραὰμ ἐπαγγειλάμενος ὁ θεός ἐπεὶ <u>κατ' οὐδενὸς εἶχεν μείζονος</u> ὀμόσαι ὤμοσεν <u>καθ' ἑαυτοῦ</u> – "for to Abraham when God made a promise since he could <u>by no one greater</u> swear, he swore <u>by himself</u>."

Hebrews 6:16: ἄνθρωποι μὲν γὰρ <u>κατὰ τοῦ μείζονος</u> ὀμνύουσιν καὶ πάσης αὐτοῖς ἀντιλογίας πέρας εἰς βεβαίωσιν ὁ ὅρκος· – "for men indeed swear <u>by one who is greater</u> and of all the oath for confirmation is to them the end of strife."

10. Genitive of Root idea (Direct Object)

Some verbs in the Greek take a genitive noun as object instead of the accusative thus in such cases, the genitive functions as the direct object in stead of an accusative. Many verbs, such as those of the five physical senses and of emotion, etc., require that their direct object be in the genitive case. These verbs commonly correspond in meaning to some other function of the genitive, e.g., separation, partitive, source, etc. The predominant uses can be grouped into four types of verbs: *sensation, emotion/volition, sharing, ruling*.[105]

Matthew 10:14: καὶ ὃς ἐὰν μὴ δέξηται ὑμᾶς μηδὲ ἀκούσῃ <u>τοὺς λόγους ὑμῶν</u> ἐξερχόμενοι τῆς οἰκίας ἢ τῆς πόλεως ἐκείνης ἐκτινάξατε τὸν κονιορτὸν τῶν ποδῶν ὑμῶν – "and whosoever shall not receive you nor hear <u>your words</u> when coming out of the house or that city shake off the dust of your feet."

Matthew 10:27: ὃ λέγω ὑμῖν ἐν τῇ σκοτίᾳ εἴπατε ἐν τῷ φωτί καὶ ὃ εἰς τὸ οὖς ἀκούετε κηρύξατε <u>ἐπὶ τῶν δωμάτων</u> – "that which I say to you in the darkness say in the light and what in the ear you hear proclaim it upon the housetops."

Luke 17:22: Εἶπεν δὲ πρὸς τοὺς μαθητάς Ἐλεύσονται ἡμέραι ὅτε ἐπιθυμήσετε μίαν <u>τῶν ἡμερῶν τοῦ υἱοῦ τοῦ ἀνθρώπου</u> ἰδεῖν καὶ οὐκ ὄψεσθε – "and he said to the disciples days shall come when you shall desire to see one of <u>the days of the Son of Man</u> and you shall not see."

Mark 10:42: ὁ δὲ Ἰησοῦς προσκαλεσάμενος αὐτοὺς λέγει αὐτοῖς Οἴδατε ὅτι οἱ δοκοῦντες ἄρχειν <u>τῶν ἐθνῶν</u> κατακυριεύουσιν <u>αὐτῶν</u> καὶ οἱ μεγάλοι αὐτῶν κατεξουσιάζουσιν <u>αὐτῶν</u> – "but Jesus having called them said to them you know they which are accounted to rule <u>over the nations</u> exercise dominion <u>over them</u> and the greater of them exercise authority <u>over them</u>."

Hebrews 2:14: ἐπεὶ οὖν τὰ παιδία κεκοινώνηκεν <u>σαρκός καὶ αἵματος</u> καὶ αὐτὸς παραπλησίως μετέσχεν <u>τῶν αὐτῶν</u> ἵνα διὰ τοῦ θανάτου καταργήσῃ τὸν τὸ κράτος ἔχοντα τοῦ θανάτου τοῦτ' ἔστιν τὸν διάβολον – "since then the children are partakers <u>of flesh and blood</u> also he himself likewise took part <u>of them</u> in order that through death the may destroy the one having power of death this one is the devil."

Ablative Case Syntactical Classification

The ablative genitive basically involves the idea of separation as Nunn observes, "In Greek, the Ablative case has always the same form as the Genitive case; ... the Ablative case denotes separation from."[106] The distinction between the genitive and the ablative is not in form but in its use for as Brooks and Winbery note, the ablative

> Indicates such things as point of departure, source, origin. Inasmuch as both the genitive and the ablative employ the same case form, one must first decide whether a word in the second inflected form is genitive or ablative. This can usually be done by asking whether the use of the word reflects kind, description, definition – in which case the word is genitive – or separation – in which case the word is ablative.[107]

---

[105] Wallace, *Greek Grammar Beyond the Basics*, 131.
[106] H. P. V. Nunn, *A Short Syntax of New Testament Greek*, 42.
[107] Brooks and Winbery, *Syntax of New Testament Greek* 21.

The idea of separation presented by the ablative can either be fixed (i.e., in a separate state) or progressing (moving away from, so as to become separated) as Dana and Mantey point out,

> Its basal significance is point of departure. This idea may be elemental in various conceptions. It is involved not only in the literal removal of one object from the vicinity of another; but in any idea which implies departure from antecedent relations, such as derivation, cause, origin and the like. It contemplates an alteration in state from the viewpoint of the original situation, as when we say h(swthri\a th=j a(marti\aj, we are considering salvation from the standpoint of man's original condition of bondage in sin."[108]

The emphasis may be on either the state resulting from the separation or the cause of separation. The uses of the ablative include:

Ablative of Separation

The genitive substantive in this case presents that from which the verb or noun is to be separated. Thus the ablative of separation "presents its simple basal significance, unaffected by any supposed idea."[109] That is this use of the ablative is the basic use of the case and indicates "the point of departure."[110]

Matthew 10:14: καὶ ὃς ἐὰν μὴ δέξηται ὑμᾶς μηδὲ ἀκούσῃ τοὺς λόγους ὑμῶν ἐξερχόμενοι τῆς οἰκίας ἢ τῆς πόλεως ἐκείνης ἐκτινάξατε τὸν κονιορτὸν <u>τῶν ποδῶν ὑμῶν</u> – "and whosoever shall not receive you nor hear your words when coming out of the house or that city shake off the dust <u>of your feet</u>."

Ephesians 2:12: ὅτι ἦτε ἐν τῷ καιρῷ ἐκείνῳ χωρὶς Χριστοῦ ἀπηλλοτριωμένοι <u>τῆς πολιτείας τοῦ Ἰσραὴλ</u> καὶ ξένοι <u>τῶν διαθηκῶν τῆς ἐπαγγελίας</u> ἐλπίδα μὴ ἔχοντες καὶ ἄθεοι ἐν τῷ κόσμῳ – "for in that season you were without Christ having been alienated <u>from the commonwealth of Israel</u> and strangers <u>from the covenant of promise</u> having no hope and without God in the world."

John 17:15: οὐκ ἐρωτῶ ἵνα ἄρῃς αὐτοὺς <u>ἐκ τοῦ κόσμου</u> ἀλλ' ἵνα τηρήσῃς αὐτοὺς <u>ἐκ τοῦ πονηροῦ</u> – "I do not ask that you take them <u>out of the world</u> but that you keep them <u>from the evil one</u>."

1 John 2:19: <u>ἐξ ἡμῶν</u> ἐξῆλθον, ἀλλ' οὐκ ἦσαν ἐξ ἡμῶν· εἰ γὰρ ἦσαν ἐξ ἡμῶν, μεμενήκεισαν ἂν μεθ' ἡμῶν· ἀλλ' ἵνα φανερωθῶσιν ὅτι οὐκ εἰσὶ πάντες ἐξ ἡμῶν. – "they went out <u>from us</u>, but they were not of us for if they were of us they would have no doubt remained with us but in order that they may be manifest that they were not all of us."

---

[108] Dana and Mantey, *A Manual of the Greek New Testament*, 81.
[109] ibid.
[110] Wallace, *Greek Grammar Beyond the Basics*, 107.

Ablative of Source

"If the word in the ablative is the source of the substantive it modifies, it is an ablative of source."[111] This indicates that the word in the ablative case indicates "the source from which the head noun is derived or depends."[112] Dana and Mantey note that

> The idea of separation may be accompanied by the implication that the original situation contributed in some way to the present character or state. That which is named in the noun modified by the ablative owes its existence in some way to that which is denoted in the ablative.[113]

The source from which something is derived expresses an idea of separation and in this case, the word 'of' could instead be translated "'*out of*', '*derived from*', '*dependent on*' or *sourced in*."[114] This category is to be distinguished from the subjective genitive in that "the subjective genitive is always used with a noun of action"[115] which is not the case for the ablative of source.

Acts 26:12: Ἐν οἷς καὶ πορευόμενος εἰς τὴν Δαμασκὸν μετ' ἐξουσίας καὶ ἐπιτροπῆς τῆς <u>παρὰ τῶν ἀρχιερέων</u> – "and in which while I was going to Damascus with authority and commission <u>from the high-priests</u>."

Mark 12:2: καὶ ἀπέστειλεν πρὸς τοὺς γεωργοὺς τῷ καιρῷ δοῦλον ἵνα <u>παρὰ τῶν γεωργῶν</u> λάβῃ ἀπὸ τοῦ καρποῦ τοῦ ἀμπελῶνος· – "and he sent to the husbandmen a servant in the season in order that he may receive <u>from the husbandmen</u> of the fruit of the vineyard."

John 1:3: πάντα δι' αὐτοῦ ἐγένετο καὶ <u>χωρὶς αὐτοῦ</u> ἐγένετο οὐδὲ ἕν ὃ γέγονεν – "through him all things were and <u>without him</u> was not made one thing that was made."

Romans 9:12: μήπω γὰρ γεννηθέντων μηδὲ πραξάντων τι ἀγαθὸν ἢ κακόν, ἵνα ἡ κατ' ἐκλογὴν τοῦ θεοῦ πρόθεσις μένῃ οὐκ ἐξ ἔργων ἀλλ' <u>ἐκ τοῦ καλοῦντος</u> – "for not yet being born neither having done what is good or evil in order that the purpose according to the election of God may remain not out of works but <u>of the one who calls</u>."

Ablative of Agency

"The word in the ablative indicates the personal agent who performs the action expressed by the passive voice or by a verbal adjective."[116] Wallace observes that this class characteristically takes verbal adjectives ending in **toj** and that in identifying it, one should "look for combinations such as **a)gaphto\j** + genitive, **didakto\j** + genitive, **e)klekto\j** + genitive."[117]

---

[111] Brooks and Winbery, *Syntax of the New Testament*, 23.
[112] Wallace, *Greek Grammar Beyond the Basics*, 109.
[113] Dana and Mantey, *A Manual Grammar of the Greek New Testament*, 82.
[114] Wallace, *Greek Grammar Beyond the Basics*, 109.
[115] Brooks and Winbery, *Syntax of the New Testament*, 23.
[116] ibid., 24.
[117] Wallace, *Greek Grammar Beyond the Basics*, 126.

2 Peter 3:2: μνησθῆναι τῶν προειρημένων ῥημάτων <u>ὑπὸ τῶν ἁγίων προφητῶν</u> καὶ τῆς τῶν ἀποστόλων ἡμῶν ἐντολῆς τοῦ κυρίου καὶ σωτῆρος – "to have in remembrance the words which were spoken before <u>by the holy prophets</u> and of the commandment of us the apostles of our lord and savior."

Luke 2:26: καὶ ἦν αὐτῷ κεχρηματισμένον <u>ὑπὸ τοῦ πνεύματος τοῦ ἁγίου</u> μὴ ἰδεῖν θάνατον πρὶν ἢ ἴδῃ τὸν Χριστὸν κυρίου – "and it had been revealed to him <u>by the Holy Spirit</u> that he will not see death before he shall have seen the Christ of the lord."

Romans 1:7: πᾶσιν τοῖς οὖσιν ἐν Ῥώμῃ <u>ἀγαπητοῖς θεοῦ</u> κλητοῖς ἁγίοις χάρις ὑμῖν καὶ εἰρήνη ἀπὸ θεοῦ πατρὸς ἡμῶν καὶ κυρίου Ἰησοῦ Χριστοῦ – "to all those who are in Rome beloved of God called to be saints grace to you and peace from God our father and the lord Jesus Christ."

1 Corinthians 2:13: ἃ καὶ λαλοῦμεν οὐκ ἐν διδακτοῖς ἀνθρωπίνης σοφίας λόγοις ἀλλ' ἐν διδακτοῖς <u>πνεύματος ἁγίου</u>, πνευματικοῖς πνευματικὰ συγκρίνοντες – "which things also we are speaking not in words taught by man's wisdom but which taught <u>by the Holy Ghost</u> comparing spiritual with spiritual."

Ablative of Means

This is used to "indicate the impersonal means used in producing the action of a verb or verbal adjective. The verb may be in any voice."[118] In this case the substantive in genitive expresses the means by which action of verb is accomplished. Dana and Mantey observe that "the expression of means is accompanied by an implication of origin or source."[119]

1 Corinthians 2:13: ἃ καὶ λαλοῦμεν οὐκ ἐν διδακτοῖς <u>ἀνθρωπίνης σοφίας</u> λόγοις ἀλλ' ἐν διδακτοῖς πνεύματος ἁγίου, πνευματικοῖς πνευματικὰ συγκρίνοντες – "which things also we are speaking not in words taught <u>by man's wisdom</u> but which taught by the Holy Ghost comparing spiritual with spiritual."

John 17:20: Οὐ περὶ τούτων δὲ ἐρωτῶ μόνον ἀλλὰ καὶ περὶ τῶν πιστευσόντων <u>διὰ τοῦ λόγου αὐτῶν</u> εἰς ἐμέ – "and I ask not concerning these alone but also concerning those who believe on me <u>through their word</u>."

Acts 8:18: θεασάμενος δὲ ὁ Σίμων ὅτι <u>διὰ τῆς ἐπιθέσεως τῶν χειρῶν τῶν ἀποστόλων</u> δίδοται τὸ πνεῦμα τὸ Ἅγιον, προσήνεγκεν αὐτοῖς χρήματα – "but when Simon saw that <u>through the laying on of hands by the apostles</u>, the Holy Ghost was given, he offered them money."

Acts 8:20: Πέτρος δὲ εἶπεν πρὸς αὐτόν Τὸ ἀργύριόν σου σὺν σοὶ εἴη εἰς ἀπώλειαν ὅτι τὴν δωρεὰν τοῦ θεοῦ ἐνόμισας <u>διὰ χρημάτων</u> κτᾶσθαι – "and Peter said to him your silver may it perish with you because you thought to obtain the gift of God <u>through money</u>."

Ablative of Comparison

"If a word in the ablative is the basis on which a comparison is made, it is an ablative of comparison. A test for this use is the ability to use the word "than" in the

---

[118] Brooks and Winbery, *Syntax of the New Testament*, 27.
[119] Dana and Mantey, *A Manual Grammar of the Greek New Testament*, 82.

translation of the word in the ablative."[120] The genitive substantive, Wallace states when comes after a comparative adjective (e.g., **plei/wn, mei/zwn**), "the comparative adjective will not be an attributive adjective. That is it will not be found in the construction article-adjective-noun."[121] The substantive in the genitive, then, is the standard (the known item[122]) against which the comparison is made.

Matt 6:25: διὰ τοῦτο λέγω ὑμῖν, μὴ μεριμνᾶτε τῇ ψυχῇ ὑμῶν τί φάγητε καὶ τί πίητε, μηδὲ τῷ σώματι ὑμῶν τί ἐνδύσησθε. οὐχὶ ἡ ψυχὴ <u>πλεῖόν ἐστι τῆς τροφῆς</u>, καὶ τὸ σῶμα <u>τοῦ ἐνδύματος</u>; – "for this cause I say to you, do not take thought for your soul what you shall eat and what you shall drink, neither for your body what you shall be clothed. Is not the soul <u>more than food</u> and the body <u>than clothing</u>?"

Mark 12:28: Καὶ προσελθὼν εἷς τῶν γραμματέων ἀκούσας αὐτῶν συζητούντων εἰδὼς ὅτι καλῶς αὐτοῖς ἀπεκρίθη ἐπηρώτησεν αὐτόν Ποία ἐστὶν πρώτη <u>πασῶν</u> ἐντολή – "and one of the scribes when he had drawn near heard them and while enquiring seeing that he answered well asked him which is the first <u>of all</u> commandment."

John 13:16: ἀμὴν ἀμὴν λέγω ὑμῖν οὐκ ἔστιν δοῦλος <u>μείζων τοῦ κυρίου</u> αὐτοῦ οὐδὲ ἀπόστολος <u>μείζων τοῦ πέμψαντος</u> αὐτόν – "amen amen I say to you <u>a slave is not greater than his lord</u> neither is an apostle <u>greater than the one who sends him</u>."

Acts 17:11: οὗτοι δὲ ἦσαν εὐγενέστεροι <u>τῶν</u> ἐν Θεσσαλονίκῃ οἵτινες ἐδέξαντο τὸν λόγον μετὰ πάσης προθυμίας τὸ καθ' ἡμέραν ἀνακρίνοντες τὰς γραφὰς εἰ ἔχοι ταῦτα οὕτως – "but these were more noble <u>than the ones</u> in Thessalonica in that they received the word with all readiness of mind searching the scriptures daily if these things were so."

Ablative of Cause

"The ablative is sometimes used to indicate the reason for an action."[123]

Luke 1:20: καὶ ἰδού, ἔσῃ σιωπῶν καὶ μὴ δυνάμενος λαλῆσαι ἄχρι ἧς ἡμέρας γένηται ταῦτα <u>ἀνθ' ὧν</u> οὐκ ἐπίστευσας τοῖς λόγοις μου οἵτινες πληρωθήσονται εἰς τὸν καιρὸν αὐτῶν – "and behold you shall be dumb and not being able to speak until the day these things come to pass <u>because</u> you did not believe my words which shall be fulfilled in their season."

Luke 19:44: καὶ ἐδαφιοῦσίν σε καὶ τὰ τέκνα σου ἐν σοὶ καὶ οὐκ ἀφήσουσιν ἐν σοὶ λίθον ἐπὶ λίθῳ· <u>ἀνθ' ὧν</u> οὐκ ἔγνως τὸν καιρὸν τῆς ἐπισκοπῆς σου – "and they shall lay you and your children with you and they shall not leave in you a stone upon a stone <u>because</u> you knew not the season of your visitation."

John 4:6: ἦν δὲ ἐκεῖ πηγὴ τοῦ Ἰακώβ ὁ οὖν Ἰησοῦς κεκοπιακὼς <u>ἐκ τῆς ὁδοιπορίας</u> ἐκαθέζετο οὕτως ἐπὶ τῇ πηγῇ· ὥρα ἦν ὡσεὶ ἕκτη – "and there was there a well of Jacob Jesus therefore being wearied <u>beacause of his journey</u> sat upon the well the hour was about the sixth."

---

[120] Brooks and Winbery, *Syntax of the New Testament*, 27.
[121] Wallace, *Greek Grammar Beyond the Basics*, 111.
[122] Wallace, *Greek Grammar Beyond the Basics*, 111.
[123] Brooks and Winbery, *Syntax of the New Testament*, 28.

Ablative of Rank

"This rare use of the ablative expresses the idea of separation in terms of rank, order, or precedence."[124]

Ephesians 1:21: <u>ὑπεράνω πάσης ἀρχῆς καὶ ἐξουσίας καὶ δυνάμεως καὶ κυριότητος καὶ παντὸς ὀνόματος</u> ὀνομαζομένου οὐ μόνον ἐν τῷ αἰῶνι τούτῳ ἀλλὰ καὶ ἐν τῷ μέλλοντι· – "<u>far above all rulers and authority and power and lordship and every name</u> being named not only in this age but in that which is to come."

Ephesians 4:6: εἷς θεὸς καὶ πατὴρ πάντων ὁ <u>ἐπὶ πάντων</u> καὶ διὰ πάντων καὶ ἐν πᾶσιν ὑμῖν – "one God and father of all who is <u>above all</u> and through all and in you all."

James 5:12: <u>Πρὸ πάντων</u> δέ ἀδελφοί μου μὴ ὀμνύετε μήτε τὸν οὐρανὸν μήτε τὴν γῆν μήτε ἄλλον τινὰ ὅρκον· ἤτω δὲ ὑμῶν τὸ Ναὶ ναὶ καὶ τὸ Οὒ οὔ ἵνα μὴ εἰς ὑπόκρισιν πέσητε – "and <u>above all</u> my brethren do not swear neither by heaven neither earth neither any other oath but let your yea be yea and your nay be nay lest you fall into condemnation."

1 Peter 4:8: <u>πρὸ πάντων</u> δὲ τὴν εἰς ἑαυτοὺς ἀγάπην ἐκτενῆ ἔχοντες ὅτι ἀγάπη καλύψει πλῆθος ἁμαρτιῶν – "and <u>above all</u> have fervent charity among yourselves because charity will hide a multitude of sins."

Colossians 1:17: καὶ αὐτός ἐστιν <u>πρὸ πάντων</u> καὶ τὰ πάντα ἐν αὐτῷ συνέστηκεν – "but he is <u>before all</u> and all things in him consist."

Ablative of Opposition

The ablative employs the preposition κατὰ or ἀπέναντι to show separation due to hostility or opposition.

Matthew 10:35: ἦλθον γὰρ διχάσαι ἄνθρωπον <u>κατὰ τοῦ πατρὸς αὐτοῦ</u> καὶ θυγατέρα <u>κατὰ τῆς μητρὸς αὐτῆς</u> καὶ νύμφην <u>κατὰ τῆς πενθερᾶς αὐτῆς</u> – "for I came to set a man at variance <u>against his father</u> and a daughter <u>against her mother</u> and daughter in law <u>against her mother in law</u>."

Matthew 5:11: Μακάριοί ἐστε ὅταν ὀνειδίσωσιν ὑμᾶς καὶ διώξωσι, καὶ εἴπωσιν πᾶν πονηρὸν ῥῆμα <u>καθ' ὑμῶν</u> ψευδόμενοι, ἕνεκεν ἐμοῦ· – "blessed are you when men reproach you and persecute and say all evil words <u>against you</u> falsely for my sake."

Matthew 12:14: οἱ δὲ Φαρισαῖοι συμβούλιον ἔλαβον <u>κατ' αὐτοῦ</u> ἐξελθόντες ὅπως αὐτὸν ἀπολέσωσιν – "and the pharisees going out took council <u>against him</u> how they may destroy him."

Ablative of Purpose

"On rare occasions the ablative may be used to express purpose. Such purpose is always expressed in terms of removing something, and this use could be included in the ablative of separation."[125]

---

[124] ibid., 29.
[125] Brooks and Winbery, *Syntax of the New Testament*, 30.

Matthew 5:11: Μακάριοί ἐστε ὅταν ὀνειδίσωσιν ὑμᾶς καὶ διώξωσι, καὶ εἴπωσιν πᾶν πονηρὸν ῥῆμα καθ᾽ ὑμῶν ψευδόμενοι, <u>ἕνεκεν ἐμοῦ</u>· – "blessed are you when men reproach you and persecute and say all evil words against you falsely <u>for my sake</u>."

Matthew 10:18: καὶ ἐπὶ ἡγεμόνας δὲ καὶ βασιλεῖς ἀχθήσεσθε <u>ἕνεκεν ἐμοῦ</u> εἰς μαρτύριον αὐτοῖς καὶ τοῖς ἔθνεσιν – "and before governors and kings you shall be brought <u>for my name's sake</u> for a witness to them and to the gentiles."

Mark 1:44: καὶ λέγει αὐτῷ Ὅρα μηδενὶ μηδὲν εἴπῃς ἀλλ᾽ ὕπαγε σεαυτὸν δεῖξον τῷ ἱερεῖ καὶ προσένεγκε <u>περὶ τοῦ καθαρισμοῦ σου</u> ἃ προσέταξεν Μωσῆς, εἰς μαρτύριον αὐτοῖς – "and he said to him see to no one you may say nothing but depart shew yourself to the priest and offer <u>for your cleansing</u> that which Moses commanded for a testimony to them."

Ablative of Exchange

"The ablative with the preposition a)nti/ may express the ideas of exchange, substitution, or succession. Such terms as "for," "in place of," in stead of," "in behalf of," and "in exchange for" may be used in the translation."[126]

Matthew 20:28: ὥσπερ ὁ υἱὸς τοῦ ἀνθρώπου οὐκ ἦλθεν διακονηθῆναι ἀλλὰ διακονῆσαι καὶ δοῦναι τὴν ψυχὴν αὐτοῦ λύτρον <u>ἀντὶ πολλῶν</u> – "even as the son of man came not to be ministered to but to minister and to give his soul a ransom <u>for many</u>."

Luke 11:11: τίνα δὲ ὑμῶν τὸν πατέρα αἰτήσει ὁ υἱὸς ἄρτον, μὴ λίθον ἐπιδώσει αὐτῷ εἰ καὶ ἰχθύν μὴ <u>ἀντὶ ἰχθύος</u> ὄφιν ἐπιδώσει αὐτῷ – "and which one of you that is a father if the son ask bread you shall give to him a stone and if a fish <u>instead of a fish</u> shall give to him a serpent."

Romans 12:17: μηδενὶ κακὸν <u>ἀντὶ κακοῦ</u> ἀποδιδόντες προνοούμενοι καλὰ ἐνώπιον πάντων ἀνθρώπων· – "to no one recompense evil <u>in exchange for evil</u> provide good things before all men."

Partitive Ablative

If the word in the ablative indicates the whole of which the word it modifies is a part, it is a partitive ablative. ... The fact that the part is derived from and in some sense separated from the whole and the fact that the use is found with the prepositions a)po/ and e)k, which are always used with the ablative, make it probable that it should be treated as ablative.[127]

The word 'of' can be substituted the words '*which is a part of*.

Luke 18:11: ὁ Φαρισαῖος σταθεὶς πρὸς ἑαυτὸν ταῦτα προσηύχετο Ὁ θεός εὐχαριστῶ σοι ὅτι οὐκ εἰμὶ ὥσπερ οἱ λοιποὶ <u>τῶν ἀνθρώπων</u> ἅρπαγες ἄδικοι μοιχοί ἢ καὶ ὡς οὗτος ὁ τελώνης· – "the pharisee stood by himself and prayed these things God I give thanks to you because I am not like <u>the remaining men</u> extortioners, unjust, adulterers or even as this tax collector."

---

[126] Brooks and Winbery, *Syntax of the New Testament*, 30.
[127] Brooks and Winbery, *Syntax of the New Testament*, 31.

John 7:48: μή τις ἐκ τῶν ἀρχόντων ἐπίστευσεν εἰς αὐτὸν ἢ ἐκ τῶν Φαρισαίων – "has any out of the rulers believed on him or out of the Pharisees?"

Matthew 6:27: τίς δὲ ἐξ ὑμῶν μεριμνῶν δύναται προσθεῖναι ἐπὶ τὴν ἡλικίαν αὐτοῦ πῆχυν ἕνα; – "and which one out of you taking thought is able to add upon his stature one cubit?"

Matthew 10:29: οὐχὶ δύο στρουθία ἀσσαρίου πωλεῖται καὶ ἓν ἐξ αὐτῶν οὐ πεσεῖται ἐπὶ τὴν γῆν ἄνευ τοῦ πατρὸς ὑμῶν – "are not two sparrows sold for a farthing yet not one out of them shall fall upon the ground without your father."

Matthew 5:18: ἀμὴν γὰρ λέγω ὑμῖν, ἕως ἂν παρέλθῃ ὁ οὐρανὸς καὶ ἡ γῆ, ἰῶτα ἓν, ἢ μία κεραία οὐ μὴ παρέλθῃ ἀπὸ τοῦ νόμου, ἕως ἂν πάντα γένηται. – "for amen I say to you, indeed until heaven and earth pass away one jot or one tittle shall never pass away from out of the law indeed until all be fulfilled."

Mark 6:43: καὶ ἦραν κλασμάτων δώδεκα κοφίνους πληρεις, καὶ ἀπὸ τῶν ἰχθύων – "and there took up twelve baskets full of fragments and of the fish."

DATIVE CASE SYNTACTICAL CLASSIFICATION

The Dative case denotes that to or for which anything is or is done. Wenham observes that "the dative is used to express the **indirect object**, the person *to* or *for* whom something is done. ... The dative can also be used to indicate a place – the so-called **locative** use. ... It can also be used for the instrument by which something is done."[128] Dana and Mantey note that "The dative, locative, and instrumental cases are all represented by the same inflectional form, but the distinction in function is very clear – much more so than the distinction between the ablative and genitive."[129] Hewett observes that

> In analyzing the uses of the third inflectional form one should bear in mind this form may convey any one of three distinct notions: (1) personal interest (the basic idea of the dative case); (2) location (in an eight case system the idea of the locative case); or (3) means (in an eight case system the basic notion of the instrumental case).[130]

The Dative as the case of personal interest, points out the person to or for whom something is done indicating the one who is concerned about or affected by the action of the verb. Such personal interest Brooks and Winbery observe that "involves either advantage or disadvantage."[131] The dative case "is primarily a case of personal relations, and it is with this in view that we must interpret it when applied to things. ... The idea o interest as applied to things become *reference*."[132] The dative has the following uses:

---

[128] Wenham, *Elements of New Testament Greek*, 45-46.
[129] Dana and Mantey, *A Manual Grammar of the Greek New Testament*, 83.
[130] Hewett, *New Testament Greek*, 201.
[131] Brooks and Winbery, *Syntax of New Testament Greek*, 31.
[132] Dana and Mantey, *A Manual Grammar of the Greek New Testament*, 83.

a. Dative of Indirect Object

This is one of the most basic and most common uses of the dative case. Nunn states that "the dative of Indirect object is used after verbs of giving showing etc."[133] It indicates an indirect object for transitive verbs the indirect object being "the person in whose interest the action is performed."[134] Wallace notes that

> The dative substantive is that to or for which the action of a verb is performed. The indirect object *will only occur with a transitive verb*. When the transitive verb is in the *active* voice, the indirect object receives the direct object ('the boy hit the ball to *me*'); when the verb is in the *passive* voice, the indirect object receives the subject of the verb ('the ball was hit to *me*'). ... The keys are (1) the verb must be transitive, and (2) if the dative can be translated with *to* or *for* it is most likely indirect object.[135]

Mark 14:11: οἱ δὲ ἀκούσαντες ἐχάρησαν καὶ ἐπηγγείλαντο αὐτῷ ἀργύριον δοῦναι καὶ ἐζήτει πῶς εὐκαίρως αὐτὸν παραδῶ – "and when they had heard rejoiced and promised to give <u>to him</u> silver and he sought how in season he may betray him."

Matthew 6:25: διὰ τοῦτο λέγω ὑμῖν, μὴ μεριμνᾶτε τῇ ψυχῇ ὑμῶν τί φάγητε καὶ τί πίητε, μηδὲ τῷ σώματι ὑμῶν τί ἐνδύσησθε. οὐχὶ ἡ ψυχὴ πλεῖόν ἐστι τῆς τροφῆς, καὶ τὸ σῶμα τοῦ ἐνδύματος; – "for this cause I say <u>to you</u>, take no thought <u>for your soul</u> what you shall eat and what you shall drink neither <u>for your body</u> what you shall be clothed. Is not the soul greater than food, and the body than raiment?"

Romans 14:4: σὺ τίς εἶ ὁ κρίνων ἀλλότριον οἰκέτην; τῷ ἰδίῳ κυρίῳ στήκει ἢ πίπτει· σταθήσεται δέ, δυνατὸς γάρ ἐστιν ὁ Θεὸς στῆσαι αὐτόν – "who are you the one judging another man's household servant? <u>To his own lord</u> he stands or falls, and he shall be established for God is able to make him stand."

John 4:10: ἀπεκρίθη Ἰησοῦς καὶ εἶπεν αὐτῇ Εἰ ᾔδεις τὴν δωρεὰν τοῦ θεοῦ καὶ τίς ἐστιν ὁ λέγων σοι, Δός μοι πιεῖν, σὺ ἂν ᾔτησας αὐτὸν καὶ ἔδωκεν ἄν σοι ὕδωρ ζῶν – "Jesus answered and said <u>to her</u> if you knew the gift of God and who it is that is saying <u>to you</u>, give <u>to me</u> to drink, indeed you would have asked him and indeed he would have given <u>to you</u> living water."

b. Dative of Advantage and Disadvantage

Grammarians consider this case as forming a specialized use of the dative of indirect object emphasizing the idea of personal interest by denoting the personal interest in the verbal action either positively (advantage) or negatively (disadvantage).[136] That is it can convey the idea of interest in terms of the person to whose advantage or disadvantage the action of the verb takes place. Brooks and Winbery write,

---

[133] Nunn, *A Short syntax of New Testament Greek*, 46.
[134] Brooks and Winbery, *Syntax of New Testament Greek*, 32.
[135] Wallace, *Greek Grammar Beyond the Basics*, 140-141
[136] Brooks and Winbery observe that "All datives of advantage or disadvantage are in fact indirect objects, and all indirect objects to a greater or lesser degree express advantage or disadvantage. ... The dative of indirect object emphasizes *to* whom something is done, the dative of advantage *for* whom, the dative of disadvantage *against* whom. [Brooks and Winbery, *Syntax of New Testament Greek*, 33.]

The dative of advantage indicates the person for whose benefit something is done. The word "for" will ordinarily be used in the translation. The dative of disadvantage indicates the person who will be adversely affected by the result of the action. The word "against" will often be used in the translation.[137]

I. **Dative of Advantage** - Indicates the meaning "*for the benefit of*" or "*in the interest of*",

2 Corinthians 5:13: εἴτε γὰρ ἐξέστημεν θεῷ· εἴτε σωφρονοῦμεν ὑμῖν – "for whether we be beside ourselves it is for God: whether we are sober minded it is for you."

Luke 21:13: ἀποβήσεται δὲ ὑμῖν εἰς μαρτύριον – "and it will turn out for you for a witness."

Acts 13:26: Ἄνδρες ἀδελφοί υἱοὶ γένους Ἀβραὰμ καὶ οἱ ἐν ὑμῖν φοβούμενοι τὸν θεόν ὑμῖν ὁ λόγος τῆς σωτηρίας ταύτης ἀπεστάλη – "men, brothers, sons of the offspring of Abraham and those among you who fear God for you the word of this salvation is sent."

II. **Dative of Disadvantage** - Can be translated "*to the detriment of*" or "*against*".

Matthew 23:31: ὥστε μαρτυρεῖτε ἑαυτοῖς ὅτι υἱοί ἐστε τῶν φονευσάντων τοὺς προφήτας – "so that you are testifying against yourselves you are sons of the ones who killed the prophets."

Mark 6:11: καὶ ὅσοι ἂν μὴ δέξωνταί ὑμᾶς μηδὲ ἀκούσωσιν ὑμῶν ἐκπορευόμενοι ἐκεῖθεν ἐκτινάξατε τὸν χοῦν τὸν ὑποκάτω τῶν ποδῶν ὑμῶν εἰς μαρτύριον αὐτοῖς ἀμὴν λέγω ὑμῖν, ἀνεκτότερον ἔσται Σοδόμοις ἢ Γομόρροις ἐν ἡμέρᾳ κρίσεως, ἢ τῇ πόλει ἐκείνῃ – "and to whosoever shall not receive you neither hear your words while going out thence shake the dust under your feet for a witness against them amen I say to you it shall be more tolerable for Sodom or Gomorrah in the day of judgment that for that city."

Romans 2:5: κατὰ δὲ τὴν σκληρότητά σου καὶ ἀμετανόητον καρδίαν θησαυρίζεις σεαυτῷ ὀργὴν ἐν ἡμέρᾳ ὀργῆς καὶ ἀποκαλύψεως δικαιοκρισίας τοῦ θεοῦ – "and according to hardness and impenitence of your heart you are treasuring up for yourself wrath against the day of wrath and revelation of righteous judgement of God."

c. Dative of Possession

This use of the dative is for the purpose of indicating the person to whom a thing belongs. "This is an idiom for which we have no exact equivalent in English. It is personal interest particularized to the point of ownership. There is in it manifest kinship

---

[137] ibid.

with the dative of indirect object."[138] Hewett adds "With the linking verbs ei)mi/, gi/nomai, and u(pa/rxw Greek will express personal interest that is, in effect, possession. ... By the use of the Dative the Greek's emphasis falls on the possessor."[139]

John 13:35: ἐν τούτῳ γνώσονται πάντες ὅτι <u>ἐμοὶ</u> μαθηταί ἐστε ἐὰν ἀγάπην ἔχητε ἐν ἀλλήλοις – "by this all men shall know that you are <u>my</u> disciples if you have love for one another."

Luke 1:7: καὶ οὐκ ἦν <u>αὐτοῖς</u> τέκνον καθότι ἡ Ἐλισάβετ ἦν στεῖρα καὶ ἀμφότεροι προβεβηκότες ἐν ταῖς ἡμέραις αὐτῶν ἦσαν – "and <u>they</u> did not have a child because Elizabeth was barren and both of them were well stricken in their days."

Mark 2:18: Καὶ ἦσαν οἱ μαθηταὶ Ἰωάννου καὶ οἱ τῶν Φαρισαίων νηστεύοντες καὶ ἔρχονται καὶ λέγουσιν αὐτῷ Διατί οἱ μαθηταὶ Ἰωάννου καὶ οἱ τῶν Φαρισαίων νηστεύουσιν οἱ δὲ <u>σοὶ</u> μαθηταὶ οὐ νηστεύουσιν – "and the disciples of John and those of the pharisees were fasting and they came and said to him why do the disciples of John and those of the pharisees fast but <u>your</u> disciples don not fast?"

Luke 4:16: Καὶ ἦλθεν εἰς τὴν Ναζαρέτ οὗ ἦν τεθραμμένος καὶ εἰσῆλθεν κατὰ τὸ εἰωθὸς <u>αὐτῷ</u> ἐν τῇ ἡμέρᾳ τῶν σαββάτων εἰς τὴν συναγωγήν καὶ ἀνέστη ἀναγνῶναι – "and he came into Nazareth where he was brought up and he entered according to <u>his</u> custom on the Sabbath day into a synagogue and he stood to read."

d. Dative of Reference or Dative of Respect

This use of the dative defines and expresses interest in a way that is similar to that of the indirect object but is more remote in that it expresses the sphere or limits in which the noun, adjective or verb are to be understood. "This use of the dative occurs mostly with things, though it may also be used with persons."[140] It reduces the force of interest to mere reference and "two things are to be observed about this use of the dative: (1) The idea of advantage or disadvantage is not prominent in it. (2) Though it may occasionally relate to persons, this use of the dative has to do mostly with things."[141] It is typically used to qualify a statement that would otherwise typically not be true. "The dative substantive is that in which something is presented as true. An author will use this dative to qualify a statement that would otherwise typically not be true."[142] Thus it acts to give a frame of reference or context to the statement with the statement often making no sense if the dative word is removed.

Romans 6:2: μὴ γένοιτο οἵτινες ἀπεθάνομεν <u>τῇ ἁμαρτίᾳ</u> πῶς ἔτι ζήσομεν ἐν αὐτῇ – "God forbid how shall we who are dead <u>to sin</u> live yet in it."

Romans 6:11: οὕτως καὶ ὑμεῖς λογίζεσθε ἑαυτοὺς νεκροὺς μὲν εἶναι <u>τῇ ἁμαρτίᾳ</u> ζῶντας δὲ <u>τῷ θεῷ</u> ἐν Χριστῷ Ἰησοῦ τῷ Κυρίῳ ἡμῶν – "likewise also reckon you yourselves dead indeed <u>to sin</u> but living <u>to God</u> in Christ Jesus our Lord."

---

[138] Dana and Mantey, *A Manual Grammar of the Greek New Testament*, 85.
[139] Hewett, *New Testament Greek*, 201
[140] Dana and Mantey, *A Manual Grammar of the Greek New Testament*, 85.
[141] Vaughan and Gideon, *A Greek grammar of the New Testament*, 50
[142] Wallace, *Greek Grammar Beyond the Basics*, 144-5

Matthew 5:3: Μακάριοι οἱ πτωχοὶ <u>τῷ πνεύματι</u>, ὅτι αὐτῶν ἐστιν ἡ βασιλεία τῶν οὐρανῶν. – "blessed are the poor <u>in spirit</u> for of theirs is the kingdom of heaven."

Matthew 5:8: Μακάριοι οἱ καθαροὶ <u>τῇ καρδίᾳ</u>, ὅτι αὐτοὶ τὸν Θεὸν ὄψονται. – "blessed are the pure <u>in heart</u> for they shall see God."

e. Dative of Root Idea or Dative of Direct Object

Certain verbs require that their direct object be in the dative case instead of the accusative, which is normally the case for direct objects. In such cases, "a dative which functions as the direct object of a verb is a dative of direct object."[143] These are verbs that usually emphasize a personal relationship "and can usually be translated with *to* or *in*."[144]

Hebrews 1:6: ὅταν δὲ πάλιν εἰσαγάγῃ τὸν πρωτότοκον εἰς τὴν οἰκουμένην λέγει Καὶ προσκυνησάτωσαν <u>αὐτῷ</u> πάντες ἄγγελοι θεοῦ – "and again when brings in the first-born to the inhabited world he says and let all the angels of God worship <u>him</u>."

Matthew 8:27: οἱ δὲ ἄνθρωποι ἐθαύμασαν λέγοντες Ποταπός ἐστιν οὗτος ὅτι καὶ οἱ ἄνεμοι καὶ ἡ θάλασσα ὑπακούουσιν <u>αὐτῷ</u> – " and the marveled saying what manner is this that the wind and the sea obey <u>him</u>?"

John 21:22: λέγει αὐτῷ ὁ Ἰησοῦς Ἐὰν αὐτὸν θέλω μένειν ἕως ἔρχομαι τί πρὸς σέ σύ ἀκολούθει <u>μοι</u> – "Jesus said to him if I desire him to abide until I come what is it to you you follow <u>me</u>."

Romans 1:8: Πρῶτον μὲν εὐχαριστῶ <u>τῷ θεῷ</u> μου διὰ Ἰησοῦ Χριστοῦ ὑπὲρ πάντων ὑμῶν ὅτι ἡ πίστις ὑμῶν καταγγέλλεται ἐν ὅλῳ τῷ κόσμῳ – "indeed first I give thanks <u>to my God</u> through Jesus Christ on behalf of you all for your faith is being declared in the whole world."

LOCATIVE CASE SYNTACTICAL CLASSIFICATION

The dative case ending can be used to refer to a place where. This is known as the locative use. The locative case answers the question "where?" Dana and Mantey write "there is no case in Greek more clearly marked in its use than the locative. Its root idea is quite distinct, and the application of the root idea in its various uses is readily discernible. … So in simplest terms we may define the locative as the case of *position*."[145] When referring to an object, the locative case refers to the setting or framework in which an action takes place thus the locative case "indicates location, place, position."[146]

a. Locative of Place

---

[143] Brooks and Winbery, *Syntax of New Testament Greek*, 37.
[144] Wallace, *Greek Grammar Beyond the Basics*, 172.
[145] Dana and Mantey, *A Manual Grammar of the Greek New Testament*, 86.
[146] Brooks and Winbery, *Syntax of New Testament Greek*, 37.

As the name implies, the word in the locative specifies "a spatial location; that is, it locates within a spot or area."[147]

Acts 14:8: Καί τις ἀνὴρ ἐν Λύστροις ἀδύνατος τοῖς ποσὶν ἐκάθητο χωλὸς ἐκ κοιλίας μητρὸς αὐτοῦ ὑπάρχων, ὃς οὐδέποτε περιεπατήκει – "and there was sitting a certain man in Lystra unable in his feet being lame from out of his mother's womb who never had walked."

James 2:25: ὁμοίως δὲ καὶ Ραὰβ ἡ πόρνη οὐκ ἐξ ἔργων ἐδικαιώθη ὑποδεξαμένη τοὺς ἀγγέλους καὶ ἑτέρᾳ ὁδῷ ἐκβαλοῦσα – "and likewise also was not Rahab the harlot justified by works when she received the messengers and sent them out by a different way?"

John 19:2 καὶ οἱ στρατιῶται πλέξαντες στέφανον ἐξ ἀκανθῶν ἐπέθηκαν αὐτοῦ τῇ κεφαλῇ καὶ ἱμάτιον πορφυροῦν περιέβαλον αὐτόν – "and the soldiers plaited a crown out of thorns and placed it on his head and cast about him a purple garment."

Hebrews 12:22: ἀλλὰ προσεληλύθατε Σιὼν ὄρει καὶ πόλει θεοῦ ζῶντος Ἰερουσαλὴμ ἐπουρανίῳ καὶ μυριάσιν ἀγγέλων – "but you have drawn near to Mount Zion and to the city of the living God the heavenly Jerusalem and to myriads of angels."

b. Locative of Time

"The locative of time is the use of the locative to indicate point of time; that is, it locates within a succession of events."[148] This use of dative expresses the time at which anything happens thus "the limits indicated by the locative may be *temporal*, ... it signifies time *at which*; i.e. point of time."[149] Brooks and Winbery note,

> theoretically, the locative is used to indicate time at which – a particular point in time, the instrumental to indicate time within which – two points of time separated by means of a period of time, and the accusative to indicate time throughout which – duration or extent of time.[150]

Matthew 16:21: Ἀπὸ τότε ἤρξατο ὁ Ἰησοῦς δεικνύειν τοῖς μαθηταῖς αὐτοῦ ὅτι δεῖ αὐτὸν ἀπελθεῖν εἰς Ἱεροσόλυμα καὶ πολλὰ παθεῖν ἀπὸ τῶν πρεσβυτέρων καὶ ἀρχιερέων καὶ γραμματέων καὶ ἀποκτανθῆναι καὶ τῇ τρίτῃ ἡμέρᾳ ἐγερθῆναι – "from that time Jesus began to shew to his disciples that it is necessary for him to go to Jerusalem and to suffer many things from the elders and high-priests and scribes and to die and on the third day to be raised."

Matthew 20:19: καὶ παραδώσουσιν αὐτὸν τοῖς ἔθνεσιν εἰς τὸ ἐμπαῖξαι καὶ μαστιγῶσαι καὶ σταυρῶσαι καὶ τῇ τρίτῃ ἡμέρᾳ ἀναστήσεται – "and they shall deliver him to the gentiles to mock him and to scourge and to crucify and on the third day he shall rise again."

---

[147] Vaughan and Gideon, *A Greek grammar of the New Testament*, 54. Dana and Mantey also state "when the limits indicated by the locative are *spatial*, we call it the locative of place." [Dana and Mantey, *A Manual Grammar of the Greek New Testament*, 87.]

[148] Vaughan and Gideon, *A Greek grammar of the New Testament*, 55.

[149] Dana and Mantey, *A Manual Grammar of the Greek New Testament*, 87.

[150] Brooks and Winbery, *Syntax of New Testament Greek*, 10.

Mark 14:30: καὶ λέγει αὐτῷ ὁ Ἰησοῦς Ἀμὴν λέγω σοι ὅτι σήμερον <u>ἐν τῇ νυκτὶ ταύτῃ</u> πρὶν ἢ δὶς ἀλέκτορα φωνῆσαι τρίς ἀπαρνήσῃ με – "and Jesus said to him amen I say to you that today <u>in this night</u> before the cock crow twice you will deny me thrice."

c. Locative of Sphere

"This is a metaphorical use of the locative in figurative expressions. The location is in a logical sphere rather than in space or time."[151] Dana and Mantey note that "The limits suggested are *logical* rather than spatial or temporal, confining one idea within the bounds of another, thus indicating the sphere within which the former idea is to be applied."[152]

Ephesians 2:11-12: Διὸ μνημονεύετε ὅτι ὑμεῖς ποτὲ τὰ ἔθνη <u>ἐν σαρκί</u> οἱ λεγόμενοι ἀκροβυστία ὑπὸ τῆς λεγομένης περιτομῆς <u>ἐν σαρκὶ</u> χειροποιήτου – "wherefore remember that you were once gentiles <u>in the flesh</u> the ones being called uncircumcision by the ones bing called circumcision <u>in the flesh</u> made by hands."

Ephesians 2:18: ὅτι δι' αὐτοῦ ἔχομεν τὴν προσαγωγὴν οἱ ἀμφότεροι <u>ἐν ἑνὶ πνεύματι</u> πρὸς τὸν πατέρα – "because through him we both have the access <u>by one Spirit</u> to the father."

Matthew 11:29: ἄρατε τὸν ζυγόν μου ἐφ' ὑμᾶς καὶ μάθετε ἀπ' ἐμοῦ ὅτι πρᾷός εἰμι καὶ ταπεινὸς <u>τῇ καρδίᾳ</u> καὶ εὑρήσετε ἀνάπαυσιν ταῖς ψυχαῖς ὑμῶν· – "take my yoke upon you and learn from me because I am meek and lowly <u>in heart</u> and you shall find rest to your souls."

Romans 4:20: εἰς δὲ τὴν ἐπαγγελίαν τοῦ θεοῦ οὐ διεκρίθη <u>τῇ ἀπιστίᾳ</u> ἀλλ' ἐνεδυναμώθη <u>τῇ πίστει</u> δοὺς δόξαν τῷ θεῷ – "and to the promise of God he wavered not <u>in unbelief</u> but he was strengthened <u>in faith</u> giving glory to God."

Hebrews 3:10: διὸ προσώχθισα τῇ γενεᾷ ἐκείνῃ, καὶ εἶπον Ἀεὶ πλανῶνται <u>τῇ καρδίᾳ</u> αὐτοὶ δὲ οὐκ ἔγνωσαν τὰς ὁδούς μου – "wherefore I was grieved with that generation and I said they are always being deceived <u>in the heart</u> and they do not know my way."

Matthew 5:8: Μακάριοι οἱ καθαροὶ <u>τῇ καρδίᾳ</u>, ὅτι αὐτοὶ τὸν Θεὸν ὄψονται. – "blessed are the pure <u>in heart</u> for they shall see God."

Hebrews 3:5: καὶ Μωσῆς μὲν πιστὸς <u>ἐν ὅλῳ τῷ οἴκῳ</u> αὐτοῦ ὡς θεράπων εἰς μαρτύριον τῶν λαληθησομένων – "and Moses was indeed faithful <u>in his whole house</u> as a servant to bear witness of the things which were to be spoken."

INSTRUMENTAL CASE SYNTACTICAL CLASSIFICATION

Instrumental use of the dative is to show the "means" or the "instrument" by which something is accomplished and it "embraces both means and association (accompaniment)."[153] The English prepositions *with*, *by*, or *by means of* can be used to translate this use.

---

[151] Brooks and Winbery, *Syntax of New Testament Greek*, 40.
[152] Dana and Mantey, *A Manual Grammar of the Greek New Testament*, 87.
[153] Vaughan and Gideon, *A Greek grammar of the New Testament*, 56.

a. Instrumental of Means

"This is the use lying closest to the root meaning of the case. It is the most prevalent use of the case in the New Testament. It is the method for expressing impersonal means while personal agent is usually expressed by u(po/ with the ablative."[154] In other words, in this case, the idea presented by the dative expresses an impersonal instrument by which or in relation to which the action of the verb takes place. This contrasts the use of u(po/ with the ablative which indicates the personal means by which something occurs. Wenham on the agent and instrument notes,

A verb in the passive will often be followed by an *agent*. Consider the sentences:

o(a)ggeloj luei ton a)postolon The angel is loosing the apostle

o(a)postoloj luetai u(po tou a)ggelou The apostle is being loosed by the angel

Both these sentences express the same idea, but they express it in different ways. It will be noticed that when a sentence in the active voice is turned into a sentence with a verb in the passive voice, as has been done in the sentences given above, the object of the first sentence, 'the apostle', becomes the subject of the second, while the subject of the first sentence, 'the angel', is introduced in the English by the preposition 'by'. But consider the sentence:

o(kosmoj threitai th| sofia| tou Qeou The world is being kept by the wisdom of God

It will be seen that the form of this sentence is the same in English as that of the second sentence above. In Greek, however, the sentences are not the same in form: the *preposition followed by a genitive* is used in the one sentence, and a simple *dative* in the other. This is because the doer of the action in the first sentence is a living person i.e. 'the angel'; but the thing that does the action in the second sentence is not a living person, but 'wisdom'. The former is spoken of as the *agent*; the latter as the *instrument*.[155]

John 13:5: εἶτα βάλλει ὕδωρ εἰς τὸν νιπτῆρα καὶ ἤρξατο νίπτειν τοὺς πόδας τῶν μαθητῶν καὶ ἐκμάσσειν <u>τῷ λεντίῳ</u> ᾧ ἦν διεζωσμένος – "after that he poured water into a bason and began to wash the feet of the disciples and to wipe them <u>with the towel</u> with which he was girded."

Romans 5:9: πολλῷ οὖν μᾶλλον δικαιωθέντες νῦν <u>ἐν τῷ αἵματι</u> αὐτοῦ σωθησόμεθα δι' αὐτοῦ ἀπὸ τῆς ὀργῆς – "much more rather now being justified <u>by his blood</u> shall we be saved from his wrath."

Ephesians 2:13: νυνὶ δὲ ἐν Χριστῷ Ἰησοῦ ὑμεῖς οἵ ποτε ὄντες μακρὰν ἐγγὺς ἐγενήθητε <u>ἐν τῷ αἵματι τοῦ Χριστοῦ</u> – "but now in Christ Jesus you who were once far have been made near <u>by the blood of Christ</u>."

Matthew 3:12: οὗ τὸ πτύον ἐν τῇ χειρὶ αὐτοῦ, καὶ διακαθαριεῖ τὴν ἅλωνα αὐτοῦ, καὶ συνάξει τὸν σῖτον αὐτοῦ εἰς τὴν ἀποθήκην, τὸ δὲ ἄχυρον κατακαύσει <u>πυρὶ</u>

---

[154] Dana and Mantey, *A Manual Grammar of the Greek New Testament*, 89.
[155] Wenham, *Elements of the New Testament Greek*, 69-70.

ἀσβέστῳ. – "whose fan is in his hand and he will thoroughly purge his floor and gather his wheat to the barn but the chaff he will burn with unquenchable fire."

Matthew 8:16: Ὀψίας δὲ γενομένης προσήνεγκαν αὐτῷ δαιμονιζομένους πολλούς· καὶ ἐξέβαλεν τὰ πνεύματα λόγῳ καὶ πάντας τοὺς κακῶς ἔχοντας ἐθεράπευσεν – "and when the evening came they brought to him many being possessed by demons and he cast out the spirits by a word and he healed all those who were having sicknesses."

b. Instrumental of Cause

It is an easy transition from the intermediary means by which a result is produced to the original factor producing it. Thus when we say, "He was destroyed by an earthquake," the mode of expression is but slightly different from saying, "He was destroyed by an assassin's dagger." The former construction agency is referred to the original cause. This is clearly instrumental, and could not be elsewhere classified.[156]

The instrumental of means expresses the cause that gives rise to a situation or as Brooks and Winbery state,

The word in the instrumental indicates what caused the action of the verb to be performed. The reference may be to an external cause and thus an occasion or to an internal cause and thus a motive. ... A test for this use is the ability to use the word "because" in the translation.[157]

Luke 15:17: εἰς ἑαυτὸν δὲ ἐλθὼν εἶπεν Πόσοι μίσθιοι τοῦ πατρός μου περισσεύουσιν ἄρτων ἐγὼ δὲ λιμῷ ἀπόλλυμαι – "and when he came to himself he said how many of the hired servants of my father have bread super abounding but I am perishing because of hunger."

2 Corinthians 2:7: ὥστε τοὐναντίον μᾶλλον ὑμᾶς χαρίσασθαι καὶ παρακαλέσαι μήπως τῇ περισσοτέρᾳ λύπῃ καταποθῇ ὁ τοιοῦτος – "so that contrawise rather you are to rejoice and comfort lest such an one should be swallowed up because of overmuch grief."

Romans 11:20: καλῶς· τῇ ἀπιστίᾳ ἐξεκλάσθησαν σὺ δὲ τῇ πίστει ἕστηκας μὴ ὑψηλοφρόνει, ἀλλὰ φοβοῦ· – "well because of unbelief they were broken of and you by faith stand be not high-minded but rather fear."

c. Instrumental of Manner

This use of the instrumental case expresses the manner or way in which something is done. It "is one of the most obvious uses of the instrumental. It is expressive of the *method by means of which* an act is achieved. It is seen frequently in adverbs of the instrumental form, such as **dhmousi/a|** *publicly* (Ac. 16:37)."[158] Thus "when the word in the instrumental presents an attendant circumstance of an action rather than the means by which it is done, it is an instrumental of manner."[159]

---

[156] Dana and Mantey, *A Manual Grammar of the Greek New Testament*, 89.
[157] Brooks and Winbery, *Syntax of New Testament Greek*, 43.
[158] Dana and Mantey, *A Manual Grammar of the Greek New Testament*, 90.
[159] Vaughan and Gideon, *A Greek grammar of the New Testament*, 57.

Ephesians 2:3: ἐν οἷς καὶ ἡμεῖς πάντες ἀνεστράφημέν ποτε <u>ἐν ταῖς ἐπιθυμίαις</u> τῆς σαρκὸς ἡμῶν ποιοῦντες τὰ θελήματα τῆς σαρκὸς καὶ τῶν διανοιῶν καὶ ἦμεν τέκνα φύσει ὀργῆς ὡς καὶ οἱ λοιποί· – "among whom also we all once had been living <u>according to the lusts</u> of our flesh doing the will of the flesh and of the mind and we were in nature children of wrath just also the remaining one."

1 Corinthians 10:30: εἰ δὲ ἐγὼ <u>χάριτι</u> μετέχω τί βλασφημοῦμαι ὑπὲρ οὗ ἐγὼ εὐχαριστῶ – "and if I am a partaker <u>according to grace</u> why am I blasphemened for that of which I give thanks?"

1 Corinthians 11:5: πᾶσα δὲ γυνὴ προσευχομένη ἢ προφητεύουσα <u>ἀκατακαλύπτῳ τῇ κεφαλῇ</u> καταισχύνει τὴν κεφαλὴν ἑαυτῆς· – "and every woman who is praying or prophesying <u>with the head uncovered</u> is dishonoring her own head."

John 3:29: ὁ ἔχων τὴν νύμφην νυμφίος ἐστίν· ὁ δὲ φίλος τοῦ νυμφίου ὁ ἑστηκὼς καὶ ἀκούων αὐτοῦ <u>χαρᾷ</u> χαίρει διὰ τὴν φωνὴν τοῦ νυμφίου αὕτη – "the one who has the bride is the bridegroom; but the friend of the bridegroom who stands and hears him rejoices <u>with joy</u> because of the voice of the bridegroom."

d. Instrumental of Measure

"The idea of instrumentality to measure is not difficult to see. Two points of time or space separated *by means of* an intervening distance. In the New Testament it is used chiefly with reference to time."[160] Concerning instrumental of measure, Brooks and Winbery note,

> The word in the instrumental indicates two points in time or space or the logical sphere which are separated by means of an interval. Unless e(te/ra| o(dw|= in James 2:25 is an example, the instrumental of measure does not occur in the New Testament with expressions of place.[161]

Acts 8:11: προσεῖχον δὲ αὐτῷ διὰ τὸ <u>ἱκανῷ χρόνῳ</u> ταῖς μαγείαις ἐξεστακέναι αὐτούς – "and they gave heed to him because he had astonished them for <u>a long time</u> by sorceries."

Luke 8:27: <u>ἐξελθόντι δὲ αὐτῷ</u> ἐπὶ τὴν γῆν ὑπήντησεν αὐτῷ ἀνήρ τις ἐκ τῆς πόλεως ὃς εἶχεν δαιμόνια ἐκ χρόνων ἱκανῶν καὶ ἱμάτιον οὐκ ἐνεδιδύσκετο, καὶ ἐν οἰκίᾳ οὐκ ἔμενεν ἀλλ᾽ ἐν τοῖς μνήμασιν – "<u>and when he came out</u> to the land there met him a certain man out of the city who was having a demon for a long time and and he wore no clothes and did not abide in a house but in the tombs."

Romans 16:25: Τῷ δὲ δυναμένῳ ὑμᾶς στηρίξαι κατὰ τὸ εὐαγγέλιόν μου καὶ τὸ κήρυγμα Ἰησοῦ Χριστοῦ κατὰ ἀποκάλυψιν μυστηρίου <u>χρόνοις αἰωνίοις</u> σεσιγημένου – "now to the one having the power to establish you according to my gospel and the preaching of Jesus Christ according to the revelation of the mystery which has been kept closed <u>since eternal time</u>."

---

[160] Dana and Mantey, *A Manual Grammar of the Greek New Testament*, 90.
[161] Brooks and Winbery, *Syntax of New Testament Greek*, 45.

e. Instrumental of Association

To have association, the second party must furnish the means of that association. However, the association is not necessarily personal, though predominantly so. In Rom. 15:27, τοῖς πνευματικοῖς ἐκοινώνησαν means literally *they had fellowship (with you) by means of your spiritual benefits*. This is clearly an example of association, though the means of association is not personal.[162]

The relationship is usually expressed by the verb with the instrumental often taking the preposition σύν.

Ephesians 2:5: καὶ ὄντας ἡμᾶς νεκροὺς <u>τοῖς παραπτώμασιν</u> συνεζωοποίησεν τῷ Χριστῷ χάριτί ἐστε σεσωσμένοι – "and when we were dead <u>in trespasses</u> he has made us alive together with Christ by grace you are saved."

John 11:31: οἱ οὖν Ἰουδαῖοι οἱ ὄντες μετ' αὐτῆς ἐν τῇ οἰκίᾳ καὶ παραμυθούμενοι αὐτὴν ἰδόντες τὴν Μαρίαν, ὅτι ταχέως ἀνέστη καὶ ἐξῆλθεν ἠκολούθησαν <u>αὐτῇ</u> λέγοντες, ὅτι ὑπάγει εἰς τὸ μνημεῖον ἵνα κλαύσῃ ἐκεῖ – "then the Jews who were with her in the house and were comforting her when they saw Mary that she stood up hastily and went out, they followed <u>with her</u> saying that she is departing to the tomb in order that she may weep there."

Romans 11:2: οὐκ ἀπώσατο ὁ θεὸς τὸν λαὸν αὐτοῦ ὃν προέγνω ἢ οὐκ οἴδατε ἐν Ἠλίᾳ τί λέγει ἡ γραφή ὡς ἐντυγχάνει <u>τῷ θεῷ</u> κατὰ τοῦ Ἰσραήλ λέγων, – "God has not cast away his people whom he foreknew or do you not know what the scripture says of Elias how he made intercession <u>with God</u> against Israel saying."

f. Instrumental of Agency

"Agency is expressed occasionally in the New Testament by the instrumental case without the use of any preposition. At such times the verb is always in the passive or middle voice."[163]

Romans 8:14: ὅσοι γὰρ <u>πνεύματι θεοῦ</u> ἄγονται οὗτοι εἰσιν υἱοὶ θεοῦ – "for as many as are led <u>by the spirit of God</u> these are the sons of God."

Galatians 5:18: εἰ δὲ <u>πνεύματι</u> ἄγεσθε οὐκ ἐστὲ ὑπὸ νόμον – "but if you are led <u>by the Spirit</u> you are not under law."

Colossians 1:16: ὅτι <u>ἐν αὐτῷ</u> ἐκτίσθη τὰ πάντα τὰ ἐν τοῖς οὐρανοῖς καὶ τὰ ἐπὶ τῆς γῆς τὰ ὁρατὰ καὶ τὰ ἀόρατα εἴτε θρόνοι εἴτε κυριότητες εἴτε ἀρχαὶ εἴτε ἐξουσίαι· τὰ πάντα δι' αὐτοῦ καὶ εἰς αὐτὸν ἔκτισται· – "for <u>by him</u> were all things created the things in heaven and the things upon the earth the things which can be seen and the things which cannot be seen whether they be thrones or lordships or rulers or authorities all things by him and for him were created."

ACCUSATIVE CASE SYNTACTICAL CLASSIFICATION

The root idea of the accusative case is that of extension and so of motion towards. The object is the name of that towards which the action of the verb goes forth. This

---

[162] Dana and Mantey, *A Manual Grammar of the Greek New Testament*, 90.
[163] Dana and Mantey, *A Manual Grammar of the Greek New Testament*, 91.

is also clearly seen from the fact that all prepositions which denote motion towards, such as ad, contra, ei)j pro/j are followed by an accusative.[164]

From this, it can be seen that the accusative indicates extent to which the action of the verb occurs. It limits the action of the verb and it is the most widely used of all the Greek cases as Dana and Mantey write,

> The accusative is probably the oldest, and is certainly the most widely used of all the Greek cases. Its function is more general than that of any other case. ... "The accusative signifies that the object referred to is considered as the point toward which something is preceding: that it is the end of the action or motion described, or space traversed in such a motion or direction." (Webster: *Syntax and Synon. of the Greek Testament*, p. 63). So the root meaning of the accusative really, embraces three ideas: the end, or direction, or extent of motion or action. But either of these ideas employed to indicate the limit of the action, and hence we may define the root meaning of the accusative as *limitation*.[165]

The uses of the accusative include:

a. Accusative of Direct Object

"The direct object is a substantive which directly and immediately receives the action of a transitive verb. If a word in the accusative functions in this way it is an accusative of direct object."[166] This is the most basic use of the accusative to express the referent about the assertion made by the verb. In this case, the noun "receives the action expressed by a transitive verb. Blass calls this use the complement of transitive verbs (Bl. 87). It refers the action of the verb to some object which is necessary to the completion of its meaning. ... It must be kept in mind in determining the accusative of direct object in Greek that many verbs which in the English are intransitive are treated as transitive in Greek."[167]

James 5:12: Πρὸ πάντων δέ ἀδελφοί μου μὴ ὀμνύετε μήτε <u>τὸν οὐρανὸν</u> μήτε <u>τὴν γῆν</u> μήτε <u>ἄλλον τινὰ ὅρκον</u>· ἤτω δὲ ὑμῶν τὸ Ναὶ ναὶ καὶ τὸ Οὒ οὒ ἵνα μὴ εἰς ὑπόκρισιν πέσητε – "and above all my brothers do not swear neither <u>by heaven</u> nor <u>the earth</u> nor <u>any other oath</u>: let your yea be yea and nay be nay lest you fall into condemnation."

John 6:27: ἐργάζεσθε μὴ <u>τὴν βρῶσιν</u> τὴν ἀπολλυμένην ἀλλὰ <u>τὴν βρῶσιν</u> τὴν μένουσαν εἰς ζωὴν αἰώνιον ἣν ὁ υἱὸς τοῦ ἀνθρώπου ὑμῖν δώσει· τοῦτον γὰρ ὁ πατὴρ ἐσφράγισεν ὁ θεός – "labour not <u>for the meat</u> which will be destroyed but <u>for the meat</u> which is abiding unto life eternal which the son of man will give to you: for him God the father has sealed."

2 Corinthians 2:11: ἵνα μὴ πλεονεκτηθῶμεν ὑπὸ τοῦ Σατανᾶ· οὐ γὰρ αὐτοῦ <u>τὰ νοήματα</u> ἀγνοοῦμεν – "lest an advantage should be gained by Satan: for we are not ignorant of his <u>devices</u>."

---

[164] Nunn, *A Short Syntax of New Testament Greek*, 39
[165] Dana and Mantey, *A Manual Grammar of The Greek New Testament*, 91-92.
[166] Brooks and Winbery, *Syntax of New Testament Greek*, 49.
[167] Dana and Mantey, *A Manual Grammar of The Greek New Testament*, 92.

CHAPTER 2: NOUN CLASIFICATIONS

John 8:46: τίς ἐξ ὑμῶν ἐλέγχει με περὶ ἁμαρτίας εἰ δὲ <u>ἀλήθειαν</u> λέγω διατί ὑμεῖς οὐ πιστεύετέ μοι – "who among you is convicting me of sins but if I say <u>truth</u> why do you not believe in me?"

John 1:14: Καὶ ὁ λόγος σὰρξ ἐγένετο καὶ ἐσκήνωσεν ἐν ἡμῖν καὶ ἐθεασάμεθα <u>τὴν δόξαν</u> αὐτοῦ δόξαν ὡς μονογενοῦς παρὰ πατρός πλήρης χάριτος καὶ ἀληθείας – "and the word was made flesh and he dwelt among us and we beheld his <u>glory</u> the glory as of the only begotten with the father full of grace and truth."

b. Cognate Accusative

"This is a special type of direct object. It differs from the ordinary object in that the verb and its object are derived from the same root. It is sometimes a device for emphasis; often, however, it is simply used for stylistic effect. Essentially the cognate accusative repeats and explains more fully the idea expressed by the verb. (Cf. English, "to do a deed," "to work a work," "to sing a song," etc.)"[168]

Mark 4:41: καὶ ἐφοβήθησαν <u>φόβον μέγαν</u> καὶ ἔλεγον πρὸς ἀλλήλους Τίς ἄρα οὗτός ἐστιν ὅτι καὶ ὁ ἄνεμος καὶ ἡ θάλασσα ὑπακούουσιν αὐτῷ – "and they feared <u>with great fear</u> and said to one another what then is this that even the wind and the sea obey him."

1 John 5:16: Ἐάν τις ἴδη τὸν ἀδελφὸν αὐτοῦ ἁμαρτάνοντα <u>ἁμαρτίαν</u> μὴ πρὸς θάνατον, αἰτήσει, καὶ δώσει αὐτῷ ζωήν, τοῖς ἁμαρτάνουσι μὴ πρὸς θάνατον. ἔστιν ἁμαρτία πρὸς θάνατον, οὐ περὶ ἐκείνης λέγω ἵνα ἐρωτήσῃ. – "if a certain man may know his brother is sinning <u>a sin</u> not to death he will ask and will give life to him, to the one sinning not to death. There is a sin to death, I do not say he shall ask concerning this."

1 Peter 5:2: ποιμάνατε τὸ ἐν ὑμῖν <u>ποίμνιον</u> τοῦ θεοῦ ἐπισκοποῦντες μὴ ἀναγκαστῶς ἀλλ ἑκουσίως μηδὲ αἰσχροκερδῶς ἀλλὰ προθύμως – "shepherd <u>the flock</u> of God among you taking oversight not by constraint but willingly neither for filthy lucre's sake but of ready mind."

Matthew 2:10: ἰδόντες δὲ τὸν ἀστέρα, ἐχάρησαν <u>χαρὰν</u> μεγάλην σφόδρα; – "and when they saw the star, they rejoiced with exceeding great <u>joy</u>."

c. Double Accusative

Some verbs may require more than one object to complete their meaning. In such cases, a double accusative is used.

The double accusative is the use of two accusatives with verbs that require more than one object (or other qualifying accusative) to complete their meaning. (1) The two accusatives may express a personal and an impersonal object (accusative of the *person* and accusative of the *thing*). ... (2) The two accusatives may express a direct object and a predicate object (the predicate object is really a sort of appositive. It

---

[168] Vaughan and Gideon, *A Greek Grammar of the New Testament*, 63. Concerning the cognate accusative, Dana and Mantey note that "the limits set by the accusative are coextensive with the significance of the verb, the use being for emphasis." [Dana and Mantey, *A Manual Grammar of The Greek New Testament*, 94.]

might be called an "object complement," because it completes the meaning of the object and specifies the same person or thing as the object.)[169]

i. A personal and impersonal object

John 14:26: ὁ δὲ παράκλητος τὸ πνεῦμα τὸ ἅγιον ὃ πέμψει ὁ πατὴρ ἐν τῷ ὀνόματί μου ἐκεῖνος <u>ὑμᾶς</u> διδάξει <u>πάντα</u> καὶ ὑπομνήσει <u>ὑμᾶς πάντα</u> ἃ εἶπον ὑμῖν – "and the comforter who is the Holy Spirit whom the father will sand in my name he will teach <u>you all things</u> and will remind <u>you all things</u> that I said to you."

Mark 6:34: καὶ ἐξελθὼν εἶδεν ὁ Ἰησοῦς πολὺν ὄχλον καὶ ἐσπλαγχνίσθη ἐπ' αὐτοῖς, ὅτι ἦσαν ὡς πρόβατα μὴ ἔχοντα ποιμένα καὶ ἤρξατο διδάσκειν <u>αὐτοὺς πολλά</u> – "and when Jesus went out, he saw much people and he was moved with compassion upon them because they were like sheep not having a shepherd and he began to teach <u>them many things</u>."

Hebrews 5:12: καὶ γὰρ ὀφείλοντες εἶναι διδάσκαλοι διὰ τὸν χρόνον πάλιν χρείαν ἔχετε τοῦ διδάσκειν <u>ὑμᾶς</u> τινὰ <u>τὰ στοιχεῖα</u> τῆς ἀρχῆς τῶν λογίων τοῦ θεοῦ καὶ γεγόνατε χρείαν ἔχοντες γάλακτος καὶ οὐ στερεᾶς τροφῆς – "for also when you ought to be teachers because of time again you have need that certain one to teach <u>you the first principles</u> of the word of God and have become one having need of milk and not of strong meat."

ii. A direct and predicate object – "the primary object may be identified as the direct object, the secondary as the double accusative. The secondary object is in apposition with the primary object, and it would be possible therefore to supply the verb "to be" in order to connect the two objects."[170]

John 15:15: οὐκέτι <u>ὑμᾶς</u> λέγω <u>δούλους</u> ὅτι ὁ δοῦλος οὐκ οἶδεν τί ποιεῖ αὐτοῦ ὁ κύριος· <u>ὑμᾶς</u> δὲ εἴρηκα <u>φίλους</u> ὅτι πάντα ἃ ἤκουσα παρὰ τοῦ πατρός μου ἐγνώρισα ὑμῖν – "no longer do I call <u>you servants</u> because the servant does not know what his lord is doing: but I have called <u>you friends</u> because all things which I heard from my father I made known to you."

John 6:15: Ἰησοῦς οὖν γνοὺς ὅτι μέλλουσιν ἔρχεσθαι καὶ ἁρπάζειν αὐτὸν ἵνα ποιήσωσιν <u>αὐτὸν, βασιλέα</u> ἀνεχώρησεν πάλιν εἰς τὸ ὄρος αὐτὸς μόνος – "then Jesus knowing that they were about to come and to seize him in order that they may make <u>him king</u> he went up again to the mountain he alone."

Matthew 22:43 λέγει αὐτοῖς Πῶς οὖν Δαβὶδ ἐν πνεύματι <u>κύριον αὐτὸν</u> καλεῖ λέγων – "and he said to them how then David by the Spirit is calling <u>him Lord</u> saying,"

d. Adverbial Accusative

The accusative may be used to express time and space and when it does, it functions as an adverb modifying the verb rather than acting as its object. Thus "the adverbial accusative is the use of the accusative to modify or limit a verb in an indirect way. "It limits by indicating a fact indirectly related to the action rather than an object

---

[169] Vaughan and Gideon, *A Greek Grammar of the New Testament*, 66.
[170] Brooks and Winbery, *Syntax of New Testament Greek*, 51.

directly affected by the action" (Dana and Mantey, p. 93). In this construction the accusative functions as an adverbial modifier."[171] The adverbial accusative can be classified as:

i. Adverbial Accusative of Measure

To indicate measure, the accusative used with verbs of activity indicates the extent to which the action of the verb is to be understood. In other words "The adverbial accusative may express *measure*, answering the questions "How far?" (accusative of extent of space) or "How long?" (accusative of extent of time). The latter is more frequent in the New Testament than the former."[172] Dana and Mantey note that

> To this adverbial accusative of measure belongs the accusative of the time during which (Mt.20:6). Sometimes the accusative is used to indicate point of time, much as the locative (Ac. 20:16), but with a sense of duration or extension not possible for the locative. When the accusative is used to indicate a point of time, it is part of a continuous period implied in the context (cf. John 4:52; Ac. 27:33; 1 Cor. 15:30). This implication is not possible for the locative.[173]

John 6:19: ἐληλακότες οὖν ὡς <u>σταδίους εἰκοσιπέντε ἢ τριάκοντα</u> θεωροῦσιν τὸν Ἰησοῦν περιπατοῦντα ἐπὶ τῆς θαλάσσης καὶ ἐγγὺς τοῦ πλοίου γινόμενον καὶ ἐφοβήθησαν – "therefore when they had rowed <u>twenty-five or thirty furlongs</u> they saw Jesus walking upon the sea and he was drawing near the boat and they feared."

Mark 14:35: καὶ προελθὼν <u>μικρὸν</u> ἔπεσεν ἐπὶ τῆς γῆς καὶ προσηύχετο ἵνα εἰ δυνατόν ἐστιν παρέλθῃ ἀπ' αὐτοῦ ἡ ὥρα – "and when he went <u>a little</u> he fell upon the ground and prayed that if it is possible the hour may pass from him."

Matthew 20:6: περὶ δὲ τὴν ἑνδεκάτην ὥραν ἐξελθὼν εὗρεν ἄλλους ἑστῶτας ἀργούς, καὶ λέγει αὐτοῖς Τί ὧδε ἑστήκατε <u>ὅλην τὴν ἡμέραν</u> ἀργοί – "and about the eleventh hour when he went out he found others standing idle and he said to them why do you stand here idle <u>the whole day</u>."

ii. Adverbial Accusative of Manner

"The word in the accusative indicates how the action of the verb takes place. This category also includes he accusative used with passive verbs."[174] In other words, when the accusative answers the question "how?" it expresses manner.

Matthew 10:8: ἀσθενοῦντας θεραπεύετε λεπροὺς καθαρίζετε νεκροὺς ἐγείρετε δαιμόνια ἐκβάλλετε· <u>δωρεὰν</u> ἐλάβετε <u>δωρεὰν</u> δότε – "heal those who are sick cleanse lepers raise dead cast out demons: <u>freely</u> you received, freely give."

Philippians 2:16: λόγον ζωῆς ἐπέχοντες εἰς καύχημα ἐμοὶ εἰς ἡμέραν Χριστοῦ ὅτι οὐκ <u>εἰς κενὸν</u> ἔδραμον οὐδὲ <u>εἰς κενὸν</u> ἐκοπίασα – "holding forth the word of life for my boasting on the day of Christ that I have not run <u>in vain</u> neither laboured <u>in vain</u>."

---

[171] Vaughan and Gideon, *A Greek Grammar of the New Testament*, 64.
[172] Vaughan and Gideon, *A Greek Grammar of the New Testament*, 64.
[173] Dana and Mantey, *A Manual Grammar of The Greek New Testament*, 93.
[174] Brooks and Winbery, *Syntax of New Testament Greek*, 55.

2 Timothy 3:8: ὃν τρόπον δὲ Ἰάννης καὶ Ἰαμβρῆς ἀντέστησαν Μωϋσεῖ οὕτως καὶ οὗτοι ἀνθίστανται τῇ ἀληθείᾳ ἄνθρωποι κατεφθαρμένοι τὸν νοῦν ἀδόκιμοι περὶ τὴν πίστιν· – "and that like Jannes and Jambres withstood Moses likewise also these withstand the truth men who have been depraved in mind reprobate concerning the faith."

iii. Adverbial Accusative of Reference or Adverbial Accusative of Respect

The adverbial accusative may express reference with an accusative plus an infinitive where the accusative functions as the subject of the infinitive where the accusative is said to be "an accusative of reference used to describe "the person connected with the action" (R–S. 97)."[175]

Philippians 1:10: εἰς τὸ δοκιμάζειν ὑμᾶς τὰ διαφέροντα ἵνα ἦτε εἰλικρινεῖς καὶ ἀπρόσκοποι εἰς ἡμέραν Χριστοῦ – "so that you may test the things which are excellent in order that you may be sincere and without offence to the day of Christ."

Ephesians 1:4: καθὼς ἐξελέξατο ἡμᾶς ἐν αὐτῷ πρὸ καταβολῆς κόσμου εἶναι ἡμᾶς ἁγίους καὶ ἀμώμους κατενώπιον αὐτοῦ ἐν ἀγάπῃ – "just as he has chosen us out in him before the foundation of the world that we may be holy and blameless before him in love."

Ephesians 4:15: ἀληθεύοντες δὲ ἐν ἀγάπῃ αὐξήσωμεν εἰς αὐτὸν τὰ πάντα ὅς ἐστιν ἡ κεφαλή ὁ Χριστός – "but speaking the truth in love may we grow up toward him in all things who is the head the Christ."

e. Accusative with Oaths

"This construction involves a verb which contains the idea of swearing (usually) an accusative of direct object, and a word in the accusative indicating the person or thing by whom or by which one swears."[176]

Mark 5:7: καὶ κράξας φωνῇ μεγάλῃ εἶπεν Τί ἐμοὶ καὶ σοί Ἰησοῦ υἱὲ τοῦ θεοῦ τοῦ ὑψίστου ὁρκίζω σε τὸν θεόν μή με βασανίσῃς – "and cried out with a great voice he said what to me and you Jesus son of the most high God, I adjure you by God do not torment me."

Acts 19:13: ἐπεχείρησαν δέ τινες ἀπὸ τῶν περιερχομένων Ἰουδαίων ἐξορκιστῶν ὀνομάζειν ἐπὶ τοὺς ἔχοντας τὰ πνεύματα τὰ πονηρὰ τὸ ὄνομα τοῦ κυρίου Ἰησοῦ λέγοντες Ὁρκίζομεν ὑμᾶς τὸν Ἰησοῦν ὃν ὁ Παῦλος κηρύσσει – "and certain of the vagabond Jews exorcists took in hand to call upon those having evil spirits by the name of the Lord Jesus saying we adjure you by Jesus whom Paul proclaims."

1 Thessalonians 5:27: ὁρκίζω ὑμᾶς τὸν κύριον ἀναγνωσθῆναι τὴν ἐπιστολὴν πᾶσιν τοῖς ἁγίοις ἀδελφοῖς – "I adjure you by the lord that this epistle be read to all the holy brothers."

---

[175] Dana and Mantey, *A Manual Grammar of The Greek New Testament*, 93.
[176] Brooks and Winbery, *Syntax of New Testament Greek*, 57.

f. Accusative Absolute

"When the word in the accusative has no direct grammatical connection with the remainder of the sentence, it is an accusative absolute (i.e., an accusative "loosed from" the rest of the sentence)."[177]

Ephesians 1:17: ἵνα ὁ θεὸς τοῦ κυρίου ἡμῶν Ἰησοῦ Χριστοῦ ὁ πατὴρ τῆς δόξης δώῃ ὑμῖν πνεῦμα σοφίας καὶ ἀποκαλύψεως ἐν ἐπιγνώσει αὐτοῦ 18 <u>πεφωτισμένους τοὺς ὀφθαλμοὺς τῆς διανοίας ὑμῶν</u> εἰς τὸ εἰδέναι ὑμᾶς τίς ἐστιν ἡ ἐλπὶς τῆς κλήσεως αὐτοῦ καὶ τίς ὁ πλοῦτος τῆς δόξης τῆς κληρονομίας αὐτοῦ ἐν τοῖς ἁγίοις – "so that the God of our Lord Jesus Christ the father of glory may give to you the spirit of wisdom and of revelation in full knowledge of him <u>the eyes of your mind being enlightened</u> so that you may know what is the hope of his calling and what is the riches of the glory of his inheritance to the saints."

1 Timothy 2:6: ὁ δοὺς ἑαυτὸν ἀντίλυτρον ὑπὲρ πάντων <u>τὸ μαρτύριον</u> καιροῖς ἰδίοις – "the one who gave himself a ransom for all <u>the testimony</u> in his own seasons."

Revelation 1:19-20: γράψον ἃ εἶδες καὶ ἃ εἰσὶν καὶ ἃ μέλλει γινέσθαι μετὰ ταῦτα 20 <u>τὸ μυστήριον</u> τῶν ἑπτὰ ἀστέρων ὧν εἶδες ἐπὶ τῆς δεξιᾶς μου καὶ τὰς ἑπτὰ λυχνίας τὰς χρυσᾶς· οἱ ἑπτὰ ἀστέρες ἄγγελοι τῶν ἑπτὰ ἐκκλησιῶν εἰσιν καὶ αἱ ἑπτὰ λυχνίαι ἃς εἶδες ἑπτὰ ἐκκλησίαι εἰσίν – "write the things yo have seen and the things which are and the things which are about to be after these things <u>the testimony</u> of the seven stars which you have seen upon my right hand and the seven lampstands of gold: these are the seven angels of the seven churches and the seven lampstands which you saw are seven churches."

g. Accusative of Purpose

"A substantive in the accusative may indicate the aim or purpose of the action of the main verb in much the same way as does i(/na with subjunctive."[178]

Acts 3:19: μετανοήσατε οὖν καὶ ἐπιστρέψατε <u>εἰς τὸ ἐξαλειφθῆναι</u> ὑμῶν τὰς ἁμαρτίας ὅπως ἂν ἔλθωσιν καιροὶ ἀναψύξεως ἀπό προσώπου τοῦ κυρίου – "repent therefore and be converted <u>in order that</u> your sins may be blotted out when seasons of revival shall come from before the lord."

Acts 4:30: ἐν τῷ τὴν χεῖρά σου ἐκτείνειν σε <u>εἰς ἴασιν</u> καὶ <u>σημεῖα</u> καὶ <u>τέρατα</u> γίνεσθαι διὰ τοῦ ὀνόματος τοῦ ἁγίου παιδός σου Ἰησοῦ – "in that to stretch out your hand <u>so that healing</u> and <u>signs</u> and <u>wonders</u> may be through the name of your holy child Jesus."

Acts 5:3: εἶπεν δὲ Πέτρος Ἀνανία διατί ἐπλήρωσεν ὁ Σατανᾶς τὴν καρδίαν σου <u>ψεύσασθαί σε τὸ πνεῦμα τὸ ἅγιον</u> καὶ νοσφίσασθαι ἀπὸ τῆς τιμῆς τοῦ χωρίου – "and Peter said Ananias why has Satan filled your heart <u>so as to lie to the Holy Spirit</u> and to keep back part of the price of the field?"

---

[177] Vaughan and Gideon, *A Greek Grammar of the New Testament*, 67.
[178] Brooks and Winbery, *Syntax of New Testament Greek*, 59.

h. Accusative of Result

"This category indicates what takes place as a result of the action of the main verb. It employs the substantive with the preposition ei)j."[179]

Romans 1:20: τὰ γὰρ ἀόρατα αὐτοῦ ἀπὸ κτίσεως κόσμου τοῖς ποιήμασιν νοούμενα καθορᾶται ἥ τε ἀΐδιος αὐτοῦ δύναμις καὶ θειότης <u>εἰς τὸ εἶναι αὐτοὺς ἀναπολογήτους</u> – "for the unseen things from the creation of the world are clearly being seen being understood by the things which are made both his eternal power and Godhead <u>so that they are without excuse</u>."

Romans 15:19: ἐν δυνάμει σημείων καὶ τεράτων ἐν δυνάμει πνεύματος θεοῦ· <u>ὥστε με</u> ἀπὸ Ἰερουσαλὴμ καὶ κύκλῳ μέχρι τοῦ Ἰλλυρικοῦ <u>πεπληρωκέναι τὸ εὐαγγέλιον</u> τοῦ Χριστοῦ – "through mighty signs and wonders by power of the Spirit of God so that from Jerusalem and regions around Illyricum <u>I have fully preached the gospel</u> of Christ."

Hebrews 13:5-6: Ἀφιλάργυρος ὁ τρόπος ἀρκούμενοι τοῖς παροῦσιν αὐτὸς γὰρ εἴρηκεν Οὐ μή σε ἀνῶ οὐδ᾽ οὐ μή σε ἐγκαταλίπω 6 <u>ὥστε θαρροῦντας ἡμᾶς λέγειν</u> Κύριος ἐμοὶ βοηθός καὶ οὐ φοβηθήσομαι τί ποιήσει μοι ἄνθρωπος – "*let your* conversation *be* without love of money being content with the things you are having for he said I will never leave you nor forsake you <u>so that we may boldly say</u> the lord is my helper and I will not fear what man will do to me."

i. Accusative of Cause

"The substantive indicates the ground or reason for the action. It answers the question, Why?"[180]

John 12:30: ἀπεκρίθη ὁ Ἰησοῦς καὶ εἶπεν Οὐ <u>δι᾽ ἐμὲ</u> αὕτη ἡ φωνὴ γέγονεν ἀλλὰ <u>δι᾽ ὑμᾶς</u> – "Jesus answered and said this voice came not <u>because of me</u> but <u>because of you</u>."

2 Corinthians 4:5: οὐ γὰρ ἑαυτοὺς κηρύσσομεν ἀλλὰ Χριστὸν Ἰησοῦν κύριον ἑαυτοὺς δὲ δούλους ὑμῶν <u>διὰ Ἰησοῦν</u> – "for we do not preach ourselves but Christ Jesus as Lord and ourselves your servants <u>because of Jesus</u>."

Acts 28:18: οἵτινες ἀνακρίναντές με ἐβούλοντο ἀπολῦσαι <u>διὰ τὸ μηδεμίαν αἰτίαν</u> θανάτου <u>ὑπάρχειν</u> ἐν ἐμοί· – "who when they had examined me intended to release me <u>because there was no cause</u> of death in me."

j. Accusative of Possession

"This rare use employs the substantive with the preposition kata/."[181]

Acts 18:15: εἰ δὲ ζήτημά ἐστιν περὶ λόγου καὶ ὀνομάτων καὶ νόμου τοῦ <u>καθ᾽ ὑμᾶς</u> ὄψεσθε αὐτοί· κριτὴς γὰρ ἐγὼ τούτων οὐ βούλομαι εἶναι – "and if it is a question of words and of names and <u>of your</u> law you will look into it yourselves: for I do not intend to be a judge of such things."

---

[179] ibid.
[180] ibid., 60.
[181] ibid., 60.

Acts 24:22: Ἀκούσας δὲ ταῦτα ὁ Φῆλιξ Ἀνεβάλετο αὐτοὺς ἀκριβέστερον εἰδὼς τὰ περὶ τῆς ὁδοῦ εἴπων, Ὅταν Λυσίας ὁ χιλίαρχος καταβῇ διαγνώσομαι <u>τὰ καθ' ὑμᾶς·</u> – "and when Felix heard these things he deferred them having more perfect knowledge concerning the way saying when Lysias the chief captain will come down I will know the uttermost <u>of your matter</u>."

Ephesians 1:15: Διὰ τοῦτο κἀγώ ἀκούσας <u>τὴν καθ' ὑμᾶς πίστιν</u> ἐν τῷ κυρίῳ Ἰησοῦ καὶ τὴν ἀγάπην τὴν εἰς πάντας τοὺς ἁγίους – "for this cause and I when I heard <u>of your faith</u> in the Lord Jesus and the love which is toward all the saints."

k. Accusative of Comparison

When used with the preposition u(pe/r, "u(pe/r always expresses comparison in terms of that which is greater."[182]

Luke 3:13: ὁ δὲ εἶπεν πρὸς αὐτούς Μηδὲν <u>πλέον παρὰ τὸ διατεταγμένον</u> ὑμῖν πράσσετε – "and he said to them do not require <u>more than that which has been appointed</u> for you."

Luke 13:2: καὶ ἀποκριθεὶς ὁ Ἰησοῦς εἶπεν αὐτοῖς Δοκεῖτε ὅτι οἱ Γαλιλαῖοι οὗτοι ἁμαρτωλοὶ <u>παρὰ πάντας τοὺς Γαλιλαίους</u> ἐγένοντο ὅτι τοιαῦτα πεπόνθασιν – "and Jesus answering said to them do you think that these Galilaeans were sinners <u>more than all the Galilaeans</u> because they have suffered such things?"

Matthew 10:24: Οὐκ ἔστιν μαθητὴς <u>ὑπὲρ τὸν διδάσκαλον</u> οὐδὲ δοῦλος <u>ὑπὲρ τὸν κύριον αὐτοῦ</u> – "the disciple is not <u>above the teacher</u> neither is the slave <u>above his lord</u>."

Matthew 10:37: Ὁ φιλῶν πατέρα ἢ μητέρα <u>ὑπὲρ ἐμὲ</u> οὐκ ἔστιν μου ἄξιος καὶ ὁ φιλῶν υἱὸν ἢ θυγατέρα <u>ὑπὲρ ἐμὲ</u> οὐκ ἔστιν μου ἄξιος· – "the one who loves father or mother <u>above me</u> is not worthy of me and the one who loves son or daughter <u>above me</u> is not worthy of me."

l. Accusative of Relationship

"On the one hand this category expresses the idea of advantage, benefit, favorable disposition, support, or friendly relationship. On the other hand this category expresses the idea of disadvantage, detriment, unfavorable disposition, opposition, or hostile relationship."[183]

Matthew 14:3: Ὁ γὰρ Ἡρῴδης κρατήσας τὸν Ἰωάννην ἔδησεν αὐτὸν καὶ ἔθετο ἐν φυλακῇ <u>διὰ Ἡρῳδιάδα</u> τὴν γυναῖκα Φιλίππου τοῦ ἀδελφοῦ αὐτοῦ· – "for when Herod had ceased John and bound him and placed him in prison <u>for the sake of Herodia</u> the wife of Philip his brother."

1 Corinthians 16:1: Περὶ δὲ τῆς λογίας τῆς <u>εἰς τοὺς ἁγίους</u> ὥσπερ διέταξα ταῖς ἐκκλησίαις τῆς Γαλατίας οὕτως καὶ ὑμεῖς ποιήσατε – "now concerning the offering <u>for the saints</u> just as I commanded the churches of Galatia so also you do."

Matthew 26:55: Ἐν ἐκείνῃ τῇ ὥρᾳ εἶπεν ὁ Ἰησοῦς τοῖς ὄχλοις Ὡς <u>ἐπὶ λῃστὴν</u> ἐξήλθετε μετὰ μαχαιρῶν καὶ ξύλων συλλαβεῖν με καθ' ἡμέραν πρὸς ὑμᾶς

---
[182] ibid., 61.
[183] ibid., 62.

ἐκαθεζόμην διδάσκων ἐν τῷ ἱερῷ καὶ οὐκ ἐκρατήσατέ με – "in that hour Jesus said to the crowd as <u>against a thief</u> you come out with swords and staves to take me I was sitting with you daily teaching in the temple and you did not take me."

Matthew 10:21: παραδώσει δὲ ἀδελφὸς ἀδελφὸν εἰς θάνατον καὶ πατὴρ τέκνον καὶ ἐπαναστήσονται τέκνα <u>ἐπὶ γονεῖς</u> καὶ θανατώσουσιν αὐτούς – "and brother shall deliver brother to death and father child and children shall rise up <u>against parents</u> and they shall kill them."

m. Predicate Accusative

A predicate accusative follows the verb "to be." A predicate accusative may be one member of a double accusative in which case the verb must be understood. This use of the accusative should be referred to as a double accusative. The present category is limited to the substantive with the preposition ei)j. sometimes the verb is expressed; sometimes it is not. The present category also expresses the idea of equivalence. It could be translated with the word "as" or with the verb 'to be'.[184]

Matthew 19:5: καὶ εἶπεν ἕνεκεν τούτου καταλείψει ἄνθρωπος τὸν πατέρα καὶ τὴν μητέρα καὶ προσκολληθήσεται τῇ γυναικὶ αὐτοῦ καὶ ἔσονται οἱ δύο <u>εἰς σάρκα μίαν</u> – "and he said for this cause a man shall leave the father and the mother and shall be joined together to his wife and they two <u>shall be one flesh</u>."

2 Corinthians 6:18: καὶ ἔσομαι ὑμῖν <u>εἰς πατέρα</u> καὶ ὑμεῖς ἔσεσθέ μοι <u>εἰς υἱοὺς καὶ θυγατέρας</u> λέγει κύριος παντοκράτωρ – "and I shall be to you <u>a father</u> and you shall be to me <u>sons and daughters</u> says the Lord almighty."

---

[184] ibid., 63.

CHAPTER III

THE SYNTAX OF THE ARTICLE

Thus since the Greek language has no "indefinite" article "a" or "an", and the absence or presence of the Greek definite article "the" is significant. Brooks and Winbery point out that

> "The basic function of the article is to point out, to draw attention to, to identify, to make definite, to define, to limit. Generally, though not always, substantives with the article are definite or generic, while those without the article are indefinite or qualitative. It would probably be an accurate summary statement to say that the presence of the article emphasizes identity, the absence of the article quality."[185]

The definite article in the Greek has varied uses and as Nunn points out,

> "As ordinarily used the definite article retains something of its original demonstrative force. Generally speaking it is used in Greek as it is in English, to denote the person or thing to whose name it is attached, is well known, has just been mentioned, or would naturally be thought of in connection with the subject which is being spoken about. ... Although the definite article is generally used in Greek where it would be used in English, this rule is by no means of universal application. The student must therefore pay most careful attention to its use; he must not think that it is used arbitrarily or without reason, because he finds it difficult to express its force in English."[186]

To show the varying uses of the article, the New Testament writers are seen carefully and skilfully using the definite article. According to Wenham, there are special uses of the article. He states,

> There are four examples of the use of the article in Greek where it is not used in English. (1) **Qeoj** usually has the article, e.g. **o(Ui(oj tou Qeou** the Son of God. (2) **a)nqrwpoj** when it refers to men as a whole class, usually has the article, e.g. **o(ui(oj tou a0nqrwpou** the son of Man **oi(ui(oi twn a)nqrwpwn** the sons of men. (3) Abstract nouns (e.g. love, truth, peace) often have the article **h(a(gaph menei** love remains. There is one important exception to this rule. It will be recalled that the function of the noun in Greek (unlike English) is indicated by case ending rather than by word order. ... (4) The name **I)hsouj** prefers the article, e.g. **o(I)hsouj lambanei ton a)rton** Jesus takes the bread.[187]

Thus in interpreting the Greek article, the basic principle to be applied is "nouns which have an article are either definite or generic; nouns without an article are indefinite ("a" or "an") or qualitative."[188] The functions of the Greek article are:

---

[185] ibid., 73.
[186] Nunn, *A Short Syntax of New Testament Greek*, 56.
[187] Wenham, *Elements of New Testament Greek*, 5-6.
[188] Vaughan and Gideon, *A Greek Grammar of the New Testament*, 79.

a. Identification

This is the basic use of the article and is similar to the English use of the article. Under this usage, the article identifies and distinguishes persons or things from others. In the case of a copulative sentence, the article may at times be used to distinguish the subject of the copulative sentence from its predicate. Wallace cautions, "unless the article fits under one of the other seven categories of the individualizing article or under the generic use (or one of the special uses), it is acceptable to list it as "the article of simple identification"."[189]

Matthew 3:3: οὗτος γάρ ἐστιν ὁ ῥηθεὶς ὑπὸ Ἠσαΐου τοῦ προφήτου, λέγοντος, Φωνὴ βοῶντος ἐν τῇ ἐρήμῳ, Ἑτοιμάσατε τὴν ὁδὸν Κυρίου, εὐθείας ποιεῖτε τὰς τρίβους αὐτοῦ. – "for this is the one who was spoken of by the prophet Isaiah saying a voice crying in the desert prepare the way of the Lord, make straight the paths of him."

Matthew 5:1: Ἰδὼν δὲ τοὺς ὄχλους, ἀνέβη εἰς τὸ ὄρος. καὶ καθίσαντος αὐτοῦ, προσῆλθον αὐτῷ οἱ μαθηταὶ αὐτοῦ, – "and when he saw the crowds, he went up to the mountain and when he sat, his disciples came to him."

Matthew 5:15: οὐδὲ καίουσι λύχνον, καὶ τιθέασιν αὐτὸν ὑπὸ τὸν μόδιον, ἀλλ' ἐπὶ τὴν λυχνίαν, καὶ λάμπει πᾶσι τοῖς ἐν τῇ οἰκίᾳ. – "neither do they light a candle and place it under the bushel, but upon the lampstand and it gives light to all that are in the house."

1 Corinthians 4:5: ὥστε μὴ πρὸ καιροῦ τι κρίνετε ἕως ἂν ἔλθῃ ὁ κύριος ὃς καὶ φωτίσει τὰ κρυπτὰ τοῦ σκότους καὶ φανερώσει τὰς βουλὰς τῶν καρδιῶν· καὶ τότε ὁ ἔπαινος γενήσεται ἑκάστῳ ἀπὸ τοῦ θεοῦ – "therefore do not judge anything before time until the Lord shall come who also will bring to light the hidden things of darkness and shall make manifest the intentions of the hearts and then the praise will be to each one from God."

b. Monadic Article

"A substantive is monadic when it is the only such thing there is."[190] This means that the monadic article points to exclusive nouns, which are irreplaceable, incomparable and inimitable.

Matthew 4:1: Τότε ὁ Ἰησοῦς ἀνήχθη εἰς τὴν ἔρημον ὑπὸ τοῦ πνεύματος, πειρασθῆναι ὑπὸ τοῦ διαβόλου. – "then Jesus was led up to the desert by the Spirit in order to be tempted by the devil."

Matthew 5:18: ἀμὴν γὰρ λέγω ὑμῖν, ἕως ἂν παρέλθῃ ὁ οὐρανὸς καὶ ἡ γῆ, ἰῶτα ἓν, ἢ μία κεραία οὐ μὴ παρέλθῃ ἀπὸ τοῦ νόμου, ἕως ἂν πάντα γένηται. – "for amen I say to you, until the heavens and the earth pass away, one jot or one tittle shall never pass away from the law, until all be fulfilled."

Mark 13:24: ἀλλ' ἐν ἐκείναις ταῖς ἡμέραις μετὰ τὴν θλῖψιν ἐκείνην ὁ ἥλιος σκοτισθήσεται καὶ ἡ σελήνη οὐ δώσει τὸ φέγγος αὐτῆς – "but in those days after that tribulation the sun shall be darkened and the moon shall not give her light."

---

[189] Wallace, *Greek Grammar Beyond the Basics*, 217.
[190] Brooks and Winbery, *Syntax of New Testament Greek*, 75.

John 1:29: Τῇ ἐπαύριον βλέπει ὁ Ἰωάννης τὸν Ἰησοῦν ἐρχόμενον πρὸς αὐτόν καὶ λέγει Ἴδε ὁ ἀμνὸς τοῦ θεοῦ ὁ αἴρων τὴν ἁμαρτίαν τοῦ κόσμου – "on the morrow, John sees Jesus coming and he says behold <u>the</u> lamb of God the one who takes away the sin of the world."

c. Anaphoric Article

The article may also be used to refer to something that has been previously mentioned. Brooks and Winbery observe that, "The article calls attention to a substantive which has been previously mentioned and which may be defined or identified or understood by recollection of the previous reference. The initial reference may or may not have the article."[191]

Matthew 2:7: Τότε Ἡρώδης λάθρα καλέσας <u>τοὺς</u> μάγους, ἠκρίβωσε παρ' αὐτῶν τὸν χρόνον τοῦ φαινομένου ἀστέρος. – "then Herod when he had called <u>the</u> Magi secretly, he enquired diligently from them the season the star was manifested." (previous mention of the Magi is in vs. 1)

John 4:9: λέγει οὖν αὐτῷ <u>ἡ</u> γυνὴ <u>ἡ</u> Σαμαρεῖτις, Πῶς σὺ Ἰουδαῖος ὢν παρ' ἐμοῦ πιεῖν αἰτεῖς οὔσης γυναικὸς Σαμαρείτιδος οὐ γὰρ συγχρῶνται Ἰουδαῖοι Σαμαρείταις – "then <u>the</u> Samaritan woman said to him how is it you being a Jew is asking to drink from me being a Samaritan woman for Jews do not have dealings with Samaritans." (previous mention of woman in vs. 7)

John 4:11: λέγει αὐτῷ <u>ἡ</u> γυνή Κύριε οὔτε ἄντλημα ἔχεις καὶ τὸ φρέαρ ἐστὶν βαθύ· πόθεν οὖν ἔχεις <u>τὸ</u> ὕδωρ <u>τὸ</u> ζῶν – "<u>The</u> woman said to him Lord you have neither a drawing vessel and the well is deep: from whence then do you have <u>the</u> living water?" (previous mention of water in vs. 10)

John 4:50: λέγει αὐτῷ ὁ Ἰησοῦς Πορεύου ὁ υἱός σου ζῇ καὶ ἐπίστευσεν <u>ὁ</u> ἄνθρωπος τῷ λόγῳ ᾧ εἶπεν αὐτῷ Ἰησοῦς καὶ ἐπορεύετο – "Jesus said to him go your son is living and <u>the</u> man believed the word which Jesus said to him and he went." (previous mention of the man is in vs. 46 – as a certain ruler)

d. Article with Abstract Nouns

"Abstract nouns are ordinarily general in their character and application, and therefore indefinite. But in Greek, when it is desired to apply the sense of an abstract noun in some special and distinct way the article accompanies it."[192] Thus the use of the article with an abstract noun serves to "objectify or personify an abstract noun"[193] and thus makes the quality of the noun to be "'tightened up,' as it were, defined more closely, distinguished from other notions."[194]

John 1:17: ὅτι ὁ νόμος διὰ Μωσέως ἐδόθη <u>ἡ</u> χάρις καὶ <u>ἡ</u> ἀλήθεια διὰ Ἰησοῦ Χριστοῦ ἐγένετο – "for the law was given through Moses <u>the</u> grace and <u>the</u> truth came through Jesus."

---

[191] Brooks and Winbery, *Syntax of New Testament Greek*, 74.
[192] Dana and Mantey, *A Manual Grammar of the Greek New Testament*, 141.
[193] Brooks and Winbery, *Syntax of New Testament Greek*, 74.
[194] Wallace, *Greek Grammar Beyond the Basics*, 226.

1 Corinthians 13:4-13: Ἡ ἀγάπη μακροθυμεῖ χρηστεύεται ἡ ἀγάπη οὐ ζηλοῖ ἡ ἀγάπη οὐ περπερεύεται οὐ φυσιοῦται – "Love suffers long, love is kind love is not envious, does not vaunt itself, is not puffed up."

1 Thessalonians 1:3: ἀδιαλείπτως μνημονεύοντες ὑμῶν τοῦ ἔργου τῆς πίστεως καὶ τοῦ κόπου τῆς ἀγάπης καὶ τῆς ὑπομονῆς τῆς ἐλπίδος τοῦ κυρίου ἡμῶν Ἰησοῦ Χριστοῦ ἔμπροσθεν τοῦ θεοῦ καὶ πατρὸς ἡμῶν – "remembering without ceasing your work of faith and your labor of love and patience of hope of our Jesus Christ before God our father."

e. Article with Proper Names

"Theoretically, a proper name should not need an article because it is by its very nature quite definite. English uses no article with proper names. Sometimes, however, Greek writers do attach the article to proper names to emphasize them."[195] Dana and Mantey note concerning the use of the article with proper nouns saying

"Thus in the New Testament, which was written for those already acquainted with the historical facts of the Christian religion, when we find o(I)hsou=j, we know immediately that it is the particular Jesus who was the Messiah and Savior. In Col. 4:1 when Paul refers to a member of the Colossian congregation who bears the name of Jesus, he significantly omits the article with I)hsou=j and adds the explanatory phrase o(lego/menoj I)ou=stoj."[196]

Acts 15:19: διὸ ἐγὼ κρίνω μὴ παρενοχλεῖν τοῖς ἀπὸ τῶν ἐθνῶν ἐπιστρέφουσιν ἐπὶ τὸν θεόν – "wherefore I judge not to trouble them from the Gentiles converted to God."

Acts 19:1: Ἐγένετο δὲ ἐν τῷ τὸν Ἀπολλῶ εἶναι ἐν Κορίνθῳ Παῦλον διελθόντα τὰ ἀνωτερικὰ μέρη ἐλθεῖν εἰς Ἔφεσον καὶ εὑρών τινας μαθητάς – "and it happened that while Apollos was in Corinth, Paul having passed through the upper coasts to come into Ephesus and finding certain disciples."

Acts 19:13: ἐπεχείρησαν δέ τινες ἀπὸ τῶν περιερχομένων Ἰουδαίων ἐξορκιστῶν ὀνομάζειν ἐπὶ τοὺς ἔχοντας τὰ πνεύματα τὰ πονηρὰ τὸ ὄνομα τοῦ κυρίου Ἰησοῦ λέγοντες Ὁρκίζομεν ὑμᾶς τὸν Ἰησοῦν ὃν ὁ Παῦλος κηρύσσει – "and certain of the vagabond Jews exorcists took upon them to call upon those having evil spirits the name of Jesus saying we adjure you by Jesus whom Paul is preaching."

f. To Show a Generic Class

When the article in the Greek is used to show distinction between classes or groups of nouns, "it may be translated as though the article were indefinite."[197] This use of the article is also known as generic use and it "comprehends a class as a single whole and sets it off in distinction from all other classes. It individualizes the group rather than a single object, and points out that group as identified by certain characteristics."[198]

---

[195] Brooks and Winbery, *Syntax of New Testament Greek*, 75.
[196] Dana and Mantey, *A Manual Grammar of the Greek New Testament*, 142.
[197] Brooks and Winbery, *Syntax of New Testament Greek*, 75.
[198] Dana and Mantey, *A Manual Grammar of the Greek New Testament*, 144.

Matthew 8:20: καὶ λέγει αὐτῷ ὁ' Ἰησοῦς <u>Αἱ</u> ἀλώπεκες φωλεοὺς ἔχουσιν καὶ <u>τὰ</u> πετεινὰ τοῦ οὐρανοῦ κατασκηνώσεις ὁ δὲ υἱὸς τοῦ ἀνθρώπου οὐκ ἔχει ποῦ τὴν κεφαλὴν κλίνη – "and Jesus said to him foxes have holes and birds of the heaven nests but the son of man does not have where he may lay his head."

Matthew 18:17: ἐὰν δὲ παρακούσῃ αὐτῶν εἰπὲ τῇ ἐκκλησίᾳ· ἐὰν δὲ καὶ τῆς ἐκκλησίας παρακούσῃ ἔστω σοι ὥσπερ <u>ὁ</u> ἐθνικὸς καὶ <u>ὁ</u> τελώνης – "and if he shall neglect them, say it to the church: and if also he shall neglect the church, let him be to you as the Gentile and the Tax-collector."

Luke 10:7: ἐν αὐτῇ δὲ τῇ οἰκίᾳ μένετε ἐσθίοντες καὶ πίνοντες τὰ παρ' αὐτῶν· ἄξιος γὰρ <u>ὁ</u> ἐργάτης τοῦ μισθοῦ αὐτοῦ ἐστιν μὴ μεταβαίνετε ἐξ οἰκίας εἰς οἰκίαν – "and in that house abide eating and drinking the things of them: for <u>the</u> workman is worthy of his reward do not go out house to house."

1 Corinthians 7:28: ἐὰν δὲ καὶ γήμῃς, οὐχ ἥμαρτες· καὶ ἐὰν γήμῃ <u>ἡ</u> παρθένος οὐχ ἥμαρτεν θλῖψιν δὲ τῇ σαρκὶ ἕξουσιν οἱ τοιοῦτοι ἐγὼ δὲ ὑμῶν φείδομαι – "but and if you marry you have not sinned and if the virgin marries she has not sinned but such ones shall have tribulation in the flesh but I spare you."

g. Bracket Use

Sometimes the article may be used with a word, phrase or clause to distinguish it from or define it in relation to the whole sentence. "In this manner the Greek article may be used together with adjectives, adverbs, pronouns, infinitives, participles, prepositional phrases, clauses, and even entire sentences. The article in such constructions gathers an expression into a single whole and points it out in a particular way."[199]

Galatians 5:14: ὁ γὰρ πᾶς νόμος ἐν ἑνὶ λόγῳ πληροῦται, ἐν <u>τῷ</u>' Ἀγαπήσεις τὸν πλησίον σου ὡς ἑαυτόν – "for the law in one word is fulfilled, in this you shall love your neighbour as yourself."

Mark 9:23: ὁ δὲ' Ἰησοῦς εἶπεν αὐτῷ <u>Τὸ</u> Εἰ δύνασαι πιστεῦσαι, πάντα δυνατὰ τῷ πιστεύοντι – "and Jesus said to him this if you are able to believe, all things are possible."

h. In Place of a Noun

"When the article stands with words which modify or phrases which serve as modifiers, it takes the place of a noun. Which noun is supplied is determined by the context and the gender of the article."[200]

1 John 2:15: Μὴ ἀγαπᾶτε τὸν κόσμον, μηδὲ <u>τὰ</u> ἐν τῷ κόσμῳ· ἐάν τις ἀγαπᾷ τὸν κόσμον, οὐκ ἔστιν ἡ ἀγάπη τοῦ πατρὸς ἐν αὐτῷ· – "do not love the world, neither <u>the things</u> in the world: if any man love the world, the love of the father is not in him"

Matthew 26:71: ἐξελθόντα δὲ αὐτὸν εἰς τὸν πυλῶνα εἶδεν αὐτὸν ἄλλη καὶ λέγει <u>τοῖς</u> ἐκεῖ καὶ Οὗτος ἦν μετὰ' Ἰησοῦ τοῦ Ναζωραίου – "and when he came out to the porch, another maid saw him and said to those who were there he also was with Jesus of Nazareth."

---

[199] Vaughan and Gideon, *A Greek Grammar of the New Testament*, 82.
[200] Brooks and Winbery, *Syntax of New Testament Greek*, 79.

i. Article with Nouns Connected by the Conjunction "kai\" (Granville Sharp Rule)

The Greek article has special use with nouns when the nouns are connected by the conjunction "kai\". These special uses would be as follows:

If both the nouns connected by **"kai\"** are of the same case and have an article, then they refer to two different persons and are separate and distinct from each other.

Acts 17:18: τινὲς δὲ τῶν Ἐπικουρείων <u>καὶ</u> <u>τῶν</u> Στωϊκῶν φιλοσόφων συνέβαλλον αὐτῷ καὶ τινες ἔλεγον Τί ἂν θέλοι ὁ σπερμολόγος οὗτος λέγειν οἱ δέ Ξένων δαιμονίων δοκεῖ καταγγελεὺς εἶναι ὅτι τὸν Ἰησοῦν καί τὴν ἀνάστασιν αὐτοῖς εὐηγγελίζετο – "certain out of <u>the</u> Epicureans and of <u>the</u> Stoics philosophers gathered together to him and certain said what does this babbler desire to say, he seems to be a setter-forth of strange gods because he preached to them Jesus and the resurrection." (the Epicureans and the stoics had opposite schools of practical philosophy and are rightly separate and distinct as in the TR)

Acts 23:7: τοῦτο δὲ αὐτοῦ λαλήσαντος, ἐγένετο στάσις <u>τῶν</u> Φαρισαίων καὶ <u>τῶν</u> Σαδδουκαίων καὶ ἐσχίσθη τὸ πλῆθος – "And when he had said this, there was a dissension between <u>the</u> Pharisees and <u>the</u> Sadducees and the multitude was divided." (the dissension between the Pharisees and Sadducees in the text affirms that they are separate and distinct as rightly conveyed by the TR)

Luke 22:4: καὶ ἀπελθὼν συνελάλησεν <u>τοῖς</u> ἀρχιερεῦσιν καὶ <u>τοῖς</u> στρατηγοῖς τὸ πῶς αὐτόν παραδῷ αὐτοῖς – "and when he went out he spoke together with <u>the</u> highpriests and <u>the</u> captains how he may deliver him to them."

If only the first noun has the article but the second noun does not then the second noun refers to the same person referred to in the first noun.

This falls under Granville Sharp's rule one that when two personal nouns of the same case are connected by the copulative "kai\", if the former has the definite article and the latter has not, they both relate to the same person. Sharp states,

"When the copulative "kai\" connects two nouns of the same case [viz. nouns (either substantive or adjective, or participles) of personal description respecting office, dignity, affinity, or connection, and attributes, properties or qualities, good or ill] if the article "o(" or any of its cases, precedes the first of the said nouns or participles, and is not repeated before the second noun or participle, the latter always relates to the same person that is expressed or described by the first noun or participle: i.e. it denotes a farther description of the first-named person."[201]

For this rule to be applied the following are to be noted:

1. The nouns must refer to persons
2. The nouns must be descriptive labels not proper names
3. Both nouns must be of the same case and singular

---

[201] Granville Sharp, *Remarks on the use of the Definite Article in the Greek Text of the New Testament containing many new proofs of the Divinity of Christ*, obtained from URL: http://www.net-magic.net/users/bmj/sharp.html

4. The first noun must be the articular one and the second noun the anarthrous one.

Sharp in page 13 of his book notes that with regard to point 2 and 3, there are exceptions in the New Testament Greek. He writes,

> there is no exception or instance of the like mode of expression, that I know of, which necessarily requires a construction different from what is here laid down, EXCEPT the nouns be *proper names, or plural in the* number, in which cases there are many exceptions; though there are not wanting examples, even of plural nouns, which are expressed agreeable to this rule.[202]

Titus 2:13: προσδεχόμενοι τὴν μακαρίαν ἐλπίδα καὶ ἐπιφάνειαν τῆς δόξης τοῦ μεγάλου θεοῦ καὶ σωτῆρος ἡμῶν Ἰησοῦ Χριστοῦ – "looking for the blessed hope and the glorious appearing of the great God even our savior Jesus Christ."

2 Corinthians 1:3: Εὐλογητὸς ὁ θεὸς καὶ πατὴρ τοῦ κυρίου ἡμῶν Ἰησοῦ Χριστοῦ ὁ πατὴρ τῶν οἰκτιρμῶν καὶ θεὸς πάσης παρακλήσεως – "blessed be God even the father of our Lord Jesus Christ the father of mercies and God of all comfort."

Ephesians 5:5: τοῦτο γὰρ ἔστε γινώσκοντες ὅτι πᾶς πόρνος ἢ ἀκάθαρτος ἢ πλεονέκτης ὅς ἐστιν εἰδωλολάτρης οὐκ ἔχει κληρονομίαν ἐν τῇ βασιλείᾳ τοῦ Χριστοῦ καὶ θεοῦ – "for knowing this that every fornicator or unclean or covetous who is an idolator has no inheritance in the kingdom of Christ even of God."

2 Peter 1:1: Συμεὼν Πέτρος δοῦλος καὶ ἀπόστολος Ἰησοῦ Χριστοῦ τοῖς ἰσότιμον ἡμῖν λαχοῦσιν πίστιν ἐν δικαιοσύνῃ τοῦ θεοῦ ἡμῶν καὶ σωτῆρος Ἰησοῦ Χριστοῦ – "Simon Peter a slave and apostle of Jesus Christ to the ones who have obtained like precious faith by the righteousness of our God even our savior Jesus Christ."

Ephesians 4:11: καὶ αὐτὸς ἔδωκεν τοὺς μὲν ἀποστόλους τοὺς δὲ προφήτας τοὺς δὲ εὐαγγελιστάς τοὺς δὲ ποιμένας καὶ διδασκάλους – "and he gave to some apostles, others prophets, others evangelists others pastors even teachers."

j. As a Pronoun

As a pronoun, the article can be used as:

Demonstrative pronoun,

Galatians 5:24: οἱ δὲ τοῦ Χριστοῦ τὴν σάρκα ἐσταύρωσαν σὺν τοῖς παθήμασιν καὶ ταῖς ἐπιθυμίαις – "but they of Christ have crucified the flesh together with the passions and the lusts."

Matthew 13:29: ὁ δέ ἔφη, Οὔ μήποτε συλλέγοντες τὰ ζιζάνια ἐκριζώσητε ἅμα αὐτοῖς τὸν σῖτον – "but he said no lest while gathering the tares you root up also the wheat."

Alternative Pronoun – i.e. used with **me/n** and **de/**.

Romans 7:25: εὐχάριστῶ τῷ θεῷ διὰ Ἰησοῦ Χριστοῦ τοῦ κυρίου ἡμῶν ἄρα οὖν αὐτὸς ἐγὼ τῷ μὲν νοῒ δουλεύω νόμῳ θεοῦ τῇ δὲ σαρκὶ νόμῳ ἁμαρτίας – "I give

---

[202] ibid.

thanks to God through Jesus Christ our Lord so therefore I myself <u>on the one hand</u> with the mind serve the law of God <u>on the other hand</u> with the flesh the law of sin."

Ephesians 4:11: καὶ αὐτὸς ἔδωκεν <u>τοὺς μὲν</u> ἀποστόλους <u>τοὺς δὲ</u> προφήτας <u>τοὺς δὲ</u> εὐαγγελιστάς <u>τοὺς δὲ</u> ποιμένας καὶ διδασκάλους – "and he gave to <u>some</u> apostles, <u>others</u> prophets, <u>others</u> evangelists <u>others</u> pastors even teachers."

Possessive pronoun

Ephesians 5:24: ἀλλ᾽ ὥσπερ ἡ ἐκκλησία ὑποτάσσεται τῷ Χριστῷ οὕτως καὶ αἱ γυναῖκες <u>τοῖς</u> ἰδίοις ἀνδράσιν ἐν παντί – "but just as the church is being subject under Christ so also the women to <u>their</u> own husbands in all things."

Matthew 7:22: πολλοὶ ἐροῦσίν μοι ἐν ἐκείνῃ τῇ ἡμέρᾳ Κύριε κύριε οὐ <u>τῷ σῷ</u> ὀνόματι προεφητεύσαμεν, καὶ <u>τῷ σῷ</u> ὀνόματι δαιμόνια ἐξεβάλομεν καὶ <u>τῷ σῷ</u> ὀνόματι δυνάμεις πολλὰς ἐποιήσαμεν – "many shall say to me in that day Lord Lord did we not prophesy in <u>your</u> name and cast out demons in <u>your</u> name and do many powerful things in <u>your</u> name?"

Relative pronoun

1 Timothy 3:13: οἱ γὰρ καλῶς διακονήσαντες βαθμὸν ἑαυτοῖς καλὸν περιποιοῦνται καὶ πολλὴν παρρησίαν ἐν πίστει <u>τῇ</u> ἐν Χριστῷ Ἰησοῦ – "for they who use the office of a deacon well purchase for themselves a good degree and much boldness in the faith <u>which</u> is in Christ Jesus."

Ephesians 1:15: Διὰ τοῦτο κἀγώ ἀκούσας τὴν καθ᾽ ὑμᾶς πίστιν ἐν τῷ κυρίῳ Ἰησοῦ καὶ τὴν ἀγάπην <u>τὴν</u> εἰς πάντας τοὺς ἁγίους – "and I because of this when I heard concerning your faith in the Lord Jesus and the love <u>which</u> is to all the saints."

k. The Definite Article used with Nouns

1. The **Articular Noun:** the definite article agrees with the noun it is attached to in case, number and gender. When attached to a noun, it makes the noun to stand out and it adds emphasis to it by either particularizing it or contrasting it thus serving to reveal the identity of the noun. For example:

Titles in Scripture are normally articular nouns which serve to identify or point to the specific nature of the noun. For example o(Qeo\j (the God) and o(I)hsou=j (the Jesus) are identifying God and Jesus as the one God of the Bible, (there are many god's), and Jesus, THE Son of God, the Savior. (Jesus was a common name among the Jews and many men were named Jesus).

Abstract nouns when attached with the article are particularized and contrasted. For example in Romans chapter 6, Paul repeatedly places the definite article before the word "sin" (a(marti/a) indicating that he is not talking in this chapter about "a sin", some "amount" of sin, or "sinning" in general, but, the sin nature which he identifies in 5:12 (Διὰ τοῦτο ὥσπερ δι᾽ ἑνὸς ἀνθρώπου <u>ἡ ἁμαρτία</u> εἰς τὸν κόσμον εἰσῆλθεν). He is contrasting our new nature and our old nature and urging us to live in the new nature.

2. The **Anarthrous Noun**: When a noun is anarthrous i.e. it does not have an article attached to it, the absence of the article serves to emphasize the quality or character of the noun in relation to its context. For example:

In 1 Timothy 3:2,12, the Greek text has no article preceding the nouns (ἐπίσκοπον ἀνεπίληπτον εἶναι μιᾶς γυναικὸς ἄνδρα). The absence of article points to the quality of the moral conduct which demands non polygamy or adultery and dedication to his wife i.e. he should be the one wife type of man.

In Romans 3:19-21, the Greek text has an interchange of (νόμος) with and without the article. The use of (ὁ νόμος) by Paul in vs. 19 and 21b distinctly and clearly points to the Old Testament Law but Paul did not place the definite article with (νόμος) in vs. 20 and 21a to indicate that he is not speaking of "the Old Testament Law", but rather he is referring to the personal quality of character and conduct manifested by men.

CHAPTER IV

THE SYNTAX OF ADJECTIVES AND PRONOUNS

THE ADJECTIVE

An adjective is "a word which modifies a noun by describing certain properties or qualities of the noun."[203] From this, because the adjective modifies and describes a noun, it must agree with the noun which it is modifying in gender, number, and case. In the Greek, the adjectives stand with respect to the noun it modifies in two position. The Greek adjective is either attributive or predicative.

The **Attributive Adjective**: an adjective is considered to be attributive i.e. descriptive of the noun giving an attribute or quality when:

1. The adjective is immediately preceded by an article
2. The article agrees with the adjective and the noun it modifies in case, gender, and number.

Hewett observes that, "When the adjective occurs with the article. i.e., in the attributive position, then the adjective is expressly qualifying or limiting the noun to which it is related to that category which is characterized by the attribute of the adjective."[204]

The **Predicative Adjective**: When the definite article "the", immediately precedes the noun, but is not placed before the adjective, but the article agrees with both the adjective and the noun being modified in case number and gender, it is called a "predicate" (statement of fact) adjective, and is stating new or additional information about the noun.

Hewett says, "When the adjective occurs without the article, i.e., in the predicate position, then the adjective is not circumscribing the meaning of the noun to which it is related, but it is expressing or asserting something about that noun and is forming a complete sentence in which "is/are" should be supplied."[205]

The difference in the "predicate" adjective and an "attribute" adjective can be seen in:

a) Its function and purpose – for the predicate, the adjective serves to reveal new information about the noun, while for the attributive, the adjective just states an attribute or quality of the noun within a larger context.
b) Its form – for the predicate, the adjective is not immediately preceded by the article while for the attributive, the adjective is always immediately preceded by the article. But it is to be noted that when the article is totally absent in the adjectival phrase, the context determines whether the adjective is attributive or predicative.

The Function of the Adjective

---

[203] Zodhiates, *The Complete Word Study New Testament*, 862.
[204] Hewett, *New testament Greek*, 22.
[205] Hewett, *New testament Greek*, 22.

The primary use of the adjective is that of description and as Dana and Mantey observe,

The genius of the adjective is description. It denotes some fact which distinguishes or qualifies a noun. ... While the genius of the adjective is description, it is not the only idiom in Greek whose distinctive character it is to perform this function. the same force belongs to the genitive, especially the genitive of description and apposition.[206]

Adjectives in their use exhibit three primary uses in which they either act as modifiers, or perform the full function of a noun. Brooks and Winbery also note that

Adjectives exist in three degrees: positives, comparatives, and superlatives. Numbers are adjectives. there is a special class of Greek adjectives which are known as verbal adjectives because they express action. They are comprised of a verb stem and the ending -toj.[207]

Adjectives can be used:

Attributively

As an attributive, the adjective acts to modify the noun directly giving an attendant description that is appended to the noun and accompanies it. Thus an adjective is said to be attributive when "it ascribes a quality to the noun which it modifies; e.g., o(a)/dikoj krith/j, the unjust judge."[208] In this form it can be seen that no complete sentence is formed just by the relationship between the noun and adjective.

a. Attributive use with article present

John 2:10: καὶ λέγει αὐτῷ Πᾶς ἄνθρωπος πρῶτον <u>τὸν καλὸν οἶνον</u> τίθησιν καὶ ὅταν μεθυσθῶσιν τότε τὸν ἐλάσσω· σὺ τετήρηκας <u>τὸν καλὸν οἶνον</u> ἕως ἄρτι. – "and he said to him every man first sets forth <u>the good wine</u> and when they have drank then the worse one: you have kept <u>the good wine</u> until now."

1 John 1:2: (καὶ ἡ ζωὴ ἐφανερώθη· καὶ ἑωράκαμεν, καὶ μαρτυροῦμεν, καὶ ἀπαγγέλλομεν ὑμῖν <u>τὴν ζωὴν τὴν αἰώνιον,</u> ἥτις ἦν πρὸς τὸν πατέρα, καὶ ἐφανερώθη ἡμῖν·) – "and the life was manifested and we beheld and we are testifying and we are announcing to you <u>the eternal life</u> which was with the father and was manifested to us."

b. Attributive use without article present

Romans 6:23: τὰ γὰρ ὀψώνια τῆς ἁμαρτίας θάνατος τὸ δὲ χάρισμα τοῦ θεοῦ <u>ζωὴ αἰώνιος</u> ἐν Χριστῷ Ἰησοῦ τῷ κυρίῳ ἡμῶν – "for the wages of sin is death but the grace-gift of God is <u>eternal life</u> in Christ Jesus our Lord."

John 1:16: καὶ ἐκ τοῦ πληρώματος αὐτοῦ <u>ἡμεῖς πάντες</u> ἐλάβομεν καὶ χάριν ἀντὶ χάριτος· – "and out of his fullness <u>we all</u> have received and grace upon grace."

Predicatively

As a predicate, the adjective is not attached to an article and its function is not to modify or modify the meaning of the noun to which it is attached to but rather it

---

[206] Dana and Mantey, *A Manual Grammar of the Greek New Testament*, 117.
[207] Brooks and Winbery, *Syntax of New Testament Greek*, 70.
[208] Dana and Mantey, *A Manual Grammar of the Greek New Testament*, 118.

serves as a complement making an assertion or expressing something about the noun. Thus unlike the attributive use of the adjective, it forms a complete sentence of which the verb "to be" is supplied in the English. Thus as Dana and Mantey note, "An adjective is in the predicate relation when it makes an assertion concerning the noun which it modifies; e.g., ο(krith/j a)/dikoj, the judge is unjust."[209]

a. Adjective used as a predicate nominative (all the beatitudes are an example of this – Matthew 5:3-10)

Matthew 5:3 Μακάριοι οἱ πτωχοὶ τῷ πνεύματι, ὅτι αὐτῶν ἐστιν ἡ βασιλεία τῶν οὐρανῶν. – "Blessed *are* the poor in spirit for theirs is the kingdom of heaven."

Matthew 5:48: ἔσεσθε οὖν ὑμεῖς τέλειοι, ὥσπερ ὁ πατὴρ ὑμῶν ὁ ἐν τοῖς οὐρανοῖς τέλειός ἐστι. – "therefore you shall be perfect just as your father who is in heaven is perfect."

Adjective used as a predicate with an attributive sense

2 Timothy 3:16: πᾶσα γραφὴ θεόπνευστος καὶ ὠφέλιμος πρὸς διδασκαλίαν πρὸς ἔλεγχον, πρὸς ἐπανόρθωσιν πρὸς παιδείαν τὴν ἐν δικαιοσύνῃ – "all scripture is God-breathed and is profitable for doctrine for correction for rebuke for instruction in righteousness."

Substantivally

The adjective when used together with an article may function as a noun and a noun may be supplied for an English translation. In its use as a substantive, Dana and Mantey write concerning the adjective that

"In this use the three genders present variation. (a.) It is so used in the masculine gender when the noun is concrete. su\ ei)= o(a(/gioj tou= qeou=. thou are the holy one of God. Jn. 6:69 (b.) The feminine gender is generally in agreement with a feminine substantive understood. e)poreu/qh ei)j th\n o)rinh/n. She went into the mountain. Lk. 1:39. This is literally rendered, She went into the mountainous, with country, xw/ran, understood. (c.) The neuter singular is ordinarily used as an abstract noun. to\ xrhsto\n tou= qeou=. The goodness of God. Rom. 2:4. Frequently a neuter substantive is implied (Mt. 10:42). Sometimes the adjective in the neuter plural refers to definite classes of things, and is to that extent concrete, as in Rom. 1:20."[210]

1 John 2:20: Καὶ ὑμεῖς χρίσμα ἔχετε ἀπὸ τοῦ ἁγίου, καὶ οἴδατε πάντα. – "and you have an anointing from the Holy one and you know all things."

Matthew 7:11: εἰ οὖν ὑμεῖς πονηροὶ ὄντες οἴδατε δόματα ἀγαθὰ διδόναι τοῖς τέκνοις ὑμῶν πόσῳ μᾶλλον ὁ πατὴρ ὑμῶν ὁ ἐν τοῖς οὐρανοῖς δώσει ἀγαθὰ τοῖς αἰτοῦσιν αὐτόν – "therefore if you being evil know to give good gifts to your children how much greater your father who is in heaven will give good things to those who ask him."

---

[209] Dana and Mantey, *A Manual Grammar of the Greek New Testament*, 118.
[210] Dana and Mantey, *A Manual Grammar of the Greek New Testament*, 118-119.

Matthew 5:45: ὅπως γένησθε υἱοὶ τοῦ πατρὸς ὑμῶν τοῦ ἐν οὐρανοῖς, ὅτι τὸν ἥλιον αὐτοῦ ἀνατέλλει ἐπὶ <u>πονηροὺς καὶ ἀγαθοὺς</u>, καὶ βρέχει ἐπὶ <u>δικαίους καὶ ἀδίκους</u>. – "then you shall be the sons of your father who is in heaven, for he causes his sun to rise upon <u>the evil ones and the good ones</u> and sends down the rain upon <u>the just ones and the unjust ones</u>."

Adverbially

"Sometimes the adjective modifies the verbal idea rather than a noun and is therefore used like an adverb. The adverbial adjective will usually be in the accusative case."[211] It is often the neuter adjective of; ἴδιον λοιπόν μικρόν μόνον ὀλίγον πολύ πρῶτον among other adjectives.

1 Corinthians 16:12: Περὶ δὲ Ἀπολλῶ τοῦ ἀδελφοῦ <u>πολλὰ</u> παρεκάλεσα αὐτὸν ἵνα ἔλθῃ πρὸς ὑμᾶς μετὰ τῶν ἀδελφῶν· καὶ πάντως οὐκ ἦν θέλημα ἵνα νῦν ἔλθῃ· ἐλεύσεται δὲ ὅταν εὐκαιρήσῃ – "Now concerning Apollos our brother, I <u>greatly</u> exhorted him that he may come to you with the brothers: but the desire was not at all that he may come now but he will come when he shall have good season."

THE PRONOUN

A pronoun is defined as a word that can be used in place of a noun.[212] Pronouns can be classified as personal, reflexive, and relative (these can only stand in place of a noun); demonstrative, relative and interrogative (these can be used either in place of nouns or adjectivally). Every pronoun represents (takes the place of) a noun and thus is "a device to render unnecessary the repetition of the noun."[213] To correctly interpret the Bible, we often must identify the noun (the antecedent) which is represented by the pronoun. Pronouns are used not to confuse but to simplify. The writer uses a pronoun because he assumes that you could figure out the antecedent. The **nearest antecedent** is often but not always the correct one and one should therefore consider other grammar rules.[214] Pronouns agree with their antecedent in gender and number, while its case is determined by how it is used in its own clause. In the Greek, the pronoun has the following uses:

Personal pronouns – these show the three persons of speech. They are called the first, second and third persons and refer to I, we; you; he, she, it, and they respectively. "In the Greek, a personal pronoun is not used as the subject of the verb, unless the author desires to be emphatic, for the simple reason that the personal endings make it unnecessary."[215]

---

[211] Brooks and Winbery, *Syntax of New Testament Greek*, 72.

[212] A pronoun is defined as "a word used to designate an object without naming it, when that which is referred to is known from the context or usage, has been already mentioned or indicated, or, being unknown, is the subject or object of inquiry." [*Oxford English Dictionary*, s.v. "pronoun."]

[213] Chamberlain, *An Exegetical Grammar of the Greek New Testament*, 44.

[214] When the noun (or other nominal) that the pronoun refers to *precedes* the pronoun, it is called the pronoun's *antecedent* (as in "**Bob** read the book. The *he* gave it to Jane"). This is the most frequent usage. When the noun comes after the pronoun, it is the pronoun's *postcedent* (as in "After *he* read the book, **Bob** gave it to Jane"). In the latter case, the pronoun may be said to be "proleptic."" [Daniel B. Wallace, *The Basics of New Testament Syntax: an Intermediate Greek Grammar*, (Grand Rapids: Zondervan Publishers, 2000), 141.]

[215] Chamberlain, *An Exegetical Grammar of the Greek New Testament*, 44.

CHAPTER 4: THE SYNTAX OF ADJECTIVES & PRONOUNS

Relative pronouns – these are pronoun that both (a) refers back to a previously mentioned noun or pronoun (often referred to as the antecedent) and (b) introduces a dependent relative clause that modifies this antecedent. Chamberlain says of the relative pronoun:

> The *relative pronoun* has the specialized function of relating clauses to clauses. The name is descriptive of the function. The relative usually agrees with its antecedent in gender and number. Sometimes the relative is attracted to the case of its antecedent e.g. Acts 3:25, where the accusative ἥν is attracted to the genitive ἧς by the antecedent, διαθήκης; but attraction does not always occur: τῳ λόγῳ ὃν εἶπεν (John 2:22).[216]

Indefinite pronouns – these pronouns are also called impersonal pronouns and are those, which are used for a person or a thing, which is not named, because one doesn't want to or does not know the name. Wallace explains that the indefinite pronoun "is used to introduce a member of a class without further identification. It is used both substantivally (as a true pronoun) and adjectivally. It can be translated *anyone, someone, a certain,* or simply a(n)."[217]

Intensive pronouns – these are pronouns which emphasises the noun that it is referring to. They are also referred to as emphatic pronouns. For example, "I myself cry," has the emphatic pronoun "myself." Without this word, the sentence can stand by itself. This pronoun "αὐτός, appears in all persons, genders and numbers. It can be recognized by the presence of another substantive or pronoun agreeing with it in case .... The degree of emphasis in the intensive must be judged by the context."[218]

Interrogative pronouns – these are pronouns are used when one wants to ask questions.

Demonstrative pronouns – these are pronouns used when one wants to show something. Examples in English include "this" and "that." Wallace writing on the demonstrative pronoun explains:

> A demonstrative pronoun is a pointer, singling out an object in a special way. The three demonstrative pronouns used in the NT are οὗτος, ἐκεῖνος and ὅδε. (This last one is rare, only occurring ten times.) ... The near-far distinctions of οὗτος and ἐκεῖνος can refer either to that which is near/far in (a) the context, (b) the writer's mind, or (c) the space or time of the writer or audience.[219]

Possessive pronouns – These are pronouns, which show possession, are called possessive pronouns.[220] Examples in English include mine, yours, and ours. Chamberlain on how possession is shown in the Greek writes,

---

[216] ibid., 49.
[217] Wallace, *The Basics of New Testament Syntax*, 154.
[218] Chamberlain, *An Exegetical Grammar of the Greek New Testament*, 46.
[219] Wallace, *The Basics of New Testament Syntax*, 144-45.
[220] "Greek does not have a distinct possessive pronoun. Instead, it usually employs either the possessive adjective (ἐμός, σός, ἡμέτερος, ὑμέτερος) or the genitive of the personal pronoun." [Wallace, *The Basics of New Testament Syntax*, 154.]

(1) There are other ways of expressing possession, such as the use of the article .... The context makes it clear to whom the article refers. (2) Another way of expressing the idea of possession is with the genitive case of the personal pronoun. (3) it will be noted that there is no possessive pronoun in the third person.[221]

Reflexive pronouns – these are pronouns showing that the same person doing the action is receiving it.[222] For example, "I shave myself;" has the reflexive pronoun "myself." Without this word, (either) the sentence cannot stand by itself (or the meaning of the sentence changes).

The *reflexive pronouns* are formed by combining the personal pronouns with the oblique cases of αὐτός. There are, it is obvious, no reflexive pronouns in the nominative. ... There are no forms of the first or second person plural reflexives in the New Testament except in ὑμῶν αὐτῶν (I Cor. 5:13; 7:35), 'yourselves.'[223]

---

[221] Chamberlain, *An Exegetical Grammar of the Greek New Testament*, 45.

[222] "The force of the reflexive is *frequently* to indicate that the subject is also the object of the action of the verb. On a broader scale, the reflexive pronoun is used to *highlight the participation of the subject* in the verbal action, as direct object, indirect object, intensifier, etc." [Wallace, *The Basics of New Testament Syntax*, 156.]

[223] Chamberlain, *An Exegetical Grammar of the Greek New Testament*, 45-46.

CHAPTER V

THE SYNTAX OF THE VERB

A verb is a word expressing action, occurrence, existence, or state of being. It is used to tell or assert something about a noun (or substantive). In the broadest sense, a verb shows 'action' Dana and Mantey define the verb as "that part of the sentence which affirms action or state of being."[224] This definition gives a general and elementary description of verbs but in the classification of the syntax of the verb in the Greek "such a definition is inadequate, however, because some nouns and some adjectives also express action."[225] Thus there is more to consider when classifying a verb. Hewett describes the nature and the formation of the Greek verb at length. He writes,

> Verbs may consist of two or three segments. All verbs have a basic segment called the stem, which identifies the word in terms of its lexical meaning and provides the basic building block on which one forms a tense or group of tenses. ... The second segment of all verbs is the sufformative. Sufformatives are letters that may be added to the right side of the stem in a variety of combinations to express the following information: 1. Person: first, second, or third. 2. Number: singular or plural. 3. Tense: past (In Greek there are four past tenses: imperfect, aorist, prefect, pluperfect), present, future. 4. Voice: active, middle or passive. 5. Mood: indicative, subjunctive, imperative or optative. The third segment that may occur as a part of the verb is the preformative. It is either a letter or letters prefixed to the stem in conjunction with certain sufformatives in order to indicate tense. In summary, by joining preformatives and sufformatives to the stems, Greek verbs convey person, number, tense, voice and mood. To parse a verb is to identify these five elements.[226]

From the above, therefore, it can be seen that in the Greek, the syntax of the Verb includes classification of voice (i.e. how the subject is related to the action of the verb. This can be presented as active, passive or middle), mood (i.e. how the idea presented by the verb is related to reality. This can be presented as a simple statement of fact, as a command, as a possibility or as a wish) and tense (i.e. what kind of action is being represented by the verb). Concerning the naming of the different classes of the Greek verb Nunn observes that,

> Many of the names given to the different forms of verbs are by no means accurate descriptions of the functions which they perform. As a rule they describe one function, and one only. Thus the Optative Mood has other functions besides expressing a wish. The Present Tense often expresses time other than present. The Subjunctive Mood is not always used in subordinate sentences. These names must therefore be

---

[224] Dana and Mantey, *A Manual Grammar of the Greek New Testament*, 154
[225] Brooks and Winbery, *Syntax of the New Testament Greek*, 82.
[226] Hewett, *New Testament Greek*, 9-10.

looked upon as being somewhat arbitrary and conventional. The functions of the various forms must be learnt from actual usage than from their names.[227]

In the Greek language the construction of the verbs clearly show who does the action, whether the statement is a command or a suggestion and whether the passage is speaking of reality or possibility.

VERB TENSES

In English grammar, tense is described in terms of time and is defined as "a deictic category which relates the time of the event/state represented by the clause to the time of the utterance (the speech moment, 'now'). Tense is expressed by the form of the finite verb."[228] thus when one thinks about tense in English, he thinks about time. In the Greek, however, the emphasis of the tense is not on time but rather Greek tense focuses on the kind of action. Simply worded, the verb expresses the state of the action. Perhaps no other language distinguishes the various relations of the verb so accurately as the Greek, because tense has had its greatest development in the Greek verb. Thus a verbal idea in the Greek presents the action in two elements (a) Kind of action and (b) time of action. The main emphasis of the verbal idea being on the kind (manner of the performance of the action) the second element of time bears directly on the action of the verb especially with the indicative mood. Otherwise time may be referred to only in describing when the action took place. As McKay puts it,

> the tenses of ancient Greek do not signal time except by implication from their relationship to their context. Most of the tenses could be used with present, past, or even future reference, depending on the time indicated mainly by other factors in the context. ... The context must be the deciding factor in every instance.[229]

The kind of action (aktionsart) of a Greek verb will generally fall into one of three categories namely (1) **Linear action**: this presents Continuous (or 'Progressive') kind of action – the action regarded as in progress, as a line. (2) **Perfective action**: this presents Completed (or 'Accomplished) kind of action, with continuing results – the action presented as perfected, which emphasizes its results or abiding state. (3) **Punctiliar action**: this presents Simple occurrence, (or 'Summary occurrence') without reference to the question of progress – the action considered in a single perspective, as a whole. Burton states,

> The action denoted by a verb may be defined by the tense of the verb (a) As respects its progress. Thus it may be represented as in progress, or as completed, or indefinitely, i.e. as a simple event without reference to progress or completion. (b) As respects its time, as past, present, or future. The tenses of the Indicative mood in general define the action of the verb in both these respects. The tenses of the other moods in general define the action of the verb only as respects its progress. ... The chief function of a Greek tense is thus not to denote time, but progress. This latter

---

[227] Nunn, *A Short Syntax of New Testament Greek*, http://www.textkit.com

[228] *Tense, Aspect and Modality I*, obtained from http://www.hfntnu.no/englesk/staff/johannesson/111gram/lect11.htm

[229] K. McKay, *A New Syntax of the Verb in New Testament Greek*, (New York: Peter Lang, 1994), 39-40.

function belongs to the tense-forms of all the moods, the former to those of the Indicative only.[230]

Thus from the explanations above, it can be seen that in the Greek, there are three basic kinds of actions as stated above and simply stated and as a rule, corresponding to these three basic tenses are the present indicative (Linear action), perfect (Perfective action), and aorist indicative (punctiliar action). Punctiliar action is denoted by the aorist tense; linear or action in progress is suggested by the present, imperfect, and future tenses; and perfective action (action in a state of completion) is denoted by the perfect, pluperfect, and future perfect tenses. And these can be represented as in the table below:

Kind of Action	***Time of Action***		
	Past	***Present***	***Future***
Punctiliar Action	Aorist tense	Present tense	Future tense
Linear Action	Imperfect	Present	Future
Perfective Action	Pluperfect	Perfect	Future Perfect

From the table above it can also be seen that the three kinds of actions as expressed in the two elements of the Greek verb. Burton summarizes it thus,

> The significance of the tenses of the Indicative mood may be stated in general as follows: -- As respects progress: The Present and Imperfect denote action in progress; the Perfect, Pluperfect, and Future Perfect denote completed action; the Aorist represents the action indefinitely as an event or single fact; the Future is used either of action in progress like the Present, or indefinitely like the Aorist. As respects time: The Present and Perfect denote present time; the Imperfect, Aorist, and Pluperfect denote past time; the Future and Future Perfect denote future time.[231]

Thus for kind, it can be said to be either Punctiliar, Linear or Perfective while for time, it can be said to be either past present of future. It is important to note that these categories are derived from a study of their usage and context as found in the Greek text mainly in the indicative mood. They did not exist by nature of some pre-set grammatical rule or principle. Therefore, the nuance of tense cannot be identified in any particular case only by the nature of the verbal idea without consideration of context factors. The nuance must be determined in the context in which the verb has been used. Concerning the tenses, Goodwin states,

> There are seven tenses – the present, imperfect, perfect, pluperfect, aorist, future and future perfect. These tenses may express two relations. They may designate the time of an action as present, past or future; and also its character as going on, finished or simply taking place. The latter relation is expressed by the tenses in all moods and in the infinitive and the participle; the former is always expressed in the

---

[230] Ernest DeWitt Burton, *Syntax of the Moods and Tenses in New Testament Greek*, (Illinois: The University of Chicago Press, 1923), 6.
[231] Ibid. 6.

indicative, and to a certain extent (to be explained below) in dependent moods and the participle. The tenses are divided into primary tenses, which denote present or future time. This distinction applies properly only to the tenses in the indicative but it mat be extended to any forms of the dependent moods which have the same distinction of time as the tenses of the indicative. The primary tenses of the indicative are the present (in its ordinary use), perfect, future, and future perfect. The secondary tenses are the imperfect, pluperfect, and aorist (in its ordinary uses).[232]

This may be represented by the table below[233]

Character/Description of Action	Past	Present	Future
Presents action as simply happening	Aorist Tense		Future tense
Presents action and time – going on	Imperfect Tense	Present Tense	
Presents action in its results	Pluperfect	Perfect Tense	Future Perfect

The Present Tense

The present tense usually denotes a continuous or linear kind of action. It shows action in progress or in a state of persistence.[234] When used in the indicative mood, it signifies action taking place in the present time. Zodhiates notes that "The present tense in the indicative mood represents contemporaneous action as opposed to action in the past of future. In moods other than in the indicative mood, it refers only to continuous or repeated action."[235] The present indicative tense in Greek can take on a wide variety of nuances. Vaughan and Gideon state,

> The present tense is the linear tense; it describes an act as in progress. The idea of time is not prominent except in the indicative, where the present tense denotes progressive or linear action in the present time. Outside of the indicative, the present speaks only of kind of action.[236]

---

[232] William Watson Goodwin, *Syntax of the Moods and Tenses of the Greek Verb*, (New York: Ginn and Company, 1897), 7.

[233] This table is adapted from W. Gunion Rutherford, *First Greek Grammar Syntax*, (London: Macmillian and Company, 1912), 83.

[234] Goodwin observes that, "The present indicative represents an action as going on at the time of speaking or writing; as γράφω I write or I am writing. An important exception occurs when the present indicative in indirect discourse denotes time which is present relatively to the leading verb." [Goodwin, *Syntax of the Moods and Tenses of the Greek Verb*, 8.]

[235] Spiros Zodhiates, *The Complete Word Study New Testament*, 867.

[236] Vaughan and Gideon, *A Greek Grammar of the New Testament*, 136. Dana and Mantey observe, "The fundamental significance of the present tense is the idea of progress. It is the linear tense. This is not, however, its exclusive significance. It is a mistake ti suppose "that the durative meaning monopolises the present stem" (M. 119). Since there is no aorist tense for present time, the present tense, as used in the indicative, must do service for both linear and punctiliar action." [Dana and Mantey, *A Manual Grammar of the Greek New Testament*, 181.]

CHAPTER 5: THE SYNTAX OF VERBS

The present tense describes the action as 1) going on, continuous or in process (durative idea) or it may describe action as 2) repeated, customary or habitual (iterative idea). Burton observes concerning the Present tense,

> The tenses of the Indicative in general denote time relative to that of speaking. Most exceptions to this rule are apparent or rhetorical rather than real and grammatical. In indirect discourse the point of view, as respects time, of the original speaking or thinking is retained. ... In conditional sentences of the second form, the tenses are properly timeless.[237]

Examples of the present tense are:

1. Descriptive Present

In this category, the action is seen as going on at the present time, and is sometimes "referred to as the progressive present of description. This use of the present describes what is now actually taking place."[238] Generally this form can be translated by the progressive form with a form of "to be" + verb form in English. Dana and Mantey note that this use "might almost be called the pictorial present since its distinctive force is to present to the mind a picture of the events as in process of occurrence."[239] Burton also notes that,

> The Progressive Present in Greek is not always best translated by what is commonly called in English the "Progressive Form." Some English verbs themselves suggest action in progress, and do not, except when there is strong emphasis on the progressive idea, use the progressive form. Thus the verb (θαυμάζω), in Gal. 1:6, is a Progressive Present, but is best translated "I marvel," the verb itself sufficiently suggesting the idea of action in progress.[240]

Matthew 8:25: καὶ προσελθόντες οἱ μαθηταὶ αὐτοῦ ἤγειραν αὐτὸν λέγοντες Κύριε σῶσον ἡμᾶς, ἀπολλύμεθα – "and his disciples coming raised him saying Lord save us, we are perishing."

Matthew 25:8: αἱ δὲ μωραὶ ταῖς φρονίμοις εἶπον, Δότε ἡμῖν ἐκ τοῦ ἐλαίου ὑμῶν ὅτι αἱ λαμπάδες ἡμῶν σβέννυνται – "and the foolish virgins said give to us of your oil because our lamps are going out."

Galatians 1:6: Θαυμάζω ὅτι οὕτως ταχέως μετατίθεσθε ἀπὸ τοῦ καλέσαντος ὑμᾶς ἐν χάριτι Χριστοῦ εἰς ἕτερον εὐαγγέλιον – "I marvel that so quickly you have been turned away from the one who called you by grace of Christ to a different gospel."

1 John 2:8: πάλιν ἐντολὴν καινὴν γράφω ὑμῖν, ὅ ἐστιν ἀληθὲς ἐν αὐτῷ, καὶ ἐν ὑμῖν, ὅτι ἡ σκοτία παράγεται, καὶ τὸ φῶς τὸ ἀληθινὸν ἤδη φαίνει. – "Again a new commandment I write to you, that which is true in him and in you for the darkness is passing away and the true light already is shining."

---

[237] E Burton, *Syntax of the Moods and Tenses in New Testament Greek*, 7.
[238] Brooks and Winbery, *Syntax of New Testament Greek*, 84.
[239] Dana and Mantey, *A Manual Grammar of the Greek New Testament*, 182.
[240] E. Burton, *Syntax of the Moods and Tenses in New Testament Greek*, 8.

2. Durative Present

Dana and Mantey write that "Sometimes the progressive present is retroactive in its application, denoting that which has begun in the past and continues in the present. ... This use is generally associated with an adverb of time, and may best be rendered by the English perfect."[241] That is this use of the tense denotes a past cation which is still in progress in the present time describing what has been and still is and thus in this the "past and the present are gathered up together in one single affirmation."[242]

John 5:6: τοῦτον ἰδὼν ὁ Ἰησοῦς κατακείμενον καὶ γνοὺς ὅτι πολὺν ἤδη χρόνον <u>ἔχει</u> λέγει αὐτῷ Θέλεις ὑγιὴς γενέσθαι – "Jesus seeing him lying and knowing that he <u>has</u> already much time he says to him do you desire to become whole?"

Luke 15:29: ὁ δὲ ἀποκριθεὶς εἶπεν τῷ πατρὶ Ἰδού, τοσαῦτα ἔτη <u>δουλεύω</u> σοι καὶ οὐδέποτε ἐντολήν σου παρῆλθον καὶ ἐμοὶ οὐδέποτε ἔδωκας ἔριφον ἵνα μετὰ τῶν φίλων μου εὐφρανθῶ· – "But he answering said to the father behold so many years <u>I have served</u> you and not at any time your commandment have I transgressed but to me not at any time did you give a kid in order that with my friends I may be merry."

Simple "Point" Present (Aoristic Present)

Nunn observes that "The present tense is occasionally used in an Aoristic sense to denote a simple event in present time, without any thought of action in progress."[243] Concerning this use of the present where no idea of duration or continuance is implied, Burton notes,

> Most frequently the action denoted by the verb is identical with the act of speaking itself, or takes place in that act. ... This usage is a distinct departure from the prevailing use of the Present tense to denote action in progress (cf. 9). There being in the Indicative no tense which represents an event as a simple fact without at the same time assigning it either to the past or the future, the Present is used for those instances (rare as compared with the cases of the Progressive Present), in which an action of present time is conceived of without reference to its progress.[244]

Matt. 5:22: Ἐγὼ δὲ <u>λέγω</u> ὑμῖν, ὅτι πᾶς ὁ ὀργιζόμενος τῷ ἀδελφῷ αὐτοῦ εἰκῇ, ἔνοχος ἔσται τῇ κρίσει. ὃς δ᾽ ἂν εἴπῃ τῷ ἀδελφῷ αὐτοῦ ῥακά, ἔνοχος ἔσται τῷ συνεδρίῳ. ὃς δ᾽ ἂν εἴπῃ μωρέ, ἔνοχος ἔσται εἰς τὴν γέενναν τοῦ πυρός. – "But <u>I say</u> to you, that whoever is angry to his brother without a cause shall be liable to the judgment and whoever shall say fool shall be liable to the fires of Gehenna."

Mark 2:5: ἰδὼν δὲ ὁ Ἰησοῦς τὴν πίστιν αὐτῶν <u>λέγει</u> τῷ παραλυτικῷ Τέκνον <u>ἀφέωνται</u> σοι αἱ ἁμαρτίαι σου – "and Jesus seeing their faith <u>he says</u> to the paralytic child your sins <u>are forgiven</u> you."

Acts 9:34: καὶ εἶπεν αὐτῷ ὁ Πέτρος Αἰνέα <u>ἰᾶταί</u> σε Ἰησοῦς ὁ Χριστός· ἀνάστηθι καὶ στρῶσον σεαυτῷ καὶ εὐθέως ἀνέστη – "and Peter said to him Aeneas Jesus Christ <u>heals</u> you be raised and spread for yourself and immediately he arose"

---

[241] Dana and Mantey, *A Manual Grammar of the Greek New Testament*, 183.
[242] Brooks and Winbery, *Syntax of New Testament Greek*, 84.
[243] Nunn, *A Short Syntax of New Testament Greek*, 67.
[244] E. Burton, *Syntax of the Moods and Tenses in New Testament Greek*, 9.

3. Iterative Present

This use of the present expresses that which recurs at successive intervals and is also referred to as present of repeated action. Brooks and Winbery state that it can be illustrated "by a series of dots (. . . . .) rather than a straight line (___). Sometimes the repetition takes the form of a local, as opposed to universal custom or practice. It is necessary to distinguish this use from those statements of universal truth called gnomic."[245]

1 Corinthians 15:31: καθ' ἡμέραν ἀποθνήσκω νὴ τὴν ἡμετέραν καύχησιν ἣν ἔχω ἐν Χριστῷ Ἰησοῦ τῷ κυρίῳ ἡμῶν – "I die daily nay your boasting which I have in Christ Jesus our Lord."

Luke 18:12: νηστεύω δὶς τοῦ σαββάτου ἀποδεκατῶ πάντα ὅσα κτῶμαι – "I fast twice a week I tithe all things as much as I possess."

4. Gnomic Present (Present of General Truth)

This use of the present expresses an action true for all time. Vaughan and Gideon note concerning this use that "Because such statements are usually axiomatic in character, the temporal element is quite remote. The gnomic present therefore does not affirm that something is happening, but that something does happen."[246] This means that the gnomic present is used in generalizations or proverbial statements and expresses universal, perpetual and timeless facts though as Vaughan and Gideon further notes further, "The historical, futuristic, and gnomic presents may be either linear or punctiliar in force, depending on the meaning of the verb and the significance of the context."[247]

John 3:35: ὁ πατὴρ ἀγαπᾷ τὸν υἱόν καὶ πάντα δέδωκεν ἐν τῇ χειρὶ αὐτοῦ – The Father loves the son and has given all things into his hand.

John 7:52: ἀπεκρίθησαν καὶ εἶπον αὐτῷ Μὴ καὶ σὺ ἐκ τῆς Γαλιλαίας εἶ ἐρεύνησον καὶ ἴδε ὅτι προφήτης ἐκ τῆς Γαλιλαίας οὐκ ἐγήγερται – "and they answered and said to him you also are not from Galilee are you? search and see that a prophet out of Galilee is not rising."

5. Conative Present (Tendential Present)

This use of the present indicates an action begun, attempted, or intended but not yet completed. It is also sometimes referred to as Inceptive, Volitive, or Tendential present. Nunn notes, "As the present tense denotes action in progress, and hence in complete, it may need to express action that is attempted or desired but not performed. This use is called the present of incomplete action or the conative present."[248]

---

[245] Brooks and Winbery, *Syntax of the New Testament Greek*, 85. - "In attempting to determine whether a present which depicts a custom or practice is iterative or gnomic, the following should be taken into consideration. If the custom or practice is local in nature and/or is confined to a comparatively brief period, the present is iterative. If the custom or practice is widespread and/or extends over a long period of time the present is gnomic. It should be remembered that the iterative present expresses linear action, the gnomic punctiliar action." [Ibid., 87.]

[246] Vaughan and Gideon, *A Greek grammar of the New Testament*, 136-37.

[247] Ibid., 137.

[248] Nunn, *A Short Syntax of New Testament Greek*, 67.

John. 10:32: ἀπεκρίθη αὐτοῖς ὁ Ἰησοῦς Πολλὰ καλὰ ἔργα ἔδειξα ὑμῖν ἐκ τοῦ πατρός μου· διὰ ποῖον αὐτῶν ἔργον <u>λιθάζετε</u> μὲ – "Jesus answered them many good works I showed you from my father for which work of them <u>are you stoning</u> me."

Romans 2:4: ἢ τοῦ πλούτου τῆς χρηστότητος αὐτοῦ καὶ τῆς ἀνοχῆς καὶ τῆς μακροθυμίας <u>καταφρονεῖς</u> ἀγνοῶν ὅτι τὸ χρηστὸν τοῦ θεοῦ εἰς μετάνοιάν σε ἄγει – "or the riches of his kindness and forbearance and long-suffering <u>you are despising</u> knowing that the kindness of God leads you to repentance."

6. Futuristic Present (Present of Anticipation)

This form of the present tense is used when a future event is thought of as certain, or near certain, to occur; especially prevalent in prophecy. Brooks and Winbery explain "The present tense is sometimes used for confident assertions about what is going to take place in the future. The event, although it has not yet occurred, is looked upon as certain that it is thought of as already occurring. The futuristic present is often used in prophecies."[249]

Matthew 26:18: ὁ δὲ εἶπεν Ὑπάγετε εἰς τὴν πόλιν πρὸς τὸν δεῖνα καὶ εἴπατε αὐτῷ Ὁ διδάσκαλος λέγει Ὁ καιρός μου ἐγγύς ἐστιν πρὸς σὲ <u>ποιῶ</u> τὸ πάσχα μετὰ τῶν μαθητῶν μου – "and he said go to the city to such a man and say to him the teacher is saying my time is near to you <u>I will make</u> the passover with my disciples."

John 21:23: ἐξῆλθεν οὖν ὁ λόγος οὗτος εἰς τοὺς ἀδελφοὺς ὅτι ὁ μαθητὴς ἐκεῖνος οὐκ <u>ἀποθνῄσκει</u> καὶ οὐκ εἶπεν αὐτῷ ὁ Ἰησοῦς ὅτι οὐκ ἀποθνῄσκει· ἀλλ' Ἐὰν αὐτὸν θέλω μένειν ἕως ἔρχομαι τί πρὸς σέ – "therefore this word went to the brothers that this disciple <u>will not die</u>, yet Jesus did not say to him that you will not die but if I desire him to remain until I come what to you?"

7. Historical Present

This use of the present tense is used when a past event is viewed with the vividness of a present occurrence; this use of the present is common to narratives and takes the third person form (either in singular or plural). Vaughan and Gideon note that this form "is very common in Mark and John."[250] Rutherford states that "in such cases, it no longer marks an action as going on, but simply as happening once for all. It is graphic or picturesque in so far as it puts a thing before the eyes of the reader."[251]

John 1:29: Τῇ ἐπαύριον <u>βλέπει</u> ὁ Ἰωάννης τὸν Ἰησοῦν ἐρχόμενον πρὸς αὐτόν καὶ <u>λέγει</u> Ἴδε ὁ ἀμνὸς τοῦ θεοῦ ὁ αἴρων τὴν ἁμαρτίαν τοῦ κόσμου – "On the morrow John <u>sees</u> Jesus coming and <u>says</u> behold the Lamb of God the one who is lifting away the sins of the world."

Mark 14:17: Καὶ ὀψίας γενομένης <u>ἔρχεται</u> μετὰ τῶν δώδεκα – "and when it was evening, he <u>comes</u> with the twelve."

---

[249] Brooks and Winbery, *Syntax of New Testament Greek*, 88.
[250] Vaughan and Gideon, *A grammar of the New Testament*, 137.
[251] W. Gunion Rutherford, *First Greek Grammar Syntax*, 85.

8. Perfective Present

This use of the present is used to express an action which begun in the past and has its results continuing in the present. This use Dana and Mantey say

> approaches its kindred tense, the perfect tense when used to denote the continuation of existing results. Here it refers to a fact which has come to be in the past but is emphasized as a present reality, ... It does approach quite closely the significance of the perfect, but stresses the continuance of the results through the present time in a way which the perfect would not do, for the perfect stresses the existence of the results but not their continuance.[252]

Brooks and Winbery observe that "The perfective present admittedly has something in common with the durative present (above). The durative present, however, emphasizes the fact that the action is still in progress, the perfective present the result or state of being of the action."[253]

1 Corinthians 11:18: πρῶτον μὲν γὰρ συνερχομένων ὑμῶν ἐν τῇ ἐκκλησίᾳ ἀκούω σχίσματα ἐν ὑμῖν ὑπάρχειν καὶ μέρος τι πιστεύω – "for indeed first when you come together in the church I hear there are divisions among you and I believe certain part."

Matthew 6:5: Καὶ ὅταν προσεύχῃ, οὐκ ἔσῃ ὥσπερ οἱ ὑποκριταὶ, ὅτι φιλοῦσιν ἐν ταῖς συναγωγαῖς καὶ ἐν ταῖς γωνίαις τῶν πλατειῶν ἑστῶτες προσεύχεσθαι, ὅπως ἂν φανῶσι τοῖς ἀνθρώποις· ἀμὴν λέγω ὑμῖν ὅτι ἀπέχουσι τὸν μισθὸν αὐτῶν. – "and when you pray do not be as the hypocrites because they love to pray standing in the synagogues and in the corners of the streets, so that they may be seen by men Amen I say to you that they have their reward."

The Imperfect Tense

The imperfect tense is the same as the present tense, except it presents the action as continual or repeated in past time with the action going on over an extended period of time. Jeremy Duff in his Elements of New Testament Greek highlights the difference between the imperfect and aorist tense. He says,

> If you want past time, there is a choice – the Imperfect carries the process aspect, and the Aorist the undefined aspect. The Aorist describes a past action without reference to continuance, repetition or completion, often but not always implying a single past action. - I untied, you untied etc. The Imperfect describes an action in the past that is viewed as a process. This itself gives rise to three different possibilities:
>
> - Continuous process gives the English translations using 'was' or 'were' – I was untying, you were untying, etc.
> - Repeated (or habitual) process gives the English translations using 'used to' – I used to untie, you used to untie, etc.

---

[252] Dana and Mantey, *A Manual Grammar of the Greek New Testament*, 182.
[253] Brooks and Winbery, *Syntax of New Testament Greek*, 90.

- Plus, the Imperfect can also be used for a process in the past that is viewed as just beginning. - I begin to untie, you begin to untie, etc. For example: Matt. 5:2: He opened his mouth (Aorist) and began to teach (Imperfect)."[254]

It can be thus seen that the Imperfect tense shows continuous action in the past without reference to the completion of the action and as Dana and Mantey observe,

The imperfect may be regarded as a sort of auxiliary to the present tense, functioning for it in the indicative to refer its significance of continuous action to past time, ... The imperfect draws the picture. It helps you to see the course of the act. It passes before the eye flowing stream of history' (R 883). That is "it dwells on the course of an event instead of merely stating its occurrence" (Goodwin: *Greek Moods and Tenses*, p. 12). The time element is more prominent in the imperfect than in the present, owing to the fact that it is exclusively an indicative tense. Since its essential force is identical with that of the present, it follows that its uses should be practically parallel.[255]

1. Descriptive Imperfect

The general characteristic use of the imperfect is to describe an action or state that is in progress in past time from the viewpoint of the speaker. This use of the imperfect is best manifested in the descriptive imperfect. Vaughan and Gideon describe this as an action "going on at some time in the past. It does not indicate whether the process was completed."[256] On its use, Wallace observes that "It speaks either of vividness or simultaneity with another action."[257]

Matthew 8:24: καὶ ἰδού, σεισμὸς μέγας ἐγένετο ἐν τῇ θαλάσσῃ ὥστε τὸ πλοῖον καλύπτεσθαι ὑπὸ τῶν κυμάτων αὐτὸς δὲ ἐκάθευδεν – "and behold a great storm was in the sea such that the boat was covered by the waves but he was sleeping."

Mark 9:31: ἐδίδασκεν γὰρ τοὺς μαθητὰς αὐτοῦ καὶ ἔλεγεν αὐτοῖς ὅτι Ὁ υἱὸς τοῦ ἀνθρώπου παραδίδοται εἰς χεῖρας ἀνθρώπων καὶ ἀποκτενοῦσιν αὐτόν καὶ ἀποκτανθεὶς τῇ τρίτῃ ἡμέρᾳ ἀναστήσεται – "for He was teaching his disciples and was saying to them "The son of man will be betrayed to the hands of man and they will kill him and being killed he will rise again on the third day."

2. Durative Imperfect

In this use, the action is portrayed as being in progress, or as occurring in the past time just as in the descriptive imperfect and many consider this part of the descriptive imperfect but with the "process as having gone on in past time up to the time denoted by the context, but without any inference as to whether or not the process has been completed."[258] Brooks and Winbery describe it at length when they state,

An act which began in the past is depicted as having continued over a period of time up to some undefined point. Presumably the action has been completed else

---

[254] Jeremy Duff, *The Elements of New Testament Greek*, (Cambridge: Cambridge University Press, 2005), 68.
[255] Dana and Mantey, *A Manual Grammar of the Greek New testament*, 186-87.
[256] Vaughan and Gideon, *A Greek Grammar of the New Testament*, 139.
[257] Wallace, *Greek Grammar Beyond the Basics*, 543.
[258] Dana and Mantey, *A Manual Grammar of the Greek New Testament*, 187.

the present tense would have been used, but there is no attempt to indicate the completion of the action, else the pluperfect tense would have been used. The term simultaneous imperfect is helpful because this use of the imperfect often refers to a parallel event, to an event which took place at the same time as some other event in the context.[259]

John 4:31: Ἐν δὲ τῷ μεταξὺ <u>ἠρώτων</u> αὐτὸν οἱ μαθηταὶ λέγοντες Ῥαββί φάγε – "in the meantime, the disciples <u>had been asking</u> him saying Rabbi eat."

Luke 2:49: καὶ εἶπεν πρὸς αὐτούς Τί ὅτι <u>ἐζητεῖτέ</u> με οὐκ ᾔδειτε ὅτι ἐν τοῖς τοῦ πατρός μου δεῖ εἶναί με – "and he said to the because of what <u>have you been seeking</u> me do you not know that in the house of my father it is necessary for me to be?"

3. Imperfect of Repeated Action

The imperfect is at times used to express an action that was repeated in past time. This use of the imperfect is by some grammarians classified in two namely (a) iterative imperfect and (b) customary imperfect. Dana and Mantey describe this use as one which describes and action that is "recurring at successive intervals in past time. The vernacular English "kept on" represents quite well the sense. It may be graphically described by a broken line (_ _ _ _ _)."[260] They state that the two are similar as Vaughan and Gideon write, "Many grammarians list, in addition to the iterative imperfect, a "customary imperfect." The English "kept on" frequently will bring out the idea, though "used to" may also express it."[261] Therefore, the iterative and customary are similar in that they describe repeated actions but are different in that the iterative is not something that regularly recurs while the customary is is used to indicate a *regularly* recurring activity in past time (habitual), or a *state* that continues for some time (general).

Iterative use:

John 19:3: καὶ <u>ἔλεγον</u> Χαῖρε ὁ βασιλεὺς τῶν Ἰουδαίων· καὶ <u>ἐδίδουν</u> αὐτῷ ῥαπίσματα – "and <u>they said</u> hail king of the Jews and <u>they gave</u> him strokes with the palm."

Customary use:

Mark 15:6: Κατὰ δὲ ἑορτὴν <u>ἀπέλυεν</u> αὐτοῖς ἕνα δέσμιον ὅνπερ ᾐτοῦντο – "and at the feast <u>he used to release</u> to them one prisoner whomever they asked."

4. Tendential Imperfect

This use of the imperfect tense occasionally portrays the action as something that was attempted, or almost done. Vaughan and Gideon note that it is used "to express an action attempted or interrupted. The inference is that the end of that action was not attained; it only tended toward realization."[262]

---

[259] Brooks and Winbery, *Syntax of New Testament Greek*, 91-92.
[260] Dana and Mantey, *A Manual Grammar of the Greek New Testament*, 188-89.
[261] Vaughan and Gideon, *A Greek Grammar of the New Testament*, 139.
[262] *Ibid*, 140.

Matthew 3:14: ὁ δὲ Ἰωάννης <u>διεκώλυεν</u> αὐτὸν, λέγων, Ἐγὼ χρείαν ἔχω ὑπὸ σοῦ βαπτισθῆναι, καὶ σὺ ἔρχῃ πρός με; – "and John <u>would have hindered</u> him saying I have need to be baptized by you and you come to me?"

Mark 15:23: καὶ <u>ἐδίδουν</u> αὐτῷ πιεῖν ἐσμυρνισμένον οἶνον· ὁ δὲ οὐκ ἔλαβεν – "and <u>they gave</u> to him to drink wine mingled with myrrh but he hid not receive."

Luke 1:59: Καὶ ἐγένετο ἐν τῇ ὀγδόῃ ἡμέρᾳ ἦλθον περιτεμεῖν τὸ παιδίον καὶ <u>ἐκάλουν</u> αὐτὸ ἐπὶ τῷ ὀνόματι τοῦ πατρὸς αὐτοῦ Ζαχαρίαν – "and it came to pass on the eigth day they came to circumcise the child and <u>they wanted to call</u> him by the name of his father Zacharias."

5. Voluntative Imperfect

Brooks and Winbery write,

> Some grammarians prefer to call this the desirederative imperfect, others the potential imperfect. Whatever the name, it expresses a present desire, wish, or disposition. The imperfect rather than the resent is used when there is need to express the desire as politely and inoffensively as possible or when there is a certain amount of hesitation due to the fact that the desire is impractical or impossible.[263]

In order to identify this class the words for wish like θελω and βουλομαι are helpful hints and the wish normally concerns the present time but the imperfect brings the idea of it being unrealistic.

Romans 9:3: <u>ηὐχόμην</u> γὰρ αὐτὸς ἐγὼ ἀνάθεμα εἶναι ἀπὸ τοῦ Χριστοῦ ὑπὲρ τῶν ἀδελφῶν μου τῶν συγγενῶν μου κατὰ σάρκα – "for I myself <u>was wishing</u> to be anathema from Christ on behalf of my brothers my kinsmen according to the flesh."

Matthew 18:33: <u>οὐκ ἔδει</u> καὶ σὲ ἐλεῆσαι τὸν σύνδουλόν σου ὡς καὶ ἐγώ σὲ ἠλέησα – "<u>was it not necessary</u> also you to have mercy on your fellow-slave as I had mercy on you?"

6. Inceptive Imperfect

The imperfect may also be used to to stress the beginning of an action. This use Vaughan and Gideon observe that "implies that the action continues, but the stress is simply on its beginning."[264] The word "began" can be used in the translation. Wallace notes that

> The difference between ingressive imperfect and the ingressive aorist is that the imperfect stresses the beginning but implies that the action continues, while the aorist stresses beginning, but does not imply that the action continues. Thus the translation for the inceptive imperfect ought to be "began doing" while inceptive aorist ought to be translated "began to do."[265]

Matthew 5:2: καὶ ἀνοίξας τὸ στόμα αὐτοῦ, ἐδίδασκεν αὐτούς, λέγων, – "and he opened his mouth and began teaching them saying,"

---

[263] Brooks and Winbery, *Syntax of the New Testament Greek*, 94.
[264] Vaughan and Gideon, *A Greek grammar of the New Testament*, 140.
[265] Wallace, *Greek Grammar Beyond the Basics*, 544.

Acts 3:8: καὶ ἐξαλλόμενος ἔστη καὶ <u>περιεπάτει</u> καὶ εἰσῆλθεν σὺν αὐτοῖς εἰς τὸ ἱερὸν περιπατῶν καὶ ἁλλόμενος καὶ αἰνῶν τὸν θεόν – "and leaping up he stood and <u>began walking</u> and went in together with them into the temple walking and leaping and praising God."

The Future Tense

The future tense in Greek is essentially the same as in English in that it describes action planned for the future but it also differs from the English future in that it usually expresses undefined or aoristic action in the future time and often speaks authoritatively about the future - not merely what is planned, but what shall actually come to pass. Wallace defines the future tense stating that

> With reference to aspect, the future seems to offer and external portrayal, something of temporal counterpart to the aorist indicative. The external portrayal "presents an occurrence in summary, viewed as a whole from the outside, without regard for the internal make-up of the occurrence." With reference to time, the future tense is always future from the speaker's presentation (or when in a participle form, in relation to the time of the main verb).[266]

The future expresses punctiliar action most of the times though it may at times indicate linear action and unlike the other tense, the element of time is more important being restricted to future time in the indicative mood. Dana and Mantey observe,

> The future is primarily an indicative tense, and hence the element of time is very pronounced. It does, however, signify to a large degree the character of the verbal idea, but instead of presenting progress as the leading idea – as do the present and imperfect – the general significance is indefinite (aoristic or punctiliar). ... As the aorist indicatives narrates an event in past time, so the future indicative expresses anticipation of an event in future time. ... Outside the indicative the future is but rarely used in the New Testament.[267]

1. Predictive Future

This is the most common and frequent use of the future tense in which the action is simply predicted that it will occur in the future. Burton observes,

> The Future Indicative is most frequently used to affirm that an action is to take place in future time. Since it does not mark the distinction between action in progress and action conceived of indefinitely without reference to its progress, it may be either aoristic or progressive.[268]

The progress or the duration of action is to be determined by the context as Vaughan and Gideon observe when they state "Whether it is punctiliar or linear must be determined by a consideration of the meaning of the verb and its context. More often than not, however, this use of the future will be punctiliar in force."[269]

---

[266] Ibid. 566-67.
[267] Dana and Mantey, *A Manual Grammar of the Greek New Testament*, 191.
[268] E. Burton, *Syntax of the Moods and Tenses in New Testament Greek*, 31.
[269] Vaughan and Gideon, *A Greek Grammar of the New Testament*, 142.

Matthew 1:21: τέξεται δὲ υἱὸν, καὶ καλέσεις τὸ ὄνομα αὐτοῦ Ἰησοῦν. αὐτὸς γὰρ σώσει τὸν λαὸν αὐτοῦ ἀπὸ τῶν ἁμαρτιῶν αὐτῶν. – "and she <u>will bear</u> a son and you will call his name Jesus for <u>he shall save</u> his people from their sins."

John 14:26: ὁ δὲ παράκλητος τὸ πνεῦμα τὸ ἅγιον ὃ πέμψει ὁ πατὴρ ἐν τῷ ὀνόματί μου ἐκεῖνος ὑμᾶς διδάξει πάντα καὶ ὑπομνήσει ὑμᾶς πάντα ἃ εἶπον ὑμῖν – "but the comforter, the Holy Spirit, the one whom the father <u>will send</u> in my name <u>he will teach</u> you all things and <u>he will remind</u> you all things which I said to you."

2. Progressive Future

This use of the future is similar to the predictive use but it differs in that this use not only states or predicts that an action will take place in the future, but it also affirms that the action will be progressive in the future. Brooks and Winbery explain that "Special emphasis is placed upon the progress of the action. ... The expression "keep on" or a similar expression may be used in the translation."[270] Thus it presents an action which will be continuous in the future.

Philippians 1:18: τί γάρ πλὴν παντὶ τρόπῳ εἴτε προφάσει εἴτε ἀληθείᾳ Χριστὸς καταγγέλλεται καὶ ἐν τούτῳ χαίρω ἀλλὰ καὶ χαρήσομαι – "for what? Yet in every way whether by pretence or by truth Christ is being proclaimed and in this I rejoice and also <u>will rejoice</u>."

Rev 9:6: καὶ ἐν ταῖς ἡμέραις ἐκείναις ζητήσουσιν οἱ ἄνθρωποι τὸν θάνατον καὶ οὐχ εὑρήσουσιν αὐτόν καὶ ἐπιθυμήσουσιν ἀποθανεῖν καὶ φεύξεται ὁ θάνατος ἀπ' αὐτῶν – "and in those days, men <u>will be seeking</u> death and they will not find it and they will be desiring to die but death will flee from them."

3. Imperative Future

In the Greek, the Future Indicative 2nd person is often used as an imperative. Wallace suggests that "The future indicative is sometimes used for a command, almost always in the OT quotations (because of a literal translation of the Hebrew)."[271]

Matthew 1:21: τέξεται δὲ υἱὸν, καὶ καλέσεις τὸ ὄνομα αὐτοῦ Ἰησοῦν. αὐτὸς γὰρ σώσει τὸν λαὸν αὐτοῦ ἀπὸ τῶν ἁμαρτιῶν αὐτῶν. – "and she will bear a son and <u>you shall call</u> his name Jesus for he shall save his people from their sins."

James 2:8: εἰ μέντοι νόμον τελεῖτε βασιλικὸν κατὰ τὴν γραφήν Ἀγαπήσεις τὸν πλησίον σου ὡς σεαυτόν καλῶς ποιεῖτε· – "if indeed you fulfil the royal law according to the scripture: <u>you shall love</u> your neighbour as yourself you do well."

The future also can be used with the negative to indicate a command prohibiting an action. This can be classified in two namely:

The prohibitive future command – uses second person future tense with οὐ

Matthew 5:21: Ἠκούσατε ὅτι ἐρρέθη τοῖς ἀρχαίοις, Οὐ φονεύσεις· ὃς δ' ἂν φονεύσῃ, ἔνοχος ἔσται τῇ κρίσει. – "you have heard that it was said by the ancients <u>you shall not murder</u> and whosoever will murder shall be liable to judgement" (see also vs. 27, 33).

---

[270] Brooks and Winbery, *Syntax of the New Testament Greek*, 96.
[271] Wallace, *Greek Grammar beyond the Basics*, 569

CHAPTER 5: THE SYNTAX OF VERBS

The future denial[272] – uses the future tense with οὐ, οὐκ, οὐχ

Matthew 10:29: οὐχὶ δύο στρουθία ἀσσαρίου πωλεῖται καὶ ἓν ἐξ αὐτῶν <u>οὐ πεσεῖται</u> ἐπὶ τὴν γῆν ἄνευ τοῦ πατρὸς ὑμῶν – "are not two sparrows sold for a farthing? and one of them shall not fall upon the ground without your father."

4. Deliberative Future

The future can also be used to cause thought and when used with questions "to consult the judgment of another person. It asks about the possibility, desirability, or necessity of a proposed action. It asks what ought to be done or what can be done."[273] This use of the future uses the negative οὐχὶ, οὐχ, οὐκ, οὐ, to ask questions expecting an affirmative or a negative answer. "Such questions may be real questions asking for information or rhetorical questions taking the place of a direct assertion. (Br. 36)."[274]

John 6:68: ἀπεκρίθη οὖν αὐτῷ Σίμων Πέτρος Κύριε πρὸς τίνα <u>ἀπελευσόμεθα</u> ῥήματα ζωῆς αἰωνίου ἔχεις – "then Simon Peter answered Lord to whom <u>shall we go</u> you have the words of life eternal."

Matthew 12:11: ὁ δὲ εἶπεν αὐτοῖς, Τίς ἔσται ἐξ ὑμῶν ἄνθρωπος ὃς ἕξει πρόβατον ἕν καὶ ἐὰν ἐμπέσῃ τοῦτο τοῖς σάββασιν εἰς βόθυνον <u>οὐχὶ κρατήσει</u> αὐτὸ καὶ ἐγερεῖ; – "and he said to them which man among you shall be who will have one sheep and if this one shall fall on the Sabbath into a pit <u>will he not lay hold on</u> it and raise it?"

5. Gnomic Future

When the future Indicative is used to state what will customarily happen in given occasions, it is termed as gnomic future. In these cases, "the element of futurity is very remote in these construction, the reference being to a general or timeless truth, valid for all times."[275] Thus what the verb offers not only holds true in the future but rather holds true at any time.

Matthew 6:24: οὐδεὶς δύναται δυσὶ κυρίοις δουλεύειν. ἢ γὰρ τὸν ἕνα <u>μισήσει</u>, καὶ τὸν ἕτερον <u>ἀγαπήσει</u>· ἢ ἑνὸς ἀνθέξεται, καὶ τοῦ ἑτέρου καταφρονήσει. οὐ δύνασθε θεῷ δουλεύειν καὶ μαμμωνᾷ. – "no one is able to serve two lords. For either <u>he will hate</u> one and <u>will love</u> another or <u>he will hold fast</u> to one and <u>will despise</u> the other. You are not able to serve God and mammon."

Romans 5:7: μόλις γὰρ ὑπὲρ δικαίου τις <u>ἀποθανεῖται</u>· ὑπὲρ γὰρ τοῦ ἀγαθοῦ τάχα τις καὶ τολμᾷ ἀποθανεῖν· – "for with difficulty one <u>will die</u> on behalf of a righteous one: for peradventure on behalf of the a good man also will venture to die."

The Aorist Tense

The aorist tense in Greek is used very commonly and may be generally represented in English by the English simple past tense (outside the indicative mood) for as Brooks and Winbery point out that,

---

[272] This denies the possibility of an event happening either totally or, as in the example presented, without certain conditions being present.

[273] Brooks and Winbery, *Syntax of the New Testament Greek*, 97.

[274] Dana and Mantey, *A Manual Grammar of the Greek New Testament*, 193.

[275] Vaughan and Gideon, *A Greek Grammar of the New Testament*, 143.

Only in the indicative mood does the aorist also indicate past time. Past time is indicated there by the augment. The absence of the augment from the aorist subjunctive, optative, imperative, infinitive, and participle is itself proof that there is not time element present in these moods and infinite verb forms.[276]

Even in participle form, the aorist participles usually suggest antecedent time to that of the main verb (i.e., past time is a relative sense). Dana and Mantey write that the aorist is "the most prevalent and the most important of the Greek tenses. It is also the most peculiar to Greek idiom. The fundamental significance of the aorist is to denote action simply as occurring, without reference to its progress."[277] Though it looks at the action of the verb without regard to its continuity but rather as a whole, the aorist may emphasize the beginning of the action, the conclusion or the action as a whole. Samuel Green writes concerning the Aorist saying,

> The Aorist Indicative in general simply names an action or state as past, leaving undetermined any question of its completedness. The Aorist is thus to be distinguished from the Imperfect, which expressly describes a past action or state as continuous and incomplete. ... The Aorist frequently puts an action into the past where there is nothing in the context to define the time referred to more precisely ... hence, in many cases, the true equivalent of the Greek Aorist is the English Perfect.[278]

This means that the aorist tense is used whenever there is no particular reason to emphasize time in the action, one looks at the action not for its duration or its abiding results but rather one looks at it as a simple statement of fact that "it happened". Hence the Aorist tense reports the simple occurrence of an action. It merely states that something happened; it tells you nothing more than the occurrence of an event. It sees the event as a single whole. The Aorist says it in the simplest way and may be likened to a snapshot (still photo) which just gives the simple fact of what was happening. The "snapshot" illustration is explained by Daniel B. Wallace:

> This contrasts with the present and imperfect, which portray the action as an ongoing process. It may be helpful to think of the aorist as taking a snapshot of the action while the imperfect (like the present) takes a motion picture, portraying the action as it unfolds. The following analogy might help.
>
> Suppose I were to take a snapshot of a student studying for a mid-term exam in intermediate Greek. Below the picture I put the caption, "Horatio Glutchstomach studied for the mid-term." From the snapshot and the caption all that one would be able to state positively is that Horatio Glutchstomach studied for the mid-term. Now in the picture you notice that Horatio has his Greek text opened before him. From this, you cannot say, "Because the picture is a snapshot rather than a movie, I know that Horatio Glutchstomach only had his Greek text opened for a split-second"! This might be true, but the snapshot does not tell you this. All you really

---

[276] Brooks and Winbery, *Syntax of the New Testament Greek*, 99.
[277] Dana and Mantey, *A Manual Grammar of the Greek New Testament*, 193.
[278] Samuel S. Green, *A Brief Introduction to New Testament Greek with vocabularies and exercises*, (London: The Religious Tract Society, 1911), 110.

know is that the student had his Greek text open. An event happened. From the picture you cannot tell for how long he had his text open. You cannot tell whether he studied for four hours straight (durative), or for eight hours, taking a ten minute break every 20 minutes (iterative). You cannot tell whether he studied successfully so as to pass the test, or whether he studied unsuccessfully. The snapshot does not tell you any of this. The snapshot by itself cannot tell if the action was momentary, "once-for-all", repeated, at regularly recurring intervals, or over a long period of time. It is obvious from this crude illustration that it would be silly to say that since I took a snapshot of Horatio studying, rather than a movie, he must have studied only for a very short time![279]

In this he shows that the Aorist Tense does not necessarily mean "completed action" nor does it necessarily mean that something has been accomplished once for all but rather it describes an event which is undefined with respect to its progress and its completion while giving you the author's perspective. The Aorist is thus the normal tense to use in Greek unless there is some special reason to use another. If one desires to emphasize the notion of linear action on the one hand or the state of completion on the other, then the Aorist is not the tense to use. Nunn observes,

The forms to which we give the name "Aorist" denoted by a simple, indefinite action, and were always used where no stress was laid on the continuity, completion, or incompletion of the action denoted by the verb. As a rule, the indicative mood of the Aorist refers to an action in past time. The idea of time is however quite secondary, and does not enter at all into the meaning of the moods of the Aorist other than the Indicative, except in reported speech. With this exception the idea of past time is only to be found in the forms of the verb which have an augment, that is to say the Imperfect, the Pluperfect, and the Aorist Indicative.[280]

1. Constantive Aorist

This use views the action as a whole and gives a summary statement of occurrence. In it the action is described as having taken place without pointing to how long it took. Dana and Mantey explain, "This use of the aorist contemplates the action in its entirety. It takes an occurrence and regardless of its extent of duration, gathers it into a single whole."[281] It describes the action as bare fact taking no interest in the internal workings of the action and can be represented by [•].

Revelation 20:4: Καὶ εἶδον θρόνους καὶ ἐκάθισαν ἐπ' αὐτούς καὶ κρίμα ἐδόθη αὐτοῖς καὶ τὰς ψυχὰς τῶν πεπελεκισμένων διὰ τὴν μαρτυρίαν Ἰησοῦ καὶ διὰ τὸν λόγον τοῦ θεοῦ καὶ οἵτινες οὐ προσεκύνησαν τῷ θηρίῳ, οὔτε τὴν εἰκόνα αὐτοῦ καὶ οὐκ ἔλαβον τὸ χάραγμα ἐπὶ τὸ μέτωπον αὐτῶν καὶ ἐπὶ τὴν χεῖρα αὐτῶν, καὶ ἔζησαν καὶ <u>ἐβασίλευσαν</u> μετὰ Χριστοῦ τὰ χίλια ἔτη – "and I saw thrones and they sat upon them and judgment was given to the and the souls of those who had been beheaded because of the testimony of Jesus and because of the word of God and those who had

---

[279] Wallace, *Greek Grammar Beyond the Basics*, 554-555.
[280] Nunn, *A Short Syntax of New Testament Greek*, 66.
[281] Dana and Mantey, *A Manual Grammar of the Greek New Testament*, 196.

not worshipped the beast neither his image and did not receive the mark upon their forehead and upon their hand and they lived and <u>reigned</u> with Christ a thousand years."

John 2:20: εἶπον οὖν οἱ Ἰουδαῖοι τεσσαράκοντα καὶ ἓξ ἔτεσιν <u>ᾠκοδομήθη</u> ὁ ναὸς οὗτος καὶ σὺ ἐν τρισὶν ἡμέραις ἐγερεῖς αὐτόν – "then the Jews said forty and six years it was necessary for this temple <u>to be built</u> and you in three days will raise it?"

2. Ingressive Aorist

The aorist tense can be and is often used to stress the beginning of an action or the entrance into a state. This use is called the ingressive use.[282] The ingressive aorist differs from the ingressive imperfect in that with the aorist, there is no implication that the action continues. Vaughan and Gideon note, "The ingressive aorist should be compared with the inceptive imperfect. The latter implies the continuance of the action; the aorist says nothing about this. The action may in fact continue, but the aorist says nothing about it."[283] Dana and Mantey explain that "The action may be regarded from the viewpoint of its initiation, which ... might be graphically represented thus: •>———."[284] Burton observes that the inceptive aorist is "The Aorist of a verb whose Present denotes a state or condition, commonly denotes the beginning of that state."[285]

John 1:14: Καὶ ὁ λόγος σὰρξ <u>ἐγένετο</u> καὶ ἐσκήνωσεν ἐν ἡμῖν καὶ ἐθεασάμεθα τὴν δόξαν αὐτοῦ δόξαν ὡς μονογενοῦς παρὰ πατρός πλήρης χάριτος καὶ ἀληθείας – "and the word <u>became</u> flesh and dwelt among us and we beheld his glory the glory as of the only begotten with the Father full of grace and truth."

2 Corinthians 8:9: γινώσκετε γὰρ τὴν χάριν τοῦ κυρίου ἡμῶν Ἰησοῦ Χριστοῦ ὅτι δι' ὑμᾶς <u>ἐπτώχευσεν</u> πλούσιος ὢν ἵνα ὑμεῖς τῇ ἐκείνου πτωχείᾳ πλουτήσητε – "for you know the grace of our lord Jesus Christ that because of you he being rich <u>became poor</u> in order that you may be rich through the poverty of that one."

3. Culminative Aorist

The aorist is not only used to show the beginning of an action but is also used to stress the cessation of an act or state. In this the conclusion or the end of the action is the focus and "certain verbs, by their very *lexical* nature, almost require this usage. For example, "he died" is hardly going to be an ingressive idea."[286] Thus this use implies that the act which is being described was already in progress and the aorist then presents the effort and progress as being successful and the action comes to a conclusion Vaughan and Gideon explain "The culminative aorist is somewhat similar to the perfect tense, but there is a difference. The culminative aorist indicates that the act or process was completed but says nothing about the continuance of results. The Perfect tense

---

[282] Burton notes that the ingressive aorist "belongs to verbs which in the Present and Imperfect denote the continuance of a state" [E. Burton, *Syntax of the Moods and Tenses in New Testament Greek*, 17.]

[283] Vaughan and Gideon, *A Greek Grammar of the New Testament*, 145.

[284] Dana and Mantey, *A Manual Grammar of the Greek New Testament*, 195.

[285] E. Burton, *Syntax of the Moods and Tenses in New Testament Greek*, 20.

[286] Wallace, *Greek Grammar Beyond the Basics*, 559.

combines both these ideas – a completed act and continuing results."²⁸⁷ The action in this case "viewed in its results ... may be indicated in the graph ———<•"²⁸⁸

Philippians 4:11: οὐχ ὅτι καθ' ὑστέρησιν λέγω ἐγὼ γὰρ <u>ἔμαθον</u> ἐν οἷς εἰμι αὐτάρκης εἶναι – "not that I speak because of need for <u>I have learned</u> in what I am to be content."

Matthew 6:6: Σὺ δὲ ὅταν προσεύχῃ, εἴσελθε εἰς τὸ ταμιεῖόν σου, καὶ <u>κλείσας</u> τὴν θύραν σου, πρόσευξαι τῷ πατρί σου τῷ ἐν τῷ κρυπτῷ· καὶ ὁ πατήρ σου ὁ βλέπων ἐν τῷ κρυπτῷ, ἀποδώσει σοι ἐν τῷ φανερῷ. – "but when you pray, enter into your chamber and <u>when you have closed</u> your door, pray to your father which in secret: and your father who is seeing in secret will reward you in the open."

5. Gnomic Aorist

The Gnomic aorist is when a timeless, general or axiomatic fact is stated using the aorist tense. This use is rendered in the English using the present tense. Wallace says, "The aorist indicative is occasionally used to present a timeless, general fact. When it does so, it does not refer to a particular event that *did* happen, but to a generic event that does happen. Normally, it is translated like a simple present tense."²⁸⁹

Galatians 5:24: οἱ δὲ τοῦ Χριστοῦ τὴν σάρκα <u>ἐσταύρωσαν</u> σὺν τοῖς παθήμασιν καὶ ταῖς ἐπιθυμίαις – but the ones belonging to Christ <u>have crucified</u> the flesh together with its passions and lusts.

1 Peter 2:24: διότι πᾶσα σὰρξ ὡς χόρτος καὶ πᾶσα δόξα ἀνθρώπου ὡς ἄνθος χόρτου· <u>ἐξηράνθη</u> ὁ χόρτος καὶ τὸ ἄνθος αὐτοῦ <u>ἐξέπεσεν</u>· – "wherefore all flesh is like grass and all glory of man as flower of grass: the grass <u>withers away</u> and the flower <u>falls out</u>."

6. Epistolary Aorist

This is the use of the aorist in the epistles in which according to Wenham, "with a pleasing courtesy the Greek writer puts himself in the position of the one who receives the letter. When the letter is received it will have been written in the past"²⁹⁰ but the author describes his letter from the audience's time frame and states a future or present in past tense. "In other words, he used the tense that would be appropriate for his readers. At the time of writing, the act was present or future, but when the letter was read, the act would be past."²⁹¹

1 John 5:13: ταῦτα <u>ἔγραψα</u> ὑμῖν τοῖς πιστεύουσιν εἰς τὸ ὄνομα τοῦ υἱοῦ τοῦ Θεοῦ, ἵνα εἰδῆτε ὅτι ζωὴν ἔχετε αἰώνιον, καὶ ἵνα πιστεύητε εἰς τὸ ὄνομα τοῦ υἱοῦ τοῦ Θεοῦ. – "these things <u>I wrote</u> to you those who believe on the name of the son of God in order that you may know that you have eternal life and that you may believe on the name of the son of God."

---

[287] Vaughan and Gideon, *A Greek Grammar of the New Testament*, 146.
[288] Dana and Mantey, *A Manual Grammar of the Greek New Testament*, 195.
[289] Wallace, *Greek Grammar Beyond the Basics*, 562.
[290] Wenham, *The Elements of new Testament* Greek, 164.
[291] Vaughan and Gideon, *A Greek Grammar of the New Testament*, 147.

Philippians 2:28: σπουδαιοτέρως οὖν <u>ἔπεμψα</u> αὐτὸν ἵνα ἰδόντες αὐτὸν πάλιν χαρῆτε κἀγὼ ἀλυπότερος ὦ. – "therefore <u>I sent</u> him more speedily in order that seeing him again you may rejoice and I may be less sorrowful."

7. Dramatic Aorist

The aorist when used to point to an event that has just happened recently expressing it vividly as if it is present; with the aim of "stating a present reality with the certitude of a past event"[292] is described as a dramatic aorist. It is a special use of the aorist tense mainly uses as "a device for emphasis. It is commonly used of a state which has just been realized, or a result which has just been accomplished, or is on the point of being accomplished."[293]

John 13:31: Ὅτε ἐξῆλθεν λέγει ὁ Ἰησοῦς Νῦν <u>ἐδοξάσθη</u> ὁ υἱὸς τοῦ ἀνθρώπου καὶ ὁ θεὸς ἐδοξάσθη ἐν αὐτῷ· – "Then when he had gone out, Jesus said now the son of man <u>is glorified</u> and God is glorified in him."

James 1:24: κατενόησεν γὰρ ἑαυτὸν καὶ ἀπελήλυθεν καὶ εὐθέως <u>ἐπελάθετο</u> ὁποῖος ἦν – "for he observes himself fully and has gone away and immediately <u>he forgets</u> what kind he was."

Luke 16:4: <u>ἔγνων</u> τί ποιήσω ἵνα ὅταν μετασταθῶ τῆς οἰκονομίας δέξωνταί με εἰς τοὺς οἴκους αὐτῶν – "<u>I know</u> what I will do that when I am put out of the stewardship they will receive me into their houses."

8. Futuristic Aorist

The aorist may be "used to describe an event that is not yet past as though it were already completed in order to stress the certainty of the event"[294] Brooks and Winbery state that this use of the aorist "involves the use of the aorist to indicate an event which has not happened but which is certain to happen that it is depicted as though it had already happened. There is a gnomic element in most futuristic aorists, but the emphasis is not on a universal truth but on a strongly anticipated occurrence."[295]

Romans 8:30: οὓς δὲ προώρισεν τούτους καὶ ἐκάλεσεν· καὶ οὓς ἐκάλεσεν τούτους καὶ ἐδικαίωσεν· οὓς δὲ ἐδικαίωσεν τούτους καὶ <u>ἐδόξασεν</u> – "and whom he predestinated these also he called: and whom he justified these also he <u>glorified</u>."

John 15:8: ἐν τούτῳ <u>ἐδοξάσθη</u> ὁ πατήρ μου ἵνα καρπὸν πολὺν φέρητε καὶ γενήσεσθε ἐμοὶ μαθηταί – "in this my Father <u>is glorified</u>, that you bear much fruit and you will become my disciples"

The Perfect Tense

The perfect is the tense of complete action. That is, it views action as a finished product and presents the picture of one at the top of the hill taking a backward look at the climb or of a runner who having run the race glances backward again. Such a person is pictured as looking back from the standpoint of one who has finished and completed

---

[292] Dana and Mantey, *A Manual Grammar of the Greek New Testament*, 198.
[293] Ibid.
[294] Wallace, *Greek Grammar Beyond the Basics*, 563.
[295] Brooks and Winbery, *Syntax of the New Testament Greek*, 103.

the race and having completed it in the past, it is the results that are continuing. Wenham gives a good explanation. he writes,

> The perfect represents a present state resulting from a past action, e.g. γέγραπται, it stands written. That is to say, the Scripture, written in the past, bears its witness now, in the present. This can be represented by: (•———) Or, if the past action was itself of extended duration before completion, by: (———•———). This use of the Greek Perfect is not altogether the same as the use of the English Perfect. Usually the English Perfect will accurately translate the Greek Perfect, and the English Past Simple will accurately translate the Greek Aorist, but by no means always. The Greek Aorist is wider in meaning than the English Past Simple, and the Greek Perfect is narrower in meaning than the English perfect.[296]

It should be noted that though the English Perfect may accurately translate the Greek Perfect, this does not mean that it is an exact equivalent of the Greek Perfect for it has no exact parallel in English. In the Greek, the perfect presents the progress of the action as completed in the past but the results of the action continuing in the present with full effect which is unlike the English perfect, which presents a completed action in the past. Burton highlights the differences as summarized in the table below[297]:

The English Perfect is used	***The Greek Perfect is used***
• of any past action between which and the time of speaking the speaker does not intend distinctly to interpose an interval. • The English Pluperfect is used to mark the fact that the event expressed by it preceded another past event indicated by the context, and this whether the earlier event is thought of as completed at the time of the later event, or only indefinitely as a simple occurrence preceding the later event! • The English Past is used of any past action between which and the moment of speaking an interval is thought of as existing. It affirms nothing respecting existing result.	• to represent an action as standing complete, i.e. as having an existing result, at the time of speaking. • The Greek Pluperfect is used to represent an action as standing complete, i.e. as having an existing result, at a point of past time indicated by the context. • The Greek Aorist is used of any past event which is conceived of simply as an event (or as entered upon, or as accomplished), regardless alike of the existence or non-existence of an interval between itself and the moment of speaking, and of the question whether it precedes or not some other past action. It affirms nothing respecting existing result.

Thus the Greek perfect tense presents action as having reached its termination and existing in its finished results. In other words, something began, happened and ended in the past, and the results of that are continuing and the abiding results in the present testify that the act or event is not nullified but rather that it stands completed in the present time. Thus the process exists in the present in a finished state in the form of

---

[296] Wenham, *Elements of New Testament Greek*, 139.
[297] The table is adapted from Burton, *Syntax of the Moods and Tenses in New Testament Greek*, 24-25.

the results. Vaughan and Gideon write that the perfect tense "represents a completed state or condition from the standpoint of present time. Thus there is a double emphasis in the perfect tense: present state resulting from past action. In this respect it may be said to combine in itself both the present and the aorist. That is to say, it is both linear and punctiliar."[298]

1. Intensive Perfect

This perfect is "used to emphasize the *results* or *present state* produced by a past action. The English present often is the best translation for such a perfect."[299]

Matthew 4:4: Ὁ δὲ ἀποκριθεὶς εἶπε, γέγραπται, Οὐκ ἐπ' ἄρτῳ μόνῳ ζήσεται ἄνθρωπος, ἀλλ' ἐπὶ παντὶ ῥήματι ἐκπορευομένῳ διὰ στόματος Θεοῦ. – "but he answering said it stands written not by bread alone shall man live but by every word coming out of the mouth of God."

1 Corinthians 15:20: Νυνὶ δὲ Χριστὸς ἐγήγερται ἐκ νεκρῶν ἀπαρχὴ τῶν κεκοιμημένων ἐγένετο – "but now Christ has risen out of the dead becoming the first fruits of those having fallen asleep."

2. Consummative Perfect

The perfect tense may be used to emphasize the completed action or the process from which a present state results. Thus when the emphasis is not on the result but the past action, the usage is referred to as consummative perfect. Dana and Mantey write,

> Here it is not the state, but a consummated process which is presented. However, we are not to suppose that the existing result is entirely out of sight, for "the writer had in mind both the past act and the present result" (Br. 38). Otherwise he would have used the aorist, which in the culminative sense denotes completed action without reference to existing results. ... we might make a graphical distinction thus: culminative aorist, presenting the fact that the process has been completed, ———•; consummative perfect, presenting the completed process, ———•.........; intensive perfect, presenting the results of the completed process, ...•———.[300]

2 Corinthians 7:3: οὐ πρὸς κατάκρισιν λέγω· προείρηκα γὰρ ὅτι ἐν ταῖς καρδίαις ἡμῶν ἐστε εἰς τὸ συναποθανεῖν καὶ συζῆν – "I do not speak to condemn for I have said before that you are in our hearts to die together and to live together."

2 Timothy 4:7: τὸν ἀγῶνα τὸν καλὸν ἠγώνισμαι τὸν δρόμον τετέλεκα τὴν πίστιν τετήρηκα· – "I have fought the good fight I have finished the course I have kept the faith."

3. Iterative Perfect

This is perfect of repeated action and presents the completed action as having occurred at repeated points in time. This use "like the consummative perfect, stresses completed action; but something either in the context or in the meaning of the word (or

---

[298] Vaughan and Gideon, *A Greek Grammar of the New Testament*, 149.
[299] Wallace, *Greek Grammar Beyond the Basics*, 574.
[300] Dana and Mantey, *A Manual Grammar of the Greek New Testament*, 202-03.

both) indicates that the character of the action was iterative. Robertson calls it the "present perfect of broken continuity" (p. 896)."[301]

1 John 1:1: ἦν ἀπ' ἀρχῆς, ὃ <u>ἀκηκόαμεν</u>, ὃ <u>ἑωράκαμεν</u> τοῖς ὀφθαλμοῖς ἡμῶν, ὃ ἐθεασάμεθα, καὶ αἱ χεῖρες ἡμῶν ἐψηλάφησαν περὶ τοῦ λόγου τῆς ζωῆς, – "that which was from the beginning which <u>we have heard</u>, which <u>we have seen</u> with our eyes, which we have beheld, which our hands have handled concerning the word of life."

John 1:18: θεὸν οὐδεὶς <u>ἑώρακεν</u> πώποτε· ὁ μονογενὴς υἱός, ὁ ὢν εἰς τὸν κόλπον τοῦ πατρὸς ἐκεῖνος ἐξηγήσατο – "no one <u>has seen</u> God at any time: the only begotten son the one who is in the bosom of the father the same has declared him."

John 5:37: καὶ ὁ πέμψας με πατὴρ αὐτὸς <u>μεμαρτύρηκεν</u> περὶ ἐμοῦ οὔτε φωνὴν αὐτοῦ <u>ἀκηκόατε</u> πώποτε οὔτε εἶδος αὐτοῦ <u>ἑωράκατε</u> – "and the father, the one who sent me, he has testified concerning me neither have you heard his voice at any time nor <u>have you seen</u> his form."

4. Dramatic Perfect

The perfect tense may also be used to express an action vividly as if it is present to the speaker. Dana and Mantey write,

> It is a rhetorical application of the perfect tense. Since the perfect represents an existing state, it may be used for the purpose of describing a fact in an unusually vivid and realistic way. The historical present and dramatic aorist are also used in a sense similar to this, but for this purpose the perfect is the most forcible of the three.[302]

This use is mainly to be determined by the context of the passage. Vaughan and Gideon observe that "The dramatic perfect occurs in narrative material and is particularly prominent in John's Gospel."[303] Brooks and Winbery note that "The perfect tense is linked indiscriminately with other tenses in such stories."[304]

James 1:24: κατενόησεν γὰρ ἑαυτὸν καὶ <u>ἀπελήλυθεν</u> καὶ εὐθέως ἐπελάθετο ὁποῖος ἦν – "for he observes himself fully and <u>has gone away</u> and immediately he forgets what kind he was."

Matthew 13:46[305]: ὃς εὑρὼν ἕνα πολύτιμον μαργαρίτην ἀπελθὼν <u>πέπρακεν</u> πάντα ὅσα εἶχεν καὶ ἠγόρασεν αὐτόν – "who when he found one pearl of great price when he went away <u>he sells</u> everything whatsoever he has and buys it,"

4. Gnomic Perfect

This use of the perfect is similar to intensive perfect. The only distinction is that this perfect does not refer to any particular event but rather states an universal truth.

---

[301] Vaughan and Gideon, *A Greek Grammar of the New Testament*, 151.
[302] Dana and Mantey, *A Manual Grammar of the Greek New Testament*, 204.
[303] Vaughan and Gideon, *A Greek Grammar of the New Testament*, 151.
[304] Brooks and Winbery, *Syntax of the New Testament Greek*, 106.
[305] Dana and Mantey explain "This passage is found the parable of the Pearl of Great Price, and the dramatic perfect as used here stresses the haste and eagerness with which the man sought to secure for himself the rich treasure he had found. In colloquial English we would say, "He goes out, and the first thing you know he's sold everything he has!" [Dana and Mantey, *A Manual Grammar of the Greek New Testament*, 205.]

Brooks and Winbery explain, "The distinctive element is the element of custom or generally accepted truth."[306]

1 Corinthians 7:39: Γυνὴ <u>δέδεται</u> νόμῳ ἐφ' ὅσον χρόνον ζῇ ὁ ἀνὴρ αὐτῆς· ἐὰν δὲ κοιμηθῇ ὁ ἀνήρ αὐτῆς ἐλευθέρα ἐστὶν ᾧ θέλει γαμηθῆναι μόνον ἐν κυρίῳ – "a woman <u>is bound</u> by law as long as her husband is living: but if her husband sleeps, she at liberty to be married by who she desires only in the lord."

James 2:10: ὅστις γὰρ ὅλον τὸν νόμον τηρήσει, πταίσει δὲ ἐν ἑνί <u>γέγονεν</u> πάντων ἔνοχος – "for whosoever will keep the whole law, but offend in one has become guilty of all."

5. Aoristic Perfect

This use of the perfect states the action of the verb as would an aorist, that is as a simple past action without a sense of its existing results. "The perfect tense is used when the action seems to be merely stated without reference to a continuing result. This differs from the consummative (above page 105) in that in the consummative the element of result is minor but still present."[307] Burton also explains, "The Perfect Indicative is sometimes used in the New Testament of a simple past fact where it is scarcely possible to suppose that the thought of existing result was in the writer's mind."[308]

Revelation 8:5: καὶ <u>εἴληφεν</u> ὁ ἄγγελος τὸ λιβανωτόν καὶ ἐγέμισεν αὐτὸ ἐκ τοῦ πυρὸς τοῦ θυσιαστηρίου καὶ ἔβαλεν εἰς τὴν γῆν καὶ ἐγένοντο φωναὶ καὶ βρονταὶ καὶ ἀστραπαὶ καὶ σεισμός – "and the angel <u>took</u> the censor and filled it from of the fire of the altar and cast into the earth and there came sounds and thunders and lightnings and earthquakes."

John 12:29: ὁ οὖν ὄχλος ὁ ἑστὼς καὶ ἀκούσας ἔλεγεν βροντὴν γεγονέναι ἄλλοι ἔλεγον Ἄγγελος αὐτῷ <u>λελάληκεν</u> – "then the crowd which was standing and hearing said thunder occurred others said an angel <u>spoke</u> to him."

The pluperfect tense

The pluperfect is the perfect projected into past time. Hewett explains,

The pluperfect tense makes the perfect tense past. It expresses action that had occurred in a past setting and the resultant effect continued up to a time that is now in the past. Both action and effect are past experiences. The pluperfect like the perfect may denote either a state that had existed up to a time in the past (cf. Jn. 18:16, 18) or a completed action (cf. Jn. 11:19).[309]

This means that the pluperfect shows an action that was completed in the past and its result existed at some time in the past. The past time in which the results continued is indicated by the context and thus its major difference with the perfect tense consists of the time factor which is essential to it. Wallace states,

The force of the pluperfect tense is that it describes an event that, completed in the past, has results that exist in the past as well (in relation to the time of speaking).

---

[306] Brooks and Winbery, *Syntax of the New Testament Greek*, 107.
[307] Ibid.
[308] E. Burton, *Syntax of the Moods and Tenses in New Testament Greek*, 39.
[309] Hewett, *New Testament Greek*, 76.

CHAPTER 5: THE SYNTAX OF VERBS

The pluperfect makes no comment about the results existing up to the time of speaking. Such results may exist at the time of speaking, or they may not; the pluperfect contributes nothing either way.[310]

Thus the pluperfect expresses continuance of the completed state in the past up to a prescribed limit in the past at some point determined by the context and the continuation of the results too are to be contemplated in past time at a point implied in the context. As regarding the relation between the perfect and the pluperfect, the pluperfect "is to the perfect tense what the imperfect is to the present. That is to say, it is an auxiliary to the perfect, differing from it only in the matter of time."[311]

1. Intensive Pluperfect

This use of the pluperfect places the emphasis on the existing results or as Dana and Mantey put it, "Here the stress is laid upon the reality of the fact, which enables it to be presented with more force than could be done with the aorist, but the only device for construing it in English is the simple past."[312]

John 1:35: Τῇ ἐπαύριον πάλιν εἱστήκει ὁ Ἰωάννης καὶ ἐκ τῶν μαθητῶν αὐτοῦ δύο – "again on the morrow John <u>was standing</u> and two out of his disciples with him."

John 18:18: <u>εἱστήκεισαν</u> δὲ οἱ δοῦλοι καὶ οἱ ὑπηρέται ἀνθρακιὰν πεποιηκότες ὅτι ψῦχος ἦν καὶ ἐθερμαίνοντο· ἦν δὲ μετ' αὐτῶν ὁ Πέτρος ἑστὼς καὶ θερμαινόμενος – "and the slaves and the officers <u>were standing</u> having made a fire of coals because it was cold and they warmed themselves: and Peter was with them standing and warming himself."

2. Consummative Pluperfect

In this use the pluperfect places emphasis on the completed action. "The pluperfect may be used to emphasize the completion of an action in past time, without focusing on the existing results. It is usually best translated as a past perfect ("had" + perfect passive participle)."[313]

John 4:18: πέντε γὰρ ἄνδρας ἔσχες καὶ νῦν ὃν ἔχεις οὐκ ἔστιν σου ἀνήρ· τοῦτο ἀληθὲς <u>εἴρηκας</u> – "for five man you have and now the one you are having is not your husband: this thing <u>you have said</u> truly."

John 9:22: ταῦτα εἶπον οἱ γονεῖς αὐτοῦ ὅτι ἐφοβοῦντο τοὺς Ἰουδαίους· ἤδη γὰρ <u>συνετέθειντο</u> οἱ Ἰουδαῖοι ἵνα ἐάν τις αὐτὸν ὁμολογήσῃ Χριστόν ἀποσυνάγωγος γένηται – "these things his parents said because they feared the Jews for already the Jews <u>had agreed</u> that if any one may confess him Christ out of the synagogue he shall be."

---

[310] Wallace, *Greek Grammar Beyond the Basics*, 583.
[311] Vaughan and Gideon, *A Greek Grammar of the New Testament*, 152.
[312] Dana and Mantey, *A Manual Grammar of the Greek New Testament*, 206.
[313] Wallace, *Greek Grammar Beyond the Basics*, 585.

VOICE

Voice is the property of the verb that indicates how the subject is related to the action (or state) expressed by the verb. Vaughan and Gideon observe that "Transitiveness, we have seen, has to do with the relation of the verbal idea to the object[314]. Voice tells how the action of the verb is related to the subject."[315] In general, the voice of the verb may indicate that the subject is *doing* the action (active)[316], *receiving* the action (passive)[317], or both *doing and receiving* (at least the results of) the action (middle)[318].

A. Active Voice

In general it can be said that in the active voice the subject *performs*, *produces*, or *experiences the action* or exists in the *state* expressed by the verb. Brooks and Winbery say, "The active voice represents the subject as producing the action, or in the case of a linking verb, as existing."[319] This use presents the simplest and most common verbal use with the relation of the subject to the verb described as direct.

1. Simple Active

This is the normal or routine use, by far the most common in which the subject performs or experiences the action. The verb may be transitive or intransitive. Dana and Mantey explain "The ordinary significance of the active voice is to describe the subject as directly performing the act affirmed."[320]

Mark 4:2: καὶ ἐδίδασκεν αὐτοὺς ἐν παραβολαῖς πολλά καὶ ἔλεγεν αὐτοῖς ἐν τῇ διδαχῇ αὐτοῦ – "and He was teaching them many things in parables and he was saying to them in his teaching."

John 2:11: Ταύτην ἐποίησεν τὴν ἀρχὴν τῶν σημείων ὁ Ἰησοῦς ἐν Κανὰ τῆς Γαλιλαίας καὶ ἐφανέρωσεν τὴν δόξαν αὐτοῦ καὶ ἐπίστευσαν εἰς αὐτὸν οἱ μαθηταὶ αὐτοῦ – "This thing is the beginning of signs Jesus did in Cana of Galilee and he manifested his glory and his disciples believed on him."

Acts 1:5: ὅτι Ἰωάννης μὲν ἐβάπτισεν ὕδατι ὑμεῖς δὲ βαπτισθήσεσθε ἐν πνεύματι ἁγίῳ οὐ μετὰ πολλὰς ταύτας ἡμέρας – "for John indeed baptized you with water but you will be baptized in the Holy Spirit not many days after these."

---

[314] "Verbs may be classified as to their nature. Viewed in this manner, they are either *transitive* or *intransitive*. Transitive verbs, sometimes called verbs of incomplete predication, are those verbs which require an object to complete their meaning. Such a verb, without its object, "creates a sense of suspense" (Dana-Mantey, p. 154). Intransitive verbs are verbs of complete predication; that is, they make complete sense without an object ('I stand'; 'The sun shines'). [Vaughan and Gideon, *A Greek Grammar of the New Testament*, 87.]

[315] Vaughan and Gideon, *A Greek Grammar of the New Testament*, 90.

[316] Hewett observes that, "A verb is said to be in the active voice when the subject performs the activity. Thus in "I throw the ball," *I*, being the actor, is the subject of an active voice verb *throw*." [Hewett, *New Testament Greek*, 11.]

[317] "The passive voice is common to both the English and Greek languages. It expresses in Greek, as in English, that the subject receives the action of the verb. ... The personal agent who actually does the action expressed by the passive constructions is often identified by using the preposition ὑπό with the genitive." [Hewett, *New Testament Greek*, 70.]

[318] "In the middle voice the subject of the verb is involved in the action, but the specific manner of involvement must be detected from the context. In some way the action is in the interest of the subject." [Hewett, *New Testament Greek*, 82.]

[319] Brooks and Winbery, *Syntax of New Testament Greek*, 110.

[320] Dana and Mantey, *A Manual Grammar of the Greek New Testament*, 156.

2. Causative Active

Sometimes the subject is not directly involved in the action, but may be said to be the ultimate source or cause of it and so as Dana and Mantey observe, the subject "is sometimes represented as related to the action through intermediary means."[321] In translation, sometimes the phrase *cause to* can be used before the verb. This usage often occurs with –ιζω verbs and Dana and Mantey further explain that

> In Hebrew we have approximately the same idiom represented in the Hiphil stem. We have it in English in such expressions as "to blow a horn," "to shine a light," "to run a horse," etc. It generally arises from the use of an intransitive verb in a transitive sense.[322]

Matthew 5:45: ὅπως γένησθε υἱοὶ τοῦ πατρὸς ὑμῶν τοῦ ἐν οὐρανοῖς, ὅτι τὸν ἥλιον αὐτοῦ <u>ἀνατέλλει</u> ἐπὶ πονηροὺς καὶ ἀγαθοὺς, καὶ <u>βρέχει</u> ἐπὶ δικαίους καὶ ἀδίκους. – "thus be the sons of your father which is in heaven for He <u>causes</u> his sun <u>to rise</u> on evil and good, and he <u>causes it to rain</u> on the righteous and unrighteous."

John 19:1: Τότε οὖν <u>ἔλαβεν</u> ὁ Πιλᾶτος τὸν Ἰησοῦν καὶ <u>ἐμαστίγωσεν</u> – "therefore when Pilate <u>took</u> Jesus and <u>scourged</u> him."

1 Corinthians 3:7: ὥστε οὔτε ὁ φυτεύων ἐστίν τι οὔτε ὁ ποτίζων ἀλλ' ὁ <u>αὐξάνων</u> θεός – "so that neither the one who plants is anything nor the one who waters but God who <u>causes to grow</u>."

B. Middle Voice

Defining the function of the middle voice is not easy because of its nuances. Generally, the middle voice describes the subject as *performing or experiencing the action* expressed by the verb in such a way that the subject participates in the results of the action in some way. Thus it may be said that the subject acts on the verb with an interest in the results of the action of the verb. Robertson notes that "The middle calls special attention to the subject ... the subject is acting in relation to himself somehow."[323] The difference between the active and middle voice is one of emphasis. The active emphasizes the *action* of the verb; the middle emphasizes the subject of the verb. Dana and Mantey explain,

> The middle voice is that use of the verb which describes the subject as *participating in the results of the action*. ... While the active voice stresses action, the middle stresses the agent. It somehow relates more intimately to the subject. Just how the action is thus related is not indicated by the middle voice, but must be detected from the context or character of the verbal idea (cf. R. 804). So "the middle is, strictly speaking, never used without some sort of reference to the subject" (Bt. 193).[324]

---

[321] ibid.
[322] ibid.
[323] Robertson, *A Grammar of the Greek New Testament*, 804.
[324] Dana and Mantey, *A Manual Grammar of the Greek New Testament*, 157.

1. Direct (Reflexive, Direct Reflexive) Middle

With the direct middle, "the subject acts on itself with reflexive force. The word "self" will be the direct object in the translation."[325] Though the direct middle presents the subject as acting directly on himself or herself with reflexive force, but "the reflexive pronoun used in English translation does not occur in the Greek."[326] The genius of the middle can most clearly be seen by this use which occurs in the New Testament with verbs whose lexical nuance includes a reflexive notion (such as putting on clothes).

Matt 27:5: καὶ ῥίψας τὰ ἀργύρια ἐν τῷ ναῷ ἀνεχώρησεν καὶ ἀπελθὼν ἀπήγξατο – "and throwing the silver in the temple he went away and hanged himself."

Mark 7:4: καὶ ἀπό ἀγορᾶς ἐὰν μὴ βαπτίσωνται οὐκ ἐσθίουσιν καὶ ἄλλα πολλά ἐστιν ἃ παρέλαβον κρατεῖν βαπτισμοὺς ποτηρίων καὶ ξεστῶν καὶ χαλκίων καὶ κλινῶν – "and from the market, unless they wash themselves they do not eat and there are many other things which they received to hold washing cups and pots and copper vessels and tables."

2 Corinthians 11:14: καὶ οὐ θαυμαστόν· αὐτὸς γὰρ ὁ Σατανᾶς μετασχηματίζεται εἰς ἄγγελον φωτός – "and it is no marvel for Satan himself transforms himself into an angel of light."

2. Indirect (Indirect Reflexive, Intensive, Dynamic) Middle

The subject acts *for* (or sometimes *by*) himself or herself, or in his or her *own interest* or as Dana and Mantey observe,

> Sometimes the middle lays stress upon the agent as producing the action rather than participating in the results. This use signifies that the action is closely related to the subject, or is related to the subject in some special and distinctive sense which the writer wishes to emphasize. The reason for the emphasis is to be inferred from the context.[327]

This is a common use of the middle in the New Testament and apart from the deponent middle, it is the most common.

Acts 5:2: καὶ ἐνοσφίσατο ἀπὸ τῆς τιμῆς συνειδυίας καὶ τῆς γυναικός αὐτοῦ, καὶ ἐνέγκας μέρος τι παρὰ τοὺς πόδας τῶν ἀποστόλων ἔθηκεν – "and he kept back part of the price his wife also being privy and bringing a certain part he placed at the feet of the apostles."

Matt 27:24: ἰδὼν δὲ ὁ Πιλᾶτος ὅτι οὐδὲν ὠφελεῖ ἀλλὰ μᾶλλον θόρυβος γίνεται λαβὼν ὕδωρ ἀπενίψατο τὰς χεῖρας ἀπέναντι τοῦ ὄχλου λέγων· Ἀθῷός εἰμι ἀπὸ τοῦ αἵματος τοῦ δικαίου τούτου· ὑμεῖς ὄψεσθε – "and Pilate seeing that it is profiting nothing but rather becoming an uproar, taking water he washed his hands before the crowd saying "I am innocent of the blood of this just man" you see to it."

3. Permissive or Causative Middle

---

[325] Brooks and Winbery, *Syntax of New Testament Greek*, 111.
[326] Hewett, *New Testament Greek*, 83.
[327] Dana and Mantey, *A Manual Grammar of the Greek New Testament*, 159.

CHAPTER 5: THE SYNTAX OF VERBS

"The middle may represent the agent as voluntarily yielding himself to the results of the action, or seeking to secure the results of the action in his own interest."³²⁸ This means that the subject *allows* something to be done *for* or *to* himself or herself or produces the action on himself or herself and as such the subject may be the source behind an action done in his or her behalf or as Brooks and Winbery put it,

> The subject permits or causes the action to take place upon itself. The subject indirectly does something to or for itself by means of someone or something else. Sometimes the words "permit" or "cause" will be used in the translation. Sometimes a passive will be used.³²⁹

Luke 2:4-5: Ἀνέβη δὲ καὶ Ἰωσὴφ ἀπὸ τῆς Γαλιλαίας ἐκ πόλεως Ναζαρὲτ εἰς τὴν Ἰουδαίαν εἰς πόλιν Δαβίδ, ἥτις καλεῖται Βηθλέεμ διὰ τὸ εἶναι αὐτὸν ἐξ οἴκου καὶ πατριᾶς Δαβίδ, 5 <u>ἀπογράψασθαι</u> σὺν Μαριὰμ τῇ μεμνηστευμένῃ αὐτῷ γυναικὶ, οὔσῃ ἐγκύῳ – "and Joseph also went up from Galilee out of the city of Nazareth into Judea to the city of David which is called Bethlehem because he was out of the house and lineage of David, <u>to be registered</u> together with Mary who was espoused to him a wife being great with child."

Acts 22:16: καὶ νῦν τί μέλλεις ἀναστὰς <u>βάπτισαι</u> καὶ <u>ἀπόλουσαι</u> τὰς ἁμαρτίας σου ἐπικαλεσάμενος τὸ ὄνομα τοῦ Κυρίου – "and now what are you about? arise <u>be baptized</u> and <u>wash away</u> your sins calling on the name of Jesus."

C. Passive Voice

In general it can be said that in the passive voice the subject *is acted upon* or *receives the action* expressed by the verb without any expression of volition implied on the part of the subject. This means that in the passive voice, the stress is on the subject receiving the action of the verb and whether the subject may or may not be aware, ow whether its volition may or may not be involved are not stressed when the passive is used but rather it simply states that the subject of the verb did not "produce the action nor participate in the action or state of being"³³⁰ Vaughan and Gideon note that

> In the passive, verbs are usually intransitive, i.e., do not take an object. ... Some verbs however, are transitive even in the passive. These ordinarily are verbs which in the active take two objects. When they become passive, the accusative of person becomes the subject and the accusative of thing is retained as the object.³³¹

1. Regular (Simple) Passive

The most common use of the passive voice is to indicate that the subject receives the action. No implication is made about cognition, volition, or cause on the part of the subject. This usage occurs both with and without and expressed agent.

Mark 4:6 ἡλίου δὲ ἀνατείλαντος <u>ἐκαυματίσθη</u> καὶ διὰ τὸ μὴ ἔχειν ῥίζαν ἐξηράνθη – "and When the sun rose, <u>it was scorched</u> and because it did not have depth, it withered."

---

³²⁸ ibid., 160.
³²⁹ Brooks and Winbery, *Syntax of New Testament Greek*, 112.
³³⁰ Brooks and Winbery, *Syntax of New Testament Greek*, 113.
³³¹ Vaughan and Gideon, *A Greek Grammar of the New Testament*, 91.

Acts 1:5: ὅτι Ἰωάννης μὲν ἐβάπτισεν ὕδατι ὑμεῖς δὲ <u>βαπτισθήσεσθε</u> ἐν πνεύματι ἁγίῳ οὐ μετὰ πολλὰς ταύτας ἡμέρας – "for John indeed baptized you with water but <u>you will be baptized</u> in the Holy Spirit not many days after these."

2. Deponent Passive

A verb that has no active *form* may be active in meaning though passive in form. In this form, the subject is presented as producing the action of the verb and is translated as though the verb was active. "Examples of deponent passive verbs are ἐβουλήθην (from βούλομαι, to wish, be willing), ἐνεθυμήθην (from ενθυμέομαι, to reflect on, to consider), ἀπεκρίθη (from ἀποκρίνομαι, to answer)."[332]

VERB MOODS

In the study of the tenses, it has been seen that there are distinct differences between English and Greek verb usage. In English, verbs emphasize the time of action - past, present, and future with their related forms while Greek verbs on the other hand emphasize the *kind* of action, with time relationships being secondary. The verb in the Greek is more concerned with the manner in which the action takes place than the time at which it occurred, and this is reflected by the tense of the verb. The Greek verb also expresses both the writer or speaker's attitude toward the action (reflected by the mood) and the writer or speaker's involvement in the action of the verb (reflected in the voice). In the Greek, the mood of the verb can represent one of two viewpoints - that which is actual and that which is possible as Dana and Mantey explain,

> In the expression of the verbal idea it is necessary to define its relation to reality: that which has, will, or does now exist. ... This *affirmation of relation to reality* is mood. Whether the verbal idea is objectively a fact or not is not the point: mood represents the way in which the matter is conceived. It represents "an attitude of mind on the part of the speaker" (M. 164).[333]

This means that when considering the mood of the verb, one is considering manner in which or the attitude with which the writer looks at the matter. Thus the different Greek moods may be represented as in the table below:

MOODS	*FORM*	*USAGE*
Indicative	Statement of action	Indicates what is true about the subject – a simple declaration of action presented as a statement of fact or as a question.
Imperative	Demand for action	Imposes a demand upon the will to do an action – this demand may be presented in the form of a command or request dependent upon the response required.

---

[332] ibid.
[333] Dana and Mantey, *A Manual Grammar of the Greek New Testament*, 165.

MOODS	FORM	USAGE
Subjunctive	possibility of action	Expresses uncertainty about something – a wish, exhortation, or conditional thought which is likely to occur depending upon conditions and/or responses stated
Optative	Request for action	Presents a polite request expressing a wish or desire without expression of the anticipated realization – often introduced by "may".

The Indicative Mood

The Indicative Mood denotes a simple assertion of fact or an interrogation. Vaughan and Gideon discuss it thus:

> The indicative is the mode of fact, or rather statement represented as fact. Robertson calls it the mode of definite assertion and explains that "it is the normal mode to use when there is no special reason for employing another mode" (*Grammar*, p. 915). Dana and Mantey describe it as "the mood of certainty" (p. 168). By far the most frequently used, the indicative states the verbal idea from the point of view of reality. However, it "does not guarantee the reality of the thing. In the nature of the case only the statement is under discussion" (Robertson, p. 915). Zerwick comments: "What matters is how the act is conceived by the speaker, not its objective nature" (p. 100).[334]

Thus from the discussion above it can be seen that as the mood of certainty, the indicative mood can state a supposition as well as make an assertion in the past, present or future. It is also clear that this certainty is not necessarily objective but rather with respect to the speaker's view of what is affirmed.[335] The Indicative mood can be classified as:

1. The Declarative Indicative

It is the statement of a simple fact. Wallace states, "The indicative is routinely used to present an assertion as a non-contingent (or unqualified) statement. This is by far the most common use."[336]

John 1:1: Ἐν ἀρχῇ <u>ἦν</u> ὁ λόγος καὶ ὁ λόγος <u>ἦν</u> πρὸς τὸν θεόν καὶ θεὸς <u>ἦν</u> ὁ λόγος – "In the beginning <u>was</u> the Word and the Word <u>was</u> with God and the Word <u>was</u> God."

John 3:36: ὁ πιστεύων εἰς τὸν υἱὸν <u>ἔχει</u> ζωὴν αἰώνιον· ὁ δὲ ἀπειθῶν τῷ υἱῷ οὐκ ὄψεται ζωήν ἀλλ' ἡ ὀργὴ τοῦ θεοῦ <u>μένει</u> ἐπ' αὐτόν – "the one who believes on the son <u>is having</u> life everlasting: but the one who is not persuaded by the son shall not see life but the wrath of God <u>is remaining</u> upon him."

---

[334] Vaughan and Gideon, *A Greek Grammar of the New Testament*, 99.

[335] Smyth states that "The indicative mood makes a simple, direct assertion of a fact; or asks a question anticipating such an assertion: ... The indicative states particular or general suppositions, makes affirmative or negative assertions, which may or may not be absolutely true." [Smyth, *Greek Grammar for Colleges*, 399.]

[336] Wallace, *Greek Grammar Beyond the Basics*, 448.

2. The Interrogative Indicative

It is the asking of a simple question. Dana and Mantey state that "The interrogative indicative assumes that there is an actual fact which may be stated in answer to the question."[337] And Wallace also notes that "The question *expects an assertion* to be made; it expects a declarative indicative in the answer. (This contrasts with the subjunctive, which asks a question of moral "oughtness" or obligation, or asks whether something is possible.)"[338]

John 1:38: στραφεὶς δὲ ὁ Ἰησοῦς καὶ θεασάμενος αὐτοὺς ἀκολουθοῦντας λέγει αὐτοῖς Τί ζητεῖτε οἱ δὲ εἶπον αὐτῷ Ῥαββί ὃ λέγεται ἑρμηνευόμενον, Διδάσκαλε ποῦ μένεις – "and Jesus turning and seeing them following says to them what <u>are you seeking?</u> and they said to him Rabbi which is to say being interpreted teacher where do you abide?"

John 1:19: Καὶ αὕτη ἐστὶν ἡ μαρτυρία τοῦ Ἰωάννου ὅτε ἀπέστειλαν οἱ Ἰουδαῖοι ἐξ Ἱεροσολύμων ἱερεῖς καὶ Λευίτας ἵνα ἐρωτήσωσιν αὐτὸν Σὺ τίς <u>εἶ</u> – "and this is the testimony of John when the Jews sent out of Jerusalem priests and levites in order that they may ask him who <u>are you</u>?"

John 11:26: καὶ πᾶς ὁ ζῶν καὶ πιστεύων εἰς ἐμὲ οὐ μὴ ἀποθάνῃ εἰς τὸν αἰῶνα· <u>πιστεύεις</u> τοῦτο – "and everyone who is living and believing on me shall never die for ever <u>do you believe</u> this thing?"

Matthew 12:10: καὶ ἰδού, ἄνθρωπος ἦν τὴν χεῖρα ἔχων ξηράν, καὶ ἐπηρώτησαν αὐτὸν λέγοντες <u>Εἰ ἔξεστιν</u> τοῖς σάββασιν θεραπεύειν ἵνα κατηγορήσωσιν αὐτοῦ – "and behold a man was having a withered hand and they asked him saying <u>is it lawful</u> to heal on the Sabbaths so that they may accuse him."

Matthew 9:28: ἐλθόντι δὲ εἰς τὴν οἰκίαν προσῆλθον αὐτῷ οἱ τυφλοί καὶ λέγει αὐτοῖς ὁ Ἰησοῦς <u>Πιστεύετε</u> ὅτι δύναμαι τοῦτο ποιῆσαι λέγουσιν αὐτῷ Ναί κύριε – "and entering into the house the blind men came to him and Jesus said to them <u>do you believe</u> that I am able to do this thing they said to him yes lord."

3. The Potential Indicative

Sometimes the idea of condition accompanies the Indicative, being supplied by the use either of ἄν or the meaning of the context. This use is classified as Potential use of the Indicative. Wallace observes, "The indicative is used with verbs of obligation, wish, or desire, followed by an infinitive. The nature of the verb root, rather than the indicative, is what makes it look like a potential mood in its semantic force."[339]

(1) Potential Indicative Expressing Command

Sometimes the second person future indicative is used to express a command. This use is classified by some grammarians as a separate class and is given the title cohortative indicative. Wallace explains "The future indicative is sometimes used for a

---

[337] Dana and Mantey, *A Manual Grammar of the Greek New Testament*, 168.
[338] Daniel B Wallace, *Greek Grammar Beyond the Basics*, 449.
[339] Ibid. 451.

command, almost always in the OT quotations (because of a literal translation of the Hebrew)."[340]

Matthew 19:18-19: λέγει αὐτῷ Ποίας ὁ δὲ Ἰησοῦς εἶπεν Τὸ <u>Οὐ φονεύσεις Οὐ μοιχεύσεις Οὐ κλέψεις Οὐ ψευδομαρτυρήσεις</u> 19 Τίμα τὸν πατέρα σου καὶ τὴν μητέρα, καί, Ἀγαπήσεις τὸν πλησίον σου ὡς σεαυτόν – "he says to him which? and Jesus says to him <u>you shall not commit murder, you shall not commit adultery, you shall not bear false witness</u> honor your father and mother and love your neighbor as yourself."

(2) Potential Indicative Expressing Obligation

This use of the indicative with verbs of obligation to claim necessity implying that "the obligation, necessity, etc., has not been lived up to."[341] "This use is most frequent with verbs whose root meaning conveys the idea of obligation."[342]

Acts 24:19: οὓς <u>δεῖ</u> ἐπὶ σοῦ παρεῖναι καὶ κατηγορεῖν εἴ τι ἔχοιεν πρός μέ – "who <u>it is necessary</u> to be before you and to accuse if they have anything against me."

1 Corinthians 4:8: ἤδη κεκορεσμένοι ἐστέ ἤδη ἐπλουτήσατε χωρὶς ἡμῶν ἐβασιλεύσατε· καὶ ὄφελόν γε <u>ἐβασιλεύσατε</u> ἵνα καὶ ἡμεῖς ὑμῖν συμβασιλεύσωμεν – "you are already full you are already become rich you have reigned without us and I would to God <u>you were reigning</u> in order that we also may reign together with you."

(3) Potential Indicative Expressing Impulse

The Indicative may be used to express a wish or some other unfulfilled event. This is used "where we might expect the optative. Most wishes expressed by the indicative are incapable of being realized, or at least there was doubt about the possibility of realization at the time they were originally expressed."[343]

Acts 25:22: Ἀγρίππας δὲ πρὸς τὸν Φῆστον ἔφη, <u>Ἐβουλόμην</u> καὶ αὐτὸς τοῦ ἀνθρώπου ἀκοῦσαι ὁ δὲ Αὔριον φησίν ἀκούσῃ αὐτοῦ – "and Agrippa said to Festus, <u>I was desiring</u> myself to hear the man and he said tomorrow you shall hear him."

Romans 9:3: <u>ηὐχόμην</u> γὰρ αὐτὸς ἐγὼ ἀνάθεμα εἶναι ἀπὸ τοῦ Χριστοῦ ὑπὲρ τῶν ἀδελφῶν μου τῶν συγγενῶν μου κατὰ σάρκα – "for I myself <u>was wishing</u> to be anathema from Christ on behalf of my brothers my kinsmen according to the flesh."

(4) Potential Indicative Expressing Condition

Brooks and Winbery note that "A condition contrary to fact is expressed by the indicative of a secondary tense. The protasis is usually introduced by , and is ordinarily found in the apodosis."[344] Wallace adds,

> This is the use of the indicative in the protasis of the conditional sentences. The conditional element is made explicit with the particle εἰ. the first class condition indicates *the assumption of truth for the sake of argument*, while the second class condition indicates *the assumption of an untruth for the sake of argument.*[345]

---

[340] Ibid. 452
[341] Vaughan and Gideon, *A Greek Grammar of the New Testament*, 101.
[342] Brooks and Winbery, *Syntax of the New Testament Greek*, 117.
[343] Ibid.
[344] ibid., 117.
[345] Wallace, *Greek Grammar Beyond the Basics*, 450.

John 8:46: τίς ἐξ ὑμῶν ἐλέγχει με περὶ ἁμαρτίας εἰ δὲ ἀλήθειαν λέγω διατί ὑμεῖς οὐ πιστεύετέ μοι – "who among you is convicting me concerning sin and if I say the truth why do you not believe me."

John 11:21: εἶπεν οὖν ἡ Μάρθα πρὸς τὸν Ἰησοῦν Κύριε εἰ ἦς ὧδε ὁ ἀδελφός μου· οὐκ ἂν ἐτεθνήκει – "then Martha said to Jesus, Lord if you were here my brother would not have died."

1 Peter 3:1: Ὁμοίως αἱ γυναῖκες ὑποτασσόμεναι τοῖς ἰδίοις ἀνδράσιν ἵνα καὶ εἴ τινες ἀπειθοῦσιν τῷ λόγῳ διὰ τῆς τῶν γυναικῶν ἀναστροφῆς ἄνευ λόγου κερδηθήσωνται – "likewise wives subjecting yourselves to your own husbands in order that also if any are not obeying by the word through the wives' behavior they may be won without the word."

The Imperative Mood

The Imperative Mood is only in the present and aorist tenses in the New Testament and there is no first person in the imperative mood. It is the mood which expresses action by the will of one person upon that of another and therefore it is the mood of strong contingency but it is also a mood which can be used to indicate possibility.[346] Hewett explains,

> Greek has two tenses in the imperative: the present and the aorist. Like the subjunctive, these refer not to time of action, but to kind of action. Again, the present expresses linear, on-going, or repeated type of activity. The aorist denotes the simple unitary act itself with nothing implied or asserted regarding the duration or the completion of the event. It does not refer to past time. Not being the indicative mood, there will be no augment.[347]

Since the present tense is basically a linear tense, the present imperative[348] has to do with action which is in progress thus it presents a continuous or repeated action; and similarly, as the aorist is punctiliar, the aorist imperative[349] presents an action that is undefined with respect to its progress, completion continuation or completion and thus has to do with action that has not yet started. Brooks and Winberry state that this mood is the furthest removed from reality as it "expresses an action or state of being which is volitionally possible, i.e. action or state which may come about as the result of

---

[346] The imperative mood is used to express possibility in the sense that the command given expresses volitional possibility and as the mood of intention, it expresses two aspects that of volition and of possibility. Wallace defines the imperative as "the mood of *intention*. It is the mood furthest removed from certainty. Ontologically, as one of the potential or oblique moods, the imperative moves into the realm of *volition* (involving the imposition of one's will upon another) and *possibility*." [Wallace, *Greek Grammar Beyond the Basics*, 485.]

[347] Hewett, *New Testament Greek*, 188.

[348] Zodhiates observes that "The present imperative occurs only in the active and middle voices in the New Testament. In the active voice, it may indicate a command to do something in the future which involves continuous or repeated action or, when it is negated, a command to stop doing something." [Zodhiates, *The Complete Word Study New Testament*, 867.]

[349] Zodhiates notes that "The aorist imperative denotes a command, a request, or entreaty. Unlike the Present Imperative (80, 81), it does not involve a command or entreaty of continuous or repetitive action. Instead, it is often used for general exhortations and for things that must be begun at that very moment." [Zodhiates, *The Complete Word Study New Testament*, 862.]

the exercise of the will. It involves the attempt of one person to exert the force of his will upon the will of another person."[350] The basic uses of the imperative:

1. The Imperative of Command.

This is the making of a direct, positive appeal to another. It is the most common use of the imperative is to express a command or an exhortation to perform an action. Dana and Mantey state, "Where one will makes a direct, positive appeal to another the imperative finds its most characteristic use. The degree of authority involved in the command, and the degree of probability that the one addressed will respond are matters but incidental to the use of the mood. The imperative itself only the appeal of the will."[351] Wallace writes,

> The imperative is most commonly used for commands, outnumbering prohibitive imperatives about five to one. The basic force of the imperative of command involves somewhat different nuances with each tense. With the aorist, the force generally is to *command the action as a whole*, without focusing on duration, repetition, etc. In keeping with its aspectual force, the aorist puts forth a *summary command*. With the *present*, the force generally is to *command the action as an ongoing process*. This is in keeping with the present's aspect, which portrays an *internal* perspective.[352]

John 21:17: λέγει αὐτῷ τὸ τρίτον Σίμων Ἰωνᾶ, φιλεῖς με ἐλυπήθη ὁ Πέτρος ὅτι εἶπεν αὐτῷ τὸ τρίτον Φιλεῖς με καὶ εἶπεν αὐτῷ Κύριε σὺ πάντα οἶδας σὺ γινώσκεις ὅτι φιλῶ σε λέγει αὐτῷ ὁ Ἰησοῦς <u>Βόσκε</u> τὰ πρόβατά μου – "thirdly he said to him Simon son of Jonas do you love me Peter was distressed that he said to him the third time do you love me and he said to him Lord you know all things you know that I love you Jesus said to him <u>feed</u> my sheep."

John 5:8: λέγει αὐτῷ ὁ Ἰησοῦς <u>ἐγεῖραι</u> <u>ἆρον</u> τὸν κράββατον σου καὶ περιπάτει – "Jesus said to him <u>arise</u> <u>lift up</u> your bed and walk."

2. The Imperative of Prohibition.

This is the use of the imperative to make a negative command. This use is almost only found in the present tense with μὴ. In this use it prohibits the continuation of an act which is in progress. Burton notes,

> Prohibitions are expressed either by the Aorist Subjunctive or by the Present Imperative, the only exceptions being a few instances of the third person Aorist Imperative with μὴ. The difference between an Aorist Subjunctive with μὴ and a Present Imperative with μὴ is in the conception of the action as respects its progress. H.A. 874. Thus (a) The Aorist Subjunctive forbids the action as a simple event with reference to the action as a whole or to its inception, and is most frequently used when the action has not been begun. ... (b) The Present Imperative (180-184) forbids the continuance of the action, most frequently when it is already in progress; in this case, it is a demand to desist from the action. ... In prohibitions, on the other

---

[350] Brooks and Winbery, *Syntax of the New Testament Greek*, 127.
[351] Dana and Mantey, *A Manual Grammar of the Greek New Testament*, 175.
[352] Wallace, *Greek Grammar Beyond the Basics*, 485.

hand, the use of the Imperative is confined almost entirely to the Present tense. A few instances only of the Aorist occur.[353]

John 14:1: Μὴ ταρασσέσθω ὑμῶν ἡ καρδία· πιστεύετε εἰς τὸν θεόν καὶ εἰς ἐμὲ πιστεύετε – "Do not let your hearts to be troubled: you believe in God believe also in in me."

John 14:27: Εἰρήνην ἀφίημι ὑμῖν εἰρήνην τὴν ἐμὴν δίδωμι ὑμῖν· οὐ καθὼς ὁ κόσμος δίδωσιν ἐγὼ δίδωμι ὑμῖν μὴ ταρασσέσθω ὑμῶν ἡ καρδία μηδὲ δειλιάτω – "peace I leave with you my peace I give to you not as the world gives I give to you do not let your hearts to be troubled neither let it to be afraid."

3. The Imperative of Entreaty.

This is the use of the imperative not to "convey the finality of command, but has the force of urgency or request"[354] Thus rather than give a direct command, the imperative is toned down to express a request for examples in prayers the aorist imperative is used to express request. Wallace notes concerning this use that,

> The imperative is often used to express a request. This is normally seen when the speaker is addressing a superior. Imperatives (almost always in the aorist tense) directed toward God in prayers fit this category. The request can be a positive one or a negative one (*please, do not* ...); in such cases the particle me precedes the verb.[355]

Matthew 14:30: βλέπων δὲ τὸν ἄνεμον ἰσχυρὸν ἐφοβήθη καὶ ἀρξάμενος καταποντίζεσθαι ἔκραξεν λέγων, Κύριε σῶσόν με – "and seeing the strong wind he feared and beginning to sink he cried saying Lord save me."

Luke 17:5: Καὶ εἶπον οἱ ἀπόστολοι τῷ κυρίῳ Πρόσθες ἡμῖν πίστιν – "and the apostles said to the Lord increase our faith."

4. The Imperative of Permission.

This use of the imperative is to express consent. The compliance may be with "an expressed desire or a manifest inclination on the part of a second party, thus involving consent as well as command"[356] but may not necessarily imply approval by the one complying as Wallace observes,

> The imperative is rarely used to connote permission or, better, *toleration*. This usage does not normally imply that some deed is optional or approved. It often views that act as a *fait accompli*. In such instances, the mood could almost be called "an imperative of resignation."[357]

The English auxiliary verb "let" can be used to make the meaning clear.

---

[353] E. Burton, *Syntax of the Moods and Tenses in New Testament Greek*, 75, 81. Most grammar books would put the prohibitions in Aorist as expressed using μὴ with the aorist subjunctive to forbid the occurrence of an action not yet begun. One of these exception which uses μὴ with the aorist imperative in the third person would be Mark 13:14-18 in which μὴ with the aorist imperative is used twice in verse 15 (μὴ καταβάτω) and 16 (μὴ ἐπιστρεψάτω).

[354] Dana and Mantey, *A Manual Grammar of the Greek New Testament*, 176.

[355] Wallace, *Greek Grammar Beyond the Basics*, 487-88.

[356] Dana and Mantey, *A Manual Grammar of the Greek New Testament*, 176.

[357] Wallace, *Greek Grammar Beyond the Basics*, 488.

1 Corinthians 7:15: εἰ δὲ ὁ ἄπιστος χωρίζεται χωριζέσθω· οὐ δεδούλωται ὁ ἀδελφὸς ἢ ἡ ἀδελφὴ ἐν τοῖς τοιούτοις· ἐν δὲ εἰρήνῃ κέκληκεν ἡμᾶς ὁ θεός – "but if the unbelieving is departing <u>let him depart</u>: the brother or sister has not been bound in such cases but God has called us to peace."

John 19:6: ὅτε οὖν εἶδον αὐτὸν οἱ ἀρχιερεῖς καὶ οἱ ὑπηρέται ἐκραύγασαν λέγοντες Σταύρωσον σταύρωσον λέγει αὐτοῖς ὁ Πιλᾶτος <u>Λάβετε</u> αὐτὸν ὑμεῖς καὶ <u>σταυρώσατε</u>· ἐγὼ γὰρ οὐχ εὑρίσκω ἐν αὐτῷ αἰτίαν – "when therefore he saw the high priests and the officer cried saying crucify crucify Pilate said to them <u>you take</u> him and <u>crucify</u>: for I do not find a fault in him."

5. Imperatives with Conjunction καὶ

The imperative can be used in conjunction with the conjunction καὶ to indicate either condition or concession.

a. Condition

When an imperative is used with the conjunction καὶ and followed by a future or subjunctive, the imperative expresses condition. Boyer says concerning the is class that,

> Probably the strangest and most controversial category of imperatives is that which seems to express some conditional element. Here it is necessary to distinguish two groups. The first is neither strange nor controversial; it includes a large number of instances (about 20) where an imperative is followed by καὶ and a future indicative verb. It says, "Do something and this will follow." This combination clearly is capable of two explanations. It could well be a simple command followed by a promise. Or it could be understood to imply that the promise is conditioned upon the doing of the thing commanded, "If you do something this will follow." Jas 4:7, 8, 10, "Resist the devil, and he will flee. . . . Draw near to God and He will draw near to you. . . . Humble yourselves. . . and He will exalt you." The familiar prayer promise, "ask. . . seek. . . knock. . ." (Matt 7:7, Luke 11:9; cf. also John 16:24), belongs here; it could mean "if you ask you will receive."[358]

Matthew 7:7: <u>Αἰτεῖτε καὶ δοθήσεται</u> ὑμῖν <u>ζητεῖτε καὶ εὑρήσετε</u> κρούετε καὶ <u>ἀνοιγήσεται</u> ὑμῖν· – "<u>ask and it shall be given</u> to you <u>seek and you shall find</u> <u>knock and it shall be open</u> to you."

b. Concession

When two imperatives are joined together using the conjunction καὶ, the first imperative expresses concession. Boyer states that:

> The second group consists of a few passages where condition has been proposed to explain a difficult passage. Each passage will be discussed briefly. Examples of this kind have been assigned to an alternate classification; ... Ephesians 4:26 The problem here is in the first word ὀργίζεσθε 'be angry'. It is an imperative. Two opposite explanations have traditionally been offered. (1) The anger here is said to

---

[358] James L. Boyer, *A Classification of Imperatives: A statistical study*, Grace Theological Journal 8.1 (1987) 35-54.

be "righteous indignation," the kind of anger God has toward sin, and which Jesus manifested on occasion. Thus the passage is a command. But it seems impossible to understand this in a good sense in a context (cf. v 31; 2:3; also Matt 5:22, Rom 12:19, Col 3:8, 1 Tim 2:8, Tit 1:7, Jas 1:19) that condemns anger and orders it to be put away. The word used here, ὀργίζω and its cognates, is never used in a good sense except in references to the anger of God and Christ. And "righteous indignation" seems never to be approved for men. In fact, the scripture says, "For the anger of man does not achieve the righteousness of God" (Jas 1:20). The righteous anger of God operates in the area of judgment, and that area is out of bounds to believers, at least for the present. Besides, if this is a command to show "righteous indignation," why is the warning added to end it before the sun goes down?   (2) Attempt is made to see here an example of some imperatival use other than command; possibly conditional, "If you do get angry don't sin by nursing it too long; don't let the sun go down on it." Or possibly it is an unwilling permission, "Be angry if you must."[359]

Ephesians 4:26: ὀργίζεσθε καὶ μὴ ἁμαρτάνετε· ὁ ἥλιος μὴ ἐπιδυέτω ἐπὶ τῷ παροργισμῷ ὑμῶν – "be angry and sin not: do not let the sun go down upon your wrath."

The Subjunctive Mood

The Subjunctive is generally called the mood of probability and its use expresses a measure of uncertainty as Wenham puts it, "the subjunctive is the mood of doubtful assertion. In nearly all its uses there is some element of indefiniteness in the sentence."[360] Thus in its use, the tenses take on a different emphasis. Dana and Mantey point out, "The Subjunctive is the Mood of mild contingency. It is the mood of probability. While the Indicative assumes reality, the subjunctive assumes unreality."[361] This mood is one of the three potential moods and is found in the present and aorist tenses only. Duff writes,

> Subjunctives occur in all three of the voices (Active, Middle or Passive), but only in the Present or the Aorist tense. Thus it is similar to the Imperative and Infinitive – indeed the difference between the Present and the Aorist in the Subjunctive is the same as in the Infinitive and Imperative (process or default). Like the Indicative it occurs in the first, second and third person, singular and plural.[362]

---

[359] Ibid.
[360] Wenham, *Elements of New Testament Greek*, 160.
[361] Dana and Mantey, *A Manual Grammar of the Greek New Testament*, 170.
[362] Duff, *Elements of New Testament Greek*, 190.

Thus the present subjunctive[363] does not indicate time of action but rather continuous or repeated action. Likewise the Aorist subjunctive[364] does not refer to time past, but rather undefined action. Wallace says,

> The subjunctive is the most common of the oblique moods in the N.T. In general, the subjunctive can be said to *represent the verbal action (or state) as uncertain but probable*. It is not correct to call this the mood of uncertainty because the optative also presents the verb as uncertain. Rather, it is better to call it the mood of *probability* so as to distinguish it from the optative. Still, this is an overly simplistic definition in light of its usage in the NT.[365]

The use of the subjunctive is mainly classified under two main headings depending on its use. They are either use of the subjunctive in (a) main clauses – independent clause or (b) subordinate clauses – dependent clauses.

(a) Subjunctive in Independent (Main) Clauses
1. The Hortatory Subjunctive

This is the use of the subjunctive where the writer exhorts others to participate in an action. In this the writer uses the first person plural exhorting others to join him in a certain action. Wallace explains,

> The subjunctive is commonly used to exhort or command oneself and one's associates. This use of the subjunctive is used "to urge some one to unite with the speaker in a course of action upon which he has already decided" (Chamberlain, 83). Since there is no first person imperative, the hortatory subjunctive is used to do roughly the same task. Thus this use of the subjunctive is an exhortation in the *first person plural*. The typical translation, rather than *we should ...*, is *let us ...*[366]

John 14:31: ἀλλ᾽ ἵνα γνῷ ὁ κόσμος ὅτι ἀγαπῶ τὸν πατέρα καὶ καθὼς ἐνετείλατο μοι ὁ πατήρ οὕτως ποιῶ Ἐγείρεσθε <u>ἄγωμεν</u> ἐντεῦθεν – "but in order that the world may know that I love the father also just as the father commanded me thus I do rise up <u>let us go</u> from hence."

Mark 12:7: ἐκεῖνοι δὲ οἱ γεωργοὶ εἶπον πρὸς ἑαυτοὺς ὅτι Οὗτός ἐστιν ὁ κληρονόμος· δεῦτε <u>ἀποκτείνωμεν</u> αὐτόν καὶ ἡμῶν ἔσται ἡ κληρονομία – "but these husbandmen said to themselves "this is the heir come <u>let us kill</u> him and the inheritance shall be ours."

Luke 2:15: Καὶ ἐγένετο ὡς ἀπῆλθον ἀπ᾽ αὐτῶν εἰς τὸν οὐρανὸν οἱ ἄγγελοι καὶ οἱ ἄνθρωποι οἱ ποιμένες εἶπον πρὸς ἀλλήλους <u>Διέλθωμεν</u> δὴ ἕως Βηθλέεμ Καὶ <u>ἴδωμεν</u> τὸ ῥῆμα τοῦτο τὸ γεγονὸς ὃ ὁ κύριος ἐγνώρισεν ἡμῖν – "and it came to pass as the angels went from them into heaven and the men, the shepherds said to one another <u>let us go</u>

---

[363] Zodhiates states that the present subjunctive tense "refers to continuous or repeated action, regardless of when the action took place. The subjunctive mood suggests that the action is subject to some condition." [Zodhiates, *The Complete Word Study New Testament*, 868.]

[364] This Zodhiates states that it "differs from the present subjunctive (psa) and the present subjunctive middle/passive (psmp) by referring to simple, undefined action, as opposed to continuous or repeated action." [Zodhiates, *The Complete Word Study New Testament*, 863.]

[365] Wallace, *Greek Grammar Beyond the Basics*, 461.

[366] Ibid., 464.

now until Bethlehem and <u>let us see</u> this thing which has come to pass that the lord has made known to us."

2. The Prohibitory Subjunctive

The Aorist Subjunctive[367] is used in the second person with μὴ. to express a prohibition or a negative command. This use presents a warning or exhortation against performing an action. Wallace explains,

> This is the use of the subjunctive is a prohibition - that is, a negative command. It is used to forbid the occurrence of an action. The structure is usually μὴ + aorist subjunctive, typically in the second person. Its force is equivalent to an imperative after me; hence, it should be translated *Do not* rather than *You should not*.[368]

Matthew 7:6: <u>Μὴ δῶτε</u> τὸ ἅγιον τοῖς κυσίν, <u>μηδὲ βάλητε</u> τοὺς μαργαρίτας ὑμῶν ἔμπροσθεν τῶν χοίρων μήποτε καταπατήσωσιν αὐτοὺς ἐν τοῖς ποσὶν αὐτῶν καὶ στραφέντες ῥήξωσιν ὑμᾶς – "<u>do not give</u> the holy thing to the dogs <u>neither cast</u> your pearls before the swine lest the trample them with their feet and turning they may tear you."

Matthew 10:5: Τούτους τοὺς δώδεκα ἀπέστειλεν ὁ Ἰησοῦς παραγγείλας αὐτοῖς λέγων, Εἰς ὁδὸν ἐθνῶν <u>μὴ ἀπέλθητε</u> καὶ εἰς πόλιν Σαμαρειτῶν <u>μὴ εἰσέλθητε</u>· – "Jesus sent these twelve commanding them saying <u>do not go</u> into the way of the gentiles and into the city of Samaritans <u>do not enter</u>."

3. The Deliberative Subjunctive

It is used in deliberate questions and in rhetorical questions having reference to the future. Brooks and Winbery explain,

> The deliberative subjunctive is used in interrogative sentences which deal with what is necessary, desirable, or possible. It is not factual information which is desired. (For this purpose the indicative would be used.) The need is for a decision about the proper course of action, concerning which the speaker or writer is uncertain. Sometimes the question is merely rhetorical; sometimes an answer is expected.[369]

Thus this use presents the speaker as deliberating or in a state of perplexity and whether the question is real or rhetorical is determined by the context as Wallace points out:

> The deliberative subjunctive asks either a *real* or *rhetorical* question. The semantics of the two are often quite different. Both imply some *doubt* about the response, but the real question is usually in the *cognitive* area (such as "How can we ... ?" in which the inquiry is about the means), while the *rhetorical* question is *volitive* (e.g., "Should we ... ?" in which the question has to do with moral obligation). Both are fairly common with first person verbs, though second and third person verbs can

---

[367] Hewett explains that "The unitary quality of the aorist expresses itself in that the action is forbidden to occur – period. ... The present tense subjunctive is not used to express prohibitions. Instead the present tense of the imperative and the negative μὴ are used. [Hewett, *New Testament Greek*, 167.]

[368] Wallace, *Greek Grammar Beyond the Basics*, 469.

[369] Brooks and Winbery, *Syntax of the New Testament Greek*, 119.

be found. The future indicative is also used in deliberate questions, though the subjunctive is more common.[370]

John 6:28: εἶπον οὖν πρὸς αὐτόν <u>Τί ποιοῦμεν</u> ἵνα ἐργαζώμεθα τὰ ἔργα τοῦ θεοῦ – "then they said to him "<u>what shall we do</u> in order that we may work the works of God?"

Romans 6:1-2: Τί οὖν ἐροῦμεν <u>ἐπιμενοῦμεν</u> τῇ ἁμαρτίᾳ ἵνα ἡ χάρις πλεονάσῃ μὴ γένοιτο οἵτινες ἀπεθάνομεν τῇ ἁμαρτίᾳ πῶς ἔτι ζήσομεν ἐν αὐτῇ – "what then shall we say <u>shall we persist</u> in sin so that grace may abound? God forbid how shall we who are dead to sin yet live in it?"

Matthew 26:54: <u>πῶς</u> οὖν <u>πληρωθῶσιν</u> αἱ γραφαὶ ὅτι οὕτως δεῖ γενέσθαι – "<u>how</u> therefore shall the scriptures <u>be fulfilled</u> that thus it is necessary to happen?"

4. The Subjunctive of Emphatic Negation

The Aorist Subjunctive is used with οὐ μὴ in the sense of emphatically denying something that is yet in the future. Vaughan and Gideon explain,

> The subjunctive in an independent clause may be used to express strong denial. (Dana and Mantey call this "emphatic negation"). The subjunctive so used occurs with οὐ μὴ and the aorist tense.[371] It is the strongest way to make a negative statement of a future occurrence.[372]

Wallace also asserts

> Emphatic negation is indicated by οὐ μὴ plus the aorist subjunctive or, less frequently, οὐ μὴ plus the future indicative. This is the strongest way to negate something in Greek. One might think that the negative with the subjunctive could not be as strong, as the negative with the indicative. However, while οὐ + the indicative denies a *certainty*, οὐ μὴ + the subjunctive denies a *potentiality*. οὐ μὴ rules out even the idea as being a possibility.[373]

Matthew 5:18: ἀμὴν γὰρ λέγω ὑμῖν, ἕως ἂν παρέλθῃ ὁ οὐρανὸς καὶ ἡ γῆ, ἰῶτα ἓν, ἢ μία κεραία <u>οὐ μὴ παρέλθῃ</u> ἀπὸ τοῦ νόμου, ἕως ἂν πάντα γένηται. – "for amen I say to you until heaven and earth shall pass away one iota or one tittle <u>shall never pass away</u> from the law until all things be."

John 6:35: εἶπεν δὲ αὐτοῖς ὁ Ἰησοῦς Ἐγώ εἰμι ὁ ἄρτος τῆς ζωῆς· ὁ ἐρχόμενος πρός με, <u>οὐ μὴ πεινάσῃ</u> καὶ ὁ πιστεύων εἰς ἐμὲ <u>οὐ μὴ διψήσῃ</u> πώποτε – "and Jesus said to them I am the bread of life, the one who comes to me <u>shall never hunger</u> and the one who believes in me <u>shall never thirst</u> at any time."

(b) Subjunctive in Dependent (Subordinate) Clauses

With regard to the use of subjunctive in subordinate clauses, Brooks and Winbery state that "the subjunctive with ἵνα to express purpose and the subjunctive with

---

[370] Wallace, *Greek Grammar Beyond the Basics*, 465.
[371] "Occasionally οὐ μὴ with a future indicative expresses strong denial." such examples would include Matthew 24:35; Mark 13:31; Luke 21:33; John 10:28.
[372] Vaughan and Gideon, *A Greek Grammar of the New Testament*, 103.
[373] Wallace, *Greek Grammar Beyond the Basics*, 468.

ἐάν to express a probable future condition are by far the most common."[374] Hewett commenting on the use of states that "any time ἵνα is encountered, think "subjunctive is following." Rarely will you be in error." Wallace concerning the use of subjunctives in subordinate clauses attests saying,

> This is the use of the subjunctive in the protasis of conditional sentences. The conditional element is made explicit by the particle ἐάν. Both the particle and the subjunctive give the condition a sense of contingency.[375] ... The single most common category of the subjunctive in the NT is after ἵνα, comprising about one third of all subjunctive instances. There are seven basic uses in this construction: Purpose, result, purpose-result, substantival, complementary, and command.[376]

1. Purpose (Final) Clause

Matthew 12:10: καὶ ἰδού, ἄνθρωπος ἦν τὴν χεῖρα ἔχων ξηράν, καὶ ἐπηρώτησαν αὐτὸν λέγοντες Εἰ ἔξεστιν τοῖς σάββασιν θεραπεύειν <u>ἵνα κατηγορήσωσιν</u> αὐτοῦ – "and behold a man was having a withered hand and they asked him saying is it lawful to heal on the Sabbaths <u>so that they may accuse</u> him."

1 John 2:1: Τεκνία μου, ταῦτα γράφω ὑμῖν, <u>ἵνα μὴ ἁμάρτητε</u>· καὶ ἐάν τις ἁμάρτῃ, παράκλητον ἔχομεν πρὸς τὸν πατέρα, Ἰησοῦν Χριστὸν δίκαιον· – "my children these things I write to you <u>in order that you sin not</u> and if any man shall sin, we have an advocate with the father Jesus Christ the righteous one."

2. Conditional Clause

John 6:51: ἐγώ εἰμι ὁ ἄρτος ὁ ζῶν ὁ ἐκ τοῦ οὐρανοῦ καταβάς· <u>ἐάν</u> τις <u>φάγῃ</u> ἐκ τούτου τοῦ ἄρτου ζήσεται εἰς τὸν αἰῶνα καὶ ὁ ἄρτος δὲ ὃν ἐγὼ δώσω ἡ σάρξ μού ἐστιν ἣν ἐγώ δώσω, ὑπὲρ τῆς τοῦ κόσμου ζωῆς – "I am the bread of life the one who descended from heaven: <u>if</u> anyone <u>eat</u> of this bread he shall live forever and even the bread that I will give is my flesh which I will give on behalf of the life of the world."

3. Result Clause

John 9:2: καὶ ἠρώτησαν αὐτὸν οἱ μαθηταὶ αὐτοῦ λέγοντες Ῥαββί τίς ἥμαρτεν οὗτος ἢ οἱ γονεῖς αὐτοῦ <u>ἵνα</u> τυφλὸς <u>γεννηθῇ</u> – "and the disciples asked him saying Rabbi who sinned this man or his parents <u>as a result he was born</u> blind."

4. Relative Clause

1 John 2:5: <u>ὃς δ' ἂν τηρῇ</u> αὐτοῦ τὸν λόγον, ἀληθῶς ἐν τούτῳ ἡ ἀγάπη τοῦ Θεοῦ τετελείωται. ἐν τούτῳ γινώσκομεν ὅτι ἐν αὐτῷ ἐσμεν. – "<u>and whosoever shall keep</u> his word truly in this the love of God is fulfilled. In this we know that we are in him."

5. Comparative Clause

1 Thessalonians 2:7: ἀλλ' ἐγενήθημεν ἤπιοι ἐν μέσῳ ὑμῶν <u>ὡς ἂν</u> τροφὸς <u>θάλπῃ</u> τὰ ἑαυτῆς τέκνα – "but we were gentle in the midst of you <u>even as</u> a nurse <u>cherishes</u> her children."

---

[374] Brooks and Winbery, *Syntax of the New Testament Greek*, 120.
[375] Wallace, *Greek Grammar Beyond the Basics*, 469.
[376] ibid., 471.

6. Indefinite Local Clause

Matthew 26:13: ἀμὴν λέγω ὑμῖν <u>ὅπου ἐὰν κηρυχθῇ</u> τὸ εὐαγγέλιον τοῦτο ἐν ὅλῳ τῷ κόσμῳ λαληθήσεται καὶ ὃ ἐποίησεν αὕτη εἰς μνημόσυνον αὐτῆς – "amen I say to you <u>wherever</u> this gospel <u>shall be preached</u> in the whole world it shall be spoken also that she did for a remembrance of her."

7. Temporal Clause

Matthew 17:9: Καὶ καταβαινόντων αὐτῶν ἀπὸ τοῦ ὄρους ἐνετείλατο αὐτοῖς ὁ Ἰησοῦς λέγων, Μηδενὶ εἴπητε τὸ ὅραμα <u>ἕως οὗ</u> ὁ υἱὸς τοῦ ἀνθρώπου ἐκ νεκρῶν <u>ἀναστῇ</u> – "and while they were descending from the mountain, Jesus commanded them saying speak the vision to no one <u>until</u> the son of man <u>be risen</u> out of the dead."

8. Concessive Clause

John 8:16: <u>καὶ ἐὰν κρίνω</u> δὲ ἐγώ ἡ κρίσις ἡ ἐμὴ ἀληθής ἐστιν ὅτι μόνος οὐκ εἰμί ἀλλ' ἐγὼ καὶ ὁ πέμψας με πατήρ – "and <u>even if I judge</u> my judgment is true because not only I but I and the father who sent me."

9. Substantival Clause

(a) Subject

Matthew 10:25: ἀρκετὸν τῷ μαθητῇ <u>ἵνα γένηται</u> ὡς ὁ διδάσκαλος αὐτοῦ καὶ ὁ δοῦλος ὡς ὁ κύριος αὐτοῦ εἰ τὸν οἰκοδεσπότην Βεελζεβοὺλ ἐκάλεσαν, πόσῳ μᾶλλον τοὺς οἰκιακοὺς αὐτοῦ – "it is enough for the disciple <u>that he may become</u> as his master and the slave as his lord if the lord of the house they called Beelzeboul how much more those of his household?"

(b) Predicate Nominative

1 John 2:27: καὶ ὑμεῖς τὸ χρίσμα ὃ ἐλάβετε ἀπ' αὐτοῦ, ἐν ὑμῖν μένει, καὶ οὐ χρείαν ἔχετε <u>ἵνα τις διδάσκῃ</u> ὑμᾶς· ἀλλ' ὡς τὸ αὐτὸ χρίσμα διδάσκει ὑμᾶς περὶ πάντων, καὶ ἀληθές ἐστι, καὶ οὐκ ἔστι ψεῦδος. Καὶ καθὼς ἐδίδαξεν ὑμᾶς, μενεῖτε ἐν αὐτῷ· – "but you have the anointing which you have received from him abiding in you and you have no need <u>that anyone teach</u> you but as the anointing teaches you concerning all things and he is true and is no lie and as he teaches you, abide in him."

(c) Object

Matthew 12:16: καὶ ἐπετίμησεν αὐτοῖς <u>ἵνα μὴ</u> φανερὸν αὐτὸν <u>ποιήσωσιν</u> – "and he charged them <u>that they may not make</u> him known."

(d) Apposition

1 John 3:11: ὅτι αὕτη ἐστὶν ἡ ἀγγελία ἣν ἠκούσατε ἀπ' ἀρχῆς, <u>ἵνα ἀγαπῶμεν ἀλλήλους</u>· – "for this is the message which you have heard from the beginning <u>that we love</u> one another."

10. Imperatival Clause

2 Corinthians 8:7: ἀλλ' ὥσπερ ἐν παντὶ περισσεύετε πίστει καὶ λόγῳ καὶ γνώσει καὶ πάσῃ σπουδῇ καὶ τῇ ἐξ ὑμῶν ἐν ἡμῖν ἀγάπῃ <u>ἵνα</u> καὶ ἐν ταύτῃ τῇ χάριτι <u>περισσεύητε</u> – "but just as in every thing you abound in faith and in word and in knowledge and in all earnestness and in your love to us <u>that</u> also in this grace <u>you may abound</u>."

The Optative Mood

According to Dana and Mantey, "The Optative Mood is the mood of strong contingency. It is the mood of possibility. It contains no definite anticipation of realization, but merely presents the action as conceivable."[377] The mood was extremely rare in the vernacular, being used less than 70 times in the New Testament. Wallace notes,

> There are less than 70 optatives in the entire NT. In general, it can be said that the optative is the mood used when a speaker wishes to portray an action as *possible*. It usually addresses cognition, but may be used to appeal to the volition. Along with the subjunctive and imperative, the optative is one of potential or oblique moods.[378]

1. The Voluntative Optative

The Optative is the mood of the verb used to express a wish. This is its most coomon use in the New Testament. Wallace writes, "This is the use of the optative in an independent clause to express an *obtainable wish* or a *prayer*. It is frequently an appeal to the *will*, in particular when used in prayers."[379] Boyer notes that "The name optative (from the Latin optari = to wish) points to one major use of the mood, to express a wish or a choice. It accounts for the majority of NT optatives (39 out of 68, or 57%). These may be grouped into six categories."[380]

Romans 6:1-2: Τί οὖν ἐροῦμεν ἐπιμενοῦμεν τῇ ἁμαρτίᾳ ἵνα ἡ χάρις πλεονάσῃ <u>μὴ γένοιτο</u> οἵτινες ἀπεθάνομεν τῇ ἁμαρτίᾳ πῶς ἔτι ζήσομεν ἐν αὐτῇ – "what then shall we say shall we persist in sin so that grace may abound? <u>God forbid</u> how shall we who are dead to sin yet live in it?"

The phrase μὴ γένοιτο is an Optative expressing a wish which strongly disapproves of some conclusion that may be derived indirectly from a question or an assertion. This is clearly seen in the use of the phrase by Paul. He mainly uses it (twelve of the fourteen times the phrase is used is by Paul) to express his disapproval of any inference which he fears may be drawn from his argument (i.e. He states in the strongest terms possible that he does not intend his words to be interpreted in the manner he fears it may be represented). Boyer notes concerning μὴ γένοιτο saying,

> Best known of optative uses, and one of the most frequent,[381] the phrase μὴ γένοιτο is an example of the volitive optative. In form it is a wish, "may it not happen." But it has become a stereotyped, idiomatic exclamation indicating revulsion and indignant, strong rejection. For this reason it is given a separate classification. The common English translation, "God forbid!" (King James Version) is not, of course, a literal translation (there is no word for God, and the verb does not mean "forbid"), but it expresses the sense accurately. Gal 6:14 is the only place where this phrase

---

[377] Dana and Mantey, *A Manual Grammar of the Greek New Testament*, 172.
[378] Wallace, *Greek Grammar Beyond the Basics*, 480.
[379] Wallace, *Greek Grammar Beyond the Basics*, 481.
[380] James L. Boyer, *The Classifications of Optatives: A Statistical Study*, Grace Theological Journal 9.1 (1988) 129-140.
[381] It occurs 15 times, all but one is in Paul: Luke 20:16; Rom 3:4, 6, 31; 6:2, 15; 7:7, 13; 9:14; 11:1, 11; 1 Cor 6:15; Gal 2:17; 3:21; 6:14.

occurs as part of a longer sentence rather than standing alone as a two-word exclamation. In every other Pauline usage, it is an appropriate negative answer to a rhetorical question. In Luke 20:16 it is also a strong reply, this time to a threat of judgment."[382]

Luke 1:38: εἶπεν δὲ Μαριάμ Ἰδού, ἡ δούλη κυρίου· <u>γένοιτό</u> μοι κατὰ τὸ ῥῆμά σου καὶ ἀπῆλθεν ἀπ' αὐτῆς ὁ ἄγγελος – "and Mary said behold the handmaid of the lord, <u>may it be</u> to me according to your word and the angel went away from her."

2. The Potential Optative[383]

The Optative with ἄν is used to express what would happen on the fulfilment of some supposed[384] condition. Wallace writes,

> This use of the optative occurs with the particle an in the apodosis of an incomplete fourth class condition. It is used to indicate a consequence in the future of an unlikely condition. There are no complete fourth class conditions in the NT. The protasis (which also uses the optative) needs to be supplied. The idea is *If he **could do** something, he **would** do this*. Only a handful of examples occur in the NT, all in Luke's writings.[385]

Luke 1:62: ἐνένευον δὲ τῷ πατρὶ αὐτοῦ τὸ τί <u>ἂν θέλοι</u> καλεῖσθαι αὐτόν – "and they made signs to his father that what <u>did he desire</u> to call him."

Acts 5:24: ὡς δὲ ἤκουσαν τοὺς λόγους τούτους ὅ τε ἱερεύς καὶ ὁ στρατηγὸς τοῦ ἱεροῦ καὶ οἱ ἀρχιερεῖς διηπόρουν περὶ αὐτῶν τί <u>ἂν γένοιτο</u> τοῦτο – "and as they heard these words, both the priest and the captain of the temple and the high priests were in doubt concerning what this thing <u>may become</u>."

3. Deliberative Optative[386]

This is the use of the optative in rhetorical questions and imply doubt in the speaker's mind. Brooks and Winbery write,

---

[382] James L. Boyer, *The Classifications of Optatives*: 129-140.

[383] The term "potential" is used in grammar to describe action which is dependent on circumstances or conditions, that which would or might happen if circumstances are right or if conditions are met. In Greek there is a potential indicative used to express a past action as dependent on past circumstances or conditions, and the potential optative used to express such actions in the future, as well as potential uses of the subjunctive in third class conditions and deliberative questions. Usually these constructions use the modal particle ἄν. [James L. Boyer, *The Classifications of Optatives*: 129-140.]

[384] Dana and Mantey observe that "These optatives occur as the fulfillment of a condition which is implied, and in the great majority of instances we can supply from the context the implied condition." [Dana and Mantey, *A Manual Grammar of the Greek New Testament*, 174.]

[385] Wallace, *Greek Grammar Beyond the Basics*, 482-83.

[386] Many grammarians classify this also under potential optative. The difference is that they label the potential optative as "potential optative in direct questions" while the deliberative optative they label as "potential optative in indirect questions". For example Boyer explains thus "*Potential Optative in Direct Questions*. Two examples are found in this category: Acts 8:31 and 17:18. Both have the particle ἄν and the sense is clearly potential. They express puzzled curiosity. Like those following, they are within a quotation, but it is a direct quotation, which would require that the original forms be preserved. *Potential Optative in Indirect Questions*. The difference between these and the preceding category is that they are in indirectly quoted questions rather than direct. This raises the question (to be discussed below) whether they should rather be classified as "oblique" optatives. They are grouped here, however, on the basis of their sense." [James L. Boyer, *The Classifications of Optatives*: 129-140.]

This use of the optative involves an indirect, rhetorical question. Indirect statements usually retain the same mood and tense which appeared in the direct statement. Therefore the indirect, rhetorical question often employs the optative because the direct question did so.[387]

Luke 1:29: ἡ δὲ ἰδοῦσα διεταράχθη ἐπὶ τῷ λόγῳ αὐτοῦ, καὶ διελογίζετο ποταπὸς <u>εἴη</u> ὁ ἀσπασμὸς οὗτος – "and when she saw him she was troubled at his word and reasoned what manner this greeting <u>may be</u>."

Luke 8:9: Ἐπηρώτων δὲ αὐτὸν οἱ μαθηταὶ αὐτοῦ λέγοντες, τίς <u>εἴη</u> ἡ παραβολὴ αὕτη – "and his disciples asked him saying what <u>might</u> this parable <u>be</u>?"

Conditional Sentences

A conditional sentence generally consists of two clauses: (1) The if-clause or <u>the protasis</u> which is used to set out beforehand, the condition and (2) The result clause or <u>the apodosis</u> which is used to set out the response that is to be given back, the conclusion, the result, the consequence. Concerning conditional sentences in the Greek, Hewett points out four classes. He says, "One element of richness in the Greek language is the variety of structures whereby one may express a conditional thought. In Greek New testament there are four."[388] A brief overview of the four classifications can be presented as:

a. Types of Conditional Sentence summarized from Robertson's *Grammar of the Greek New Testament*[389]:

Classifications of Conditional sentences:
- Reality (Determined as fulfilled): Assumes the condition to be a reality and the conclusion follows logically and naturally from that assumption.
- Unreality (Determined as Unfilled): The premise is assumed to be contrary to fact. The thing itself may be true, but it is treated as untrue.
- Probability (Undetermined, but with the Prospect of Determination): Uses in the condition clause the mode of expectation, the subjunctive. It is not determined as is true of the 1st and 2nd class conditions.
- Possibility (Remote Prospect of Determination): Uses optative in the protasis denoting that the condition is undetermined with less likelihood of determination than is true of the 3rd class with the subjunctive.

"The point about all 4 classes to note it that the form of the condition has to do only with the statement, not with the absolute truth or certainty of the matter…We must distinguish always therefore between the fact and the statement of fact. The conditional sentence deals only with the statement"

Suppositions from the 4 classes of conditional sentences:
- 1st class condition: Premise as a supposition from the viewpoint of reality, or premise based on fact.

---

[387] Brooks and Winbery, *Syntax of the New Testament Greek*, 125.
[388] Hewett, *New Testament Greek*, 33.
[389] Robertson, *A Grammar of the Greek New testament in the Light of Historical Research*, 1005

- 2ⁿᵈ class condition: Premise, which is contrary to fact.
- 3ʳᵈ class condition: Premise which is more probable future, premise of probability.
- 4ᵗʰ class condition: Premise of less probability in a future condition often the information contained in the premise is a wish without any implication.

b. Types of Conditional Sentence summarized from Chamberlain's *Exegetical Grammar*:[390]

- 1ˢᵗ Class Conditions – (1) The protasis will always have the indicative mood, and will usually be introduced by εἰ. It may use any of the tenses. (2) The apodosis (conclusion) may have any tense and any mode. It may be a statement or a question.
- 2ⁿᵈ Class Conditions – (1) The protasis will always have the indicative mood, and will be introduced by εἰ. The tense will always be a past tense: imperfect, aorist, and pluperfect. (2) The apodosis will take a past tense of the indicative. Usually an will occur in the apodosis to mark this condition off from a 1ˢᵗ class condition. (3) If the condition refers to present time, the imperfect is used (4) If the condition refers to past time, usually the aorist tense is used (5) If it is desired to express continued action in past time, the imperfect must be used.
- 3ʳᵈ Class Conditions – (1) The protasis will have always have the subjunctive mood, and will usually be introduced by ἐάν but occasionally by εἰ. (2) Since the subjunctive mode alone is used, the tense is limited to present and aorist. (3) The apodosis may have any mode or any tense. (4) It may make a statement, ask a question, or give a command.
- 4ᵗʰ Class Conditions – (1) The protasis has the optative mood, and is introduced by εἰ. (2) It may use either the present or the aorist tense. (3) The apodosis has the optative mood, and the modal ἄν.

Conditional sentences are classified as:

1. First Class – Condition of Reality

This condition is sometimes referred to as a simple condition, condition of fact, or condition of reality. In this class, the condition presented in the protasis is regarded as true. This class takes the form of the particle εἰ + the present indicative in the protasis as Green writes, "a condition is assumed as ground of assertion ... in such cases if is expressed by εἰ with the indicative followed by the indicative."[391] Thus this case can be represented by "εἰ"(if) + indicative mood verb = True. Wallace explains, "The first class condition indicates *the assumption of truth for the sake of argument*. The normal idea, then, is *if – and let us assume that this is true for the sake of argument – then ...*"[392]

This means that the speaker or writer assumes the condition to be true. The "if" condition in the protasis is merely stated as true for the sake of argument. It is stated in

---

[390] Chamberlain, *An Exegetical Grammar of the Greek New Testament*, 195-200.
[391] Green, *A Brief Introduction to New Testament Greek with vocabularies and exercises*, 111.
[392] Wallace, *Greek Grammar Beyond the Basics*, 690.

the indicative mood (the mood of fact) thus the writer presents the condition as true for the sake of argument and in taking a statement which he knows to be false (but which his opponents believe is true) and assumes that it is true the writer shows the absurd and illogical conclusions that follow. Thus whether the protasis is really true must be determined by the context and by common sense.

1 Corinthians 15:19-20: εἰ ἐν τῇ ζωῇ ταύτῃ ἠλπικότες ἐσμὲν ἐν Χριστῷ μόνον ἐλεεινότεροι πάντων ἀνθρώπων ἐσμέν 20 Νυνὶ δὲ Χριστὸς ἐγήγερται ἐκ νεκρῶν ἀπαρχὴ τῶν κεκοιμημένων ἐγένετο – "if in this life we have hope in Christ only then we are of all men most miserable but now Christ is raised from the dead, he became the firstfruits of those who have fallen asleep."

2. Second Class – Condition of Unreality[393]

This condition is sometimes referred to as condition contrary to fact, or condition of assumed unreality in which the "if" statement in the protasis is assumed as as untrue. Green writes that, "the condition is viewed as impossible or unfulfilled the reference being in the past ... here if is expressed by εἰ with the past indicative followed by the past indicative with ἄν."[394] This is represented by "εἰ" (if) + "μὴ" (not) = False. Wallace explains,

> The second class condition indicates *the assumption of an untruth (for the sake of argument)*. For this reason it is appropriately called the "contrary to fact" condition (or the *unreal* condition). It might be better to call it *presumed* contrary to fact, however, since sometimes it presents a condition that is true, even though the speaker assumes it to be untrue (e.g., Luke 7:39).[395]

In the second class conditional sentence, the speaker assumes the condition to be untrue and this assumption is used by the speaker to show what would have happened if conditions had been different. Boyer explains that the second class condition "states a condition which as a matter of fact has not been met and follows with a statement of what would have been true if it had. An extended paraphrase in English would be, "If this were the case, which it is not, then this would have been true, which as a matter of fact, is not." The term "contrary to fact" therefore is an accurate descriptive name for this type."[396]

John 8:42: εἶπεν οὖν αὐτοῖς ὁ Ἰησοῦς Εἰ ὁ θεὸς πατὴρ ὑμῶν ἦν ἠγαπᾶτε ἂν ἐμέ ἐγὼ γὰρ ἐκ τοῦ θεοῦ ἐξῆλθον καὶ ἥκω· οὐδὲ γὰρ ἀπ' ἐμαυτοῦ ἐλήλυθα ἀλλ' ἐκεῖνός με ἀπέστειλεν – "therefore Jesus says to them if God was your father, then you would love me for I proceeded and am come from God for neither came I of myself but he sent me."

---

[393] "Second class conditional sentences occur less frequently than other types in the NT; there are only 47 examples. Called by some "Contrary to Fact" or "Unreal",2 by others "Determined as Unfulfilled,") ... Second class conditions are more formally structured than either of the other types. Both first and third class show a characteristic structure only in the protasis, but the second class shows a distinctive pattern in both the protasis and apodosis; indeed, it is the apodosis which clearly identifies it." [James L. Boyer, *Second Class Conditions in New Testament Greek*, Grace Theological Journal 3.1 (1982) 81-88.]

[394] Green, *A Brief Introduction to New Testament Greek with vocabularies and exercises*, 111.

[395] Wallace, *Greek Grammar Beyond the Basics*, 694.

[396] Boyer, *Second Class Conditions in New Testament Greek*, 83.

3. Third Class – Condition of Assumed Probability

This condition is sometimes referred to as future condition. It is used to express possibility in which though the protasis "if" has not happened yet, it may happen, but when it does then the apodosis will be the result. Green writes, "the condition itself is regarded as doubtful ... in such sentences if is expressed by ἐάν with subjunctive, followed by the indicative, generally future."[397] Thus this is represented by - "ἐάν" + subjunctive mood verb = Maybe yes, maybe no. Wallace observes,

> The third class condition often presents the condition as *uncertain of fulfillment, but still likely*. There are, however, many exceptions to this ... The *third* class condition encompasses a broad range of potentialities in Koine Greek. It depicts what is *likely to occur* in the *future*, what could *possibly occur*, or even what is only *hypothetical* and will not occur.[398]

The third class conditional sentence points out what results are expected to be achieved or realized if the future condition stated in the protasis is met. The writer or speaker knows that at the present time the condition has not been fulfilled and is still future, but the possibility of the condition being realized is there and there is an expectation that the condition will be fulfilled although there is some uncertainty or doubt in the writer's mind as to whether the condition will be met. Boyer observes, "Since the use of the subjunctive distinguishes this class from the others, it seems obvious that the basic significance must be seen in the meaning of the subjunctive mood."[399]

Revelation 22:18-19: Συμμαρτυροῦμαι γὰρ παντὶ ἀκούοντι τοὺς λόγους τῆς προφητείας τοῦ βιβλίου τούτου, <u>ἐάν τις ἐπιτιθῇ</u> πρὸς ταῦτα, ἐπιθήσει ὁ θεὸς ἐπ᾽ αὐτὸν τὰς πληγὰς τὰς γεγραμμένας ἐν βιβλίῳ τούτῳ 19 καὶ <u>ἐάν τις ἀφαιρῇ</u> ἀπὸ τῶν λόγων βίβλου τῆς προφητείας ταύτης ἀφαιρήσει ὁ θεὸς τὸ μέρος αὐτοῦ ἀπὸ βίβλου τῆς ζωῆς καὶ ἐκ τῆς πόλεως τῆς ἁγίας καὶ τῶν γεγραμμένων ἐν βιβλίῳ τούτῳ – "for I testify together with everyone who is hearing these words of the prophecy of this book, <u>If anyone adds</u> to these things God will add upon him the plagues which have been written in this book and <u>if anyone takes away</u> from the words of this book of this prophecy God will take away his part from the book of life and from the holy city and from the things which have been written in this book."

4. Fourth Class Condition – Condition of Assumed Possibility

This condition is expresses a wish or desire that is even less probable than the third class. The protasis presents a condition that has not happened yet, the fulfilment of a fourth class condition is merely possible. Wallace states, "The fourth class condition indicates a *possible* condition in the future, usually a remote possibility ... There are no complete fourth class conditions in the NT"[400] Thus this is represented in the Greek by "εἰ" + optative mood verb = Wish/desire.

---

[397] Green, *A Brief Introduction to New Testament Greek with vocabularies and exercises*, 111.
[398] Wallace, *Greek Grammar Beyond the Basics*, 696.
[399] James L. Boyer, *Third (and Fourth) Class Conditions*, Grace Theological Journal 3.2 (1982) 163-75.
[400] Wallace, *Greek Grammar Beyond the Basics*, 699.

1 Pet 3:14: ἀλλ' <u>εἰ</u> καὶ <u>πάσχοιτε</u> διὰ δικαιοσύνην μακάριοι τὸν δὲ φόβον αὐτῶν μὴ φοβηθῆτε μηδὲ ταραχθῆτε – "but if you may suffer because of righteousness you are blessed and do not be afraid of their terror neither be troubled."

CHAPTER VI

THE SYNTAX OF VERBAL FORMS: INFINITIVES AND PARTICIPLES

The infinitive

The infinitive is a verbal noun. Wallace defines it as:

The infinitive is an indeclinable verbal noun. As such it participates in some of the features of the verb and some of the noun. Like a *verb*, the infinitive has tense and voice, but not person or mood. Its number is always singular. Like the oblique moods (i.e., non-indicative moods), the infinitive is normally negated by μὴ or οὐ. Like a *noun*, the infinitive can have many of the case functions that an ordinary noun can have. Although technically infinitives do not have gender, frequently the neuter singular article is attached to them.[401]

From this it can be stated that the infinitive is used both as a verb and as a noun. When it is used as a noun or as a verb it takes on some of the characteristics of verbs or nouns as Wallace pointed above, when it is used as a noun, though it always takes the neuter gender singular number, it can have many of the case functions and be used with most of the prepositions. When used as a verb, it takes tense and person but no mood. this means that the infinitive in the present tense present a durative idea (i.e. on-going or linear action in the past, present or future depending on the context) and when in the aorist, it presents an undefined idea (i.e. unitary or single event).[402] Nunn observes,

The Infinitive partakes of the nature both of a verb and a noun. As a verb it has a subject expressed or understood, and it may have an object, it is qualified by adverbs and has tense and voice. As a noun it may stand as the subject or object of another verb, it may be in apposition to another noun or pronoun, or it may be governed by a preposition. The subject of the Infinitive is properly in the Accusative case. The use of the Greek Infinitive is much wider than that of the English Infinitive. It is sometimes translated by the English Infinitive or by the English verbal noun in *ing*, and sometimes by the English Indicative, Subjunctive, or even Imperative mood.[403]

Thus the characteristics of an infinitive can be tabled as below:

Infinitive's characteristics as a Noun	*Infinitive's characteristics as verb*
It has case relations	It has voice[404]

---

[401] ibid., 588.

[402] Duff explains that "The **difference between the Present and Aorist Infinitive** is the same as between the Present and Aorist Imperative – the Aorist is the default, undefined, aspect; the present is process (either continuous or repeated). [Duff, *The Elements of New Testament Greek*, 82.]

[403] Nunn, *A Short Syntax of New Testament Greek*, 87.

[404] "All three voices, the active, the middle, and the passive, occur and function as in the other moods and participles." [Hewett, *New Testament Greek*, 175.]

Infinitive's characteristics as a Noun	Infinitive's characteristics as verb
It is used as a subject	It has tense[405]
It is used as an object	It takes an object
It is found in apposition..	It is qualified by adverbs
It takes an article[406]	
It is qualified by adjectives	

The Infinitive is widely used in the New Testament. Its dual nature enables it to perform in a variety of functions. Vaughan and Gideon note concerning its use,

> The use of the infinitive in Greek is much wider than the use of the infinitive in English. ... 1. It may be used as *a noun* element in the sentence. That is to say, the infinitive sometimes performs the typical noun functions of subject, object, appositive, and modifier. ... 2. It may be used as *the equivalent of an adverbial clause*. As such the infinitive may express purpose, result, time, or cause. ... 3. It may be used as *an independent element*, as in the greetings of letters and in the expression of a command. In these constructions it is equivalent to a principal clause or an independent sentence.[407]

1. The Verbal Infinitive

The verbal Infinitive is the adverbial function of the infinitive. Boyer notes concerning this class that "In many instances the infinitive is used, in effect, as a subordinate adverbial clause which usually expresses time but may also express cause, purpose or result."[408] Thus the verbal infinitive can used to indicate:

1. Purpose

The infinitive can be used to indicate the purpose of the main verb. This use of the infinitive makes use of: (a) simple infinitive with verbs of motions[409] (b) infinitive with the genitive article τοῦ (c) infinitive with εἰς τό (d) infinitive with πρὸς τό. Wallace

---

[405] Hewett observes that "The Greek infinitive occurs in the present, future, aorist and perfect tenses. As in the subjunctive mood and the participle, tense does not indicate time of action, except the future, where an anticipation of action is to be felt. Rather, tense in the infinitive indicates the kind of action." [Hewett, *New Testament Greek*, 174.]

[406] "Like any noun the infinitive may be used with an article. It will only use the neuter gender and only the singular number." [Hewett, *New Testament Greek*, 175.]

[407] Vaughan and Gideon, *A Greek grammar of the New Testament*, 184-86

[408] James L. Boyer, *The Classification of Infinitives a statistical study*, Grace Theological Journal 6.1 (1985) 3-27.

[409] Boyer points out that "Verbs found with an infinitive of purpose are (a) 'to send': ἀποστέλλω (19), ἐξαποστέλλω (2), πέμπω (4); (b) 'to give': δίδωμι (17), παραδίδωμι (3); (c) 'to choose': ἐκλέγομαι (4), προχειρίζομαι (3); (d) more than 40 others with three or less infinitives involved; and (e) a special category of intransitive verbs of motion: 'to go' or 'to come'; compounds of βαίνω (13), ἔρχομαι and its compounds (79), πορεύομαι and its compounds (12), compounds of ἄγω (5); verbs meaning 'to be present, to have come', ἥκω (2), παραγίνομαι (2), πάρειμι (1); and miscellaneous intransitive verbs of motion (19)." [Boyer, *The Classification of Infinitives* 11.]

writes that (e) infinitive with ὥστε (f) infinitive with ὡς "The infinitive is used to indicate the purpose or goal of the action or state of its controlling verb. It answers the question "Why?" in that it looks ahead to the anticipated and intended result."[410]

John 21:3: λέγει αὐτοῖς Σίμων Πέτρος Ὑπάγω <u>ἁλιεύειν</u> λέγουσιν αὐτῷ Ἐρχόμεθα καὶ ἡμεῖς σὺν σοί ἐξῆλθον καὶ ἀνέβησαν εἰς τὸ πλοῖον εὐθὺς, καὶ ἐν εἴνη τῇ νυκτὶ ἐπίασαν οὐδέν – "Simon Peter said to them I go <u>to fish</u> they said to him we come also with you they went out and the entered into a boat straight away and that night they caught nothing."

Matthew 13:3: καὶ ἐλάλησεν αὐτοῖς πολλὰ ἐν παραβολαῖς λέγων, Ἰδού, ἐξῆλθεν ὁ σπείρων <u>τοῦ σπείρειν</u> – "and he spoke to them many things in parables saying, behold a sower went out <u>to sow</u>."

Matthew 27:31: καὶ ὅτε ἐνέπαιξαν αὐτῷ ἐξέδυσαν αὐτὸν τὴν χλαμύδα καὶ ἐνέδυσαν αὐτὸν τὰ ἱμάτια αὐτοῦ καὶ ἀπήγαγον αὐτὸν <u>εἰς τὸ σταυρῶσαι</u> – "and when they had mocked him they stripped the robe of him and clothed him with his garment and led him <u>to be crucified</u>."

Matthew 23:5: πάντα δὲ τὰ ἔργα αὐτῶν ποιοῦσιν <u>πρὸς τὸ θεαθῆναι</u> τοῖς ἀνθρώποις· πλατύνουσιν δὲ τὰ φυλακτήρια αὐτῶν καὶ μεγαλύνουσιν τὰ κράσπεδα τῶν ἱματίων αὐτῶν – "but all of their works they <u>in order to be seen</u> by men and they widen their phylacteries and enlarge the borders of their garments."

2. Result

This is the use of the infinitive to indicate the results of the action of the main verb. Wallace explains,

> The infinitive of result indicates the outcome produced by the controlling verb. In this respect it is similar to the infinitive of purpose, but the former puts an emphasis on intention while the latter places the emphasis on effort. A number of instances are difficult to distinguish, leaving room for exegetical discussion. As a general guideline, however, if in doubt, label a given infinitive as purpose (it occurs almost four times as often as result).[411]

Romans 7:3: ἄρα οὖν ζῶντος τοῦ ἀνδρὸς μοιχαλὶς χρηματίσει ἐὰν γένηται ἀνδρὶ ἑτέρῳ· ἐὰν δὲ ἀποθάνῃ ὁ ἀνήρ ἐλευθέρα ἐστὶν ἀπὸ τοῦ νόμου <u>τοῦ μὴ εἶναι</u> αὐτὴν μοιχαλίδα γενομένην ἀνδρὶ ἑτέρῳ – "therefore then while the husband is living, she will be called an adulteress if she be with another man but if the husband be dead, she is free from the law <u>that she may not be</u> an adulteress being with another man."

Acts 5:3: εἶπεν δὲ Πέτρος Ἀνανία διατί ἐπλήρωσεν ὁ Σατανᾶς τὴν καρδίαν σου <u>ψεύσασθαί</u> σε τὸ πνεῦμα τὸ ἅγιον καὶ νοσφίσασθαι ἀπὸ τῆς τιμῆς τοῦ χωρίου – "and Peter said Ananias why has Satan filled your heart <u>so that you lie</u> to the Holy Spirit and to keep back for yourself from the price of the land?"

---

[410] Wallace, *Greek Grammar Beyond the Basics*, 590.
[411] Wallace, *Greek Grammar Beyond the Basics*, 592.

Romans 1:20: τὰ γὰρ ἀόρατα αὐτοῦ ἀπὸ κτίσεως κόσμου τοῖς ποιήμασιν νοούμενα καθορᾶται ἥ τε ἀΐδιος αὐτοῦ δύναμις καὶ θειότης <u>εἰς τὸ εἶναι</u> αὐτοὺς ἀναπολογήτους – "for the hidden things of him from the creation of the world the things made being understood being clearly seen both his eternal power and Godhead <u>so that they are</u> without excuse."

3. Temporal

The temporal use of the infinitive indicates time that is relative to the time of the action of the main verb. This use may either be antecedent contemporaneous or subsequent time. Wallace explains, "This use of the infinitive indicates a temporal relationship between its action and the action of the controlling verb. It answers the question "When?""[412] Although the infinitive in itself does not contain temporal significance, yet within given contexts it can be used to bring out temporal meanings. Hewett explains,

> Although infinitives per se express no specific time, in conjunction with various prepositions they become idiomatic phrases having the following time significance. *Simultaneous time.* ἐν τῷ and the infinitive have this task 55 times. ... Always determine the temporal setting of the main verb. Then cast that idiom accordingly. *Antecedent or subsequent time.* Antecedent time is expressed by πρίν or πρὶν ἤ (either means before) and the infinitive (cf. Mt. 26:34). Subsequent time may be expressed by μετὰ τό and the infinitive (cf. Acts 1:3).[413]

Antecedent Time

Matthew 6:8: μὴ οὖν ὁμοιωθῆτε αὐτοῖς· οἶδε γὰρ ὁ πατὴρ ὑμῶν ὧν χρείαν ἔχετε, <u>πρὸ τοῦ ὑμᾶς αἰτῆσαι</u> αὐτόν. – "therefore do not be like them for your father knows which needs you have <u>before you ask</u> him."

John 8:58: εἶπεν αὐτοῖς ὅ Ἰησοῦς Ἀμὴν ἀμὴν λέγω ὑμῖν <u>πρὶν Ἀβραὰμ γενέσθαι</u> ἐγὼ εἰμί – "Jesus said to them amen amen I say to you <u>before Abraham was</u> I am."

Contemporaneous (Simultaneous Time)

Matthew 13:4: καὶ <u>ἐν τῷ σπείρειν</u> αὐτὸν ἃ μὲν ἔπεσεν παρὰ τὴν ὁδόν, καὶ ἦλθεν τὰ πετεινὰ καὶ κατέφαγεν αὐτά – "and <u>while he sowed</u>, some fell along the wayside, and the birds came and devoured them."

Subsequent Time

Mark 14:28: ἀλλὰ <u>μετὰ τὸ ἐγερθῆναί</u> με προάξω ὑμᾶς εἰς τὴν Γαλιλαίαν – "but <u>after I am raised</u> I will go before you into Galilee."

Future Time

Acts 8:40: Φίλιππος δὲ εὑρέθη εἰς Ἄζωτον· καὶ διερχόμενος εὐηγγελίζετο τὰς πόλεις πάσας <u>ἕως τοῦ ἐλθεῖν</u> αὐτὸν εἰς Καισάρειαν – "and Philip was found in Azotus and while passing through he preached in all the cities <u>until he came</u> to Caesarea."

4. Cause

Causal Infinitive, Wallace defines as the use of the infinitive to indicate "the reason for the action of the controlling verb. In this respect, it answers the question

---
[412] Ibid., 594
[413] Hewett, *New Testament Greek*, 181-82.

"Why?" Unlike the infinitive of purpose, however, the causal infinitive gives a *retrospective* answer (i.e., it looks back to the ground or reason), while the purpose infinitive gives *prospective* answer (looking forward to the intended result)."[414] Brooks and Winbery note that "The idea of cause is often expressed by διὰ τό with the infinitive and rarely by τῷ with the infinitive and ἕνεκεν τοῦ with the infinitive (one time each in the New Testament)."[415]

Matthew 13:5-6: ἄλλα δὲ ἔπεσεν ἐπὶ τὰ πετρώδη ὅπου οὐκ εἶχεν γῆν πολλήν, καὶ εὐθέως ἐξανέτειλεν <u>διὰ τὸ μὴ ἔχειν</u> βάθος γῆς· 6 ἡλίου δὲ ἀνατείλαντος ἐκαυματίσθη καὶ <u>διὰ τὸ μὴ ἔχειν</u> ῥίζαν ἐξηράνθη – "and others fell upon the stony places where they had not much earth and straightway sprang up <u>because they had not</u> depth of earth and the sun rising up scorched and <u>because they had not</u> root it withered."

John 2:24: αὐτὸς δὲ ὁ Ἰησοῦς οὐκ ἐπίστευεν ἑαυτὸν αὐτοῖς <u>διὰ τὸ αὐτὸν γινώσκειν</u> πάντας – "but Jesus himself did not commit himself to them <u>because he knew</u> all."

1. Infinitive of Command

Dana and Mantey say "It is the only independent use of the Greek infinitive, and is not of very frequent occurrence. ... The construction suggests a close kinship between the infinitive and imperative."[416] Burton adds, "The Infinitive without the article is occasionally used to express a command or exhortation. This is the only use of the Infinitive as a principal verb."[417]

Romans 12:15: <u>χαίρειν</u> μετὰ χαιρόντων καὶ <u>κλαίειν</u> μετὰ κλαιόντων – "<u>rejoice</u> with those who are rejoicing and <u>weep</u> with those who are weeping."

2. Infinitive Absolute

When the infinitive stands out of connection in a sentence, it can be said to be an infinitive absolute. This usage is mainly found in greetings.

James 1:1: Ἰάκωβος θεοῦ καὶ κυρίου Ἰησοῦ Χριστοῦ δοῦλος ταῖς δώδεκα φυλαῖς ταῖς ἐν τῇ διασπορᾷ <u>χαίρειν</u> – "James a slave of God and the lord Jesus Christ to the twelve tribes to them in the dispersion <u>greetings</u>."

3. The Substantival Infinitive

This second use of the infinitive in a sentence construction is that of a noun. Wenham states that "The infinitive is a neuter verbal noun. As a noun it may stand as the subject or object of another verb"[418]

1. Subject

On the use of the Infinitive as a subject, Wallace observes, "An infinitive or an infinitive phrase sometimes functions as the subject of a finite verb. This category includes instances where the infinitive occurs with impersonal verbs such as δεῖ, ἔξεστιν,

---

[414] Wallace, *Greek Grammar Beyond the Basics*, 596.
[415] Brooks and Winbery, *Syntax of the new Testament Greek*, 138.
[416] Dana and Mantey, *A Manual Grammar of the Greek New Testament*, 216.
[417] E. Burton, *Syntax of the Moods and Tenses In New Testament Greek*, 146.
[418] Wenham, *Elements of New Testament Greek*, 84.

δοκεῖ etc."⁴¹⁹ William Goodwin explains the use of the infinitive as a subject stating that the infinitive may form the subject of impersonal verbs, other infinitives (in which it is classified as a subject accusative since the subject of the infinitive is in the accusative). He explains that:

> The infinitive may be the subject nominative of a finite verb, or the subject accusative of another infinitive. It is especially common as subject of an impersonal verb or of ἐστί. It may also be a predicate nominative or accusative, and it may stand in apposition to a noun in the nominative or accusative.⁴²⁰

Subject of Finite Verbs:

Philippians 1:21: ἐμοὶ γὰρ <u>τὸ ζῆν</u> Χριστὸς καὶ <u>τὸ ἀποθανεῖν</u> κέρδος – "for to me <u>to live</u> is Christ and <u>to die</u> is gain."⁴²¹

Subject of Impersonal Verbs:

Matthew 12:10: καὶ ἰδού, ἄνθρωπος ἦν τὴν χεῖρα ἔχων ξηράν, καὶ ἐπηρώτησαν αὐτὸν λέγοντες Εἰ ἔξεστιν τοῖς σάββασιν <u>θεραπεύειν</u> ἵνα κατηγορήσωσιν αὐτοῦ – "and behold a man was there having a withered hand and they asked him saying "is it lawful <u>to heal</u> on the Sabbath" in order that they may accuse him."

Subject Accusatives of another Infinitive:

Mark 8:31: Καὶ ἤρξατο διδάσκειν αὐτοὺς ὅτι δεῖ τὸν υἱὸν τοῦ ἀνθρώπου πολλὰ <u>παθεῖν</u> καὶ <u>ἀποδοκιμασθῆναι</u> ἀπὸ τῶν πρεσβυτέρων καὶ ἀρχιερέων καὶ γραμματέων καὶ <u>ἀποκτανθῆναι</u> καὶ μετὰ τρεῖς ἡμέρας <u>ἀναστῆναι</u>· – "and he began to teach that it is necessary the Son of Man <u>to suffer</u> many things and <u>to be rejected</u> of the elders and chief-priests and scribes and <u>to be killed</u> and after three days <u>to rise again</u>."⁴²²

Apposition to a Noun:

1 Thessalonians 4:3: τοῦτο γάρ ἐστιν θέλημα τοῦ θεοῦ ὁ ἁγιασμὸς ὑμῶν <u>ἀπέχεσθαι</u> ὑμᾶς ἀπὸ τῆς πορνείας – "for this is the will of God your sanctification <u>that you abstain</u> from fornication."

2. Object

The infinitive or an infinitive phrase may sometimes be employed to function as the direct object of a finite verb.⁴²³ Hewett says that in this use, "The infinitive simply

---

⁴¹⁹ Wallace, *Greek Grammar Beyond the Basics*, 600.

⁴²⁰ Goodwin, *Syntax of Moods and Tenses of the Greek Verbs*, 299.

⁴²¹ Hewett explains the use of the infinitive in this example that "The article may be prefaced to the infinitive and used as the subject of sentences that do not use impersonal verbs. ... τὸ is a pointer, almost a demonstrative, drawing attention to the two infinitives and indicating that they are to be considered as subjects in the nominative case." [Hewett, *New Testament Greek*, 179.]

⁴²² The infinitives underlined form the subject of the infinitive διδάσκειν "to teach". Since the word son in phrase the Son of Man "τὸν υἱὸν τοῦ ἀνθρώπου" which forms the subject of the underlined infinitives is in the accusative, when considered together with the infinitives underlined, they form the subject of the infinitive διδάσκειν "to teach".

⁴²³ Brooks and Winbery explain that "certain verbs which cannot take a direct object as such but which require an infinitive to complete their meaning." [Brooks and Winbery, *Syntax of the new Testament Greek*, 140.]

fills out the thought expressed by the main verb. In this sense it is a complement, not in a grammatical sense."[424] Goodwin classifies it thus

The infinitive may the object of a verb, generally appearing as the accusative of direct object, sometimes as the accusative of kindred meaning. Here belong (1) the infinitive after verbs of *wishing, commanding*, and the like (not in indirect discourse), and (2) the infinitive in indirect discourse as the object of the verbs of saying and thinking.[425]

Infinitive as Direct Object of a Finite Verb:

Mark 10:38: ὁ δὲ Ἰησοῦς εἶπεν αὐτοῖς Οὐκ οἴδατε τί αἰτεῖσθε δύνασθε <u>πιεῖν</u> τὸ ποτήριον ὃ ἐγὼ πίνω καί τὸ βάπτισμα ὃ ἐγὼ βαπτίζομαι <u>βαπτισθῆναι</u> – "and Jesus said to them you know not what you are asking are you able <u>to drink</u> the cup which i drink and the baptism I am being baptized with are you able <u>to be baptized</u>?"

Matthew 7:11: εἰ οὖν ὑμεῖς πονηροὶ ὄντες οἴδατε δόματα ἀγαθὰ <u>διδόναι</u> τοῖς τέκνοις ὑμῶν πόσῳ μᾶλλον ὁ πατὴρ ὑμῶν ὁ ἐν τοῖς οὐρανοῖς δώσει ἀγαθὰ τοῖς αἰτοῦσιν αὐτόν – "therefore if you being evil know <u>to give</u> good gifts to your children how much more your father who is in heaven will give good things to those asking him."

Infinitive in Indirect Discourse:

Matthew 16:13: Ἐλθὼν δὲ ὁ Ἰησοῦς εἰς τὰ μέρη Καισαρείας τῆς Φιλίππου ἠρώτα τοὺς μαθητὰς αὐτοῦ λέγων, Τίνα με λέγουσιν οἱ ἄνθρωποι <u>εἶναι</u> τὸν υἱὸν τοῦ ἀνθρώπου – "and when Jesus came to region of Caesarea Philippi he asked his disciples saying who do men say that I the Son of man <u>am</u>?"

Infinitive as an Indirect Object:

Luke 10:40: ἡ δὲ Μάρθα περιεσπᾶτο περὶ πολλὴν διακονίαν· ἐπιστᾶσα δὲ εἶπεν Κύριε οὐ μέλει σοι ὅτι ἡ ἀδελφή μου μόνην με κατέλιπεν <u>διακονεῖν</u> εἰπὲ οὖν αὐτῇ ἵνα μοι συναντιλάβηται – "but Martha was distracted with much serving and coming up she said Lord is it not a care to you that my sister has left me alone <u>to serve</u> say to her therefore that she may help me."

Infinitive Complement:

Matthew 3:11: Ἐγὼ μὲν βαπτίζω ὑμᾶς ἐν ὕδατι εἰς μετάνοιαν· ὁ δὲ ὀπίσω μου ἐρχόμενος, ἰσχυρότερός μου ἐστίν, οὗ οὐκ εἰμὶ <u>ἱκανὸς</u> τὰ ὑποδήματα <u>βαστάσαι</u>, αὐτὸς ὑμᾶς βαπτίσει ἐν πνεύματι ἁγίῳ καὶ πυρί. – "I indeed baptize you with water to repentance but the one who is coming before me who is stronger than me whose shoelace I am not <u>worthy to loose</u> he will baptize you with the Holy Spirit and with fire."

1. Modifier

The infinitive may be used as a modifier of which use Brooks and Winbery write that it "may modify nouns or adjectives. When it modifies a noun it functions as

---

[424] Hewett, *New Testament Greek*, 179. Dana and Mantey explain this further stating that "This is in line with the fundamental relationship of the object to its verb, for a substantive object is essentially the complement of the verbal idea." [Dana and Mantey, *A Manual Grammar of the Greek New Testament*, 217.]

[425] Goodwin, *Syntax of Moods and Tenses of the Greek Verbs*, 300.

an adjective or a substantive in the genitive case ... or it may modify the noun by being in apposition with it"[426]

Luke 2:1: Ἐγένετο δὲ ἐν ταῖς ἡμέραις ἐκείναις ἐξῆλθεν δόγμα παρὰ Καίσαρος Αὐγούστου <u>ἀπογράφεσθαι</u> πᾶσαν τὴν οἰκουμένην – "and it came to pass in those days a decree went out from Caesar Augustus <u>to register</u> all the world."

John 1:12: ὅσοι δὲ ἔλαβον αὐτόν ἔδωκεν αὐτοῖς ἐξουσίαν τέκνα θεοῦ <u>γενέσθαι</u> τοῖς πιστεύουσιν εἰς τὸ ὄνομα αὐτοῦ – "and as many as received him to them he gave authority <u>to become</u> the children of God to the ones believing on his name."

THE PARTICIPLE

A participle is considered a "verbal adjective". In English, the participle is formed by adding "-ing" to the verb in forming the present participle and "-ed" to the verb in forming the past participle. Thus the the Present participle may be presented as "After <u>eating</u>, I will go to bed." while the Past participle as "<u>Moved</u> by the sermon, they all began to cry." In English, the present participle with the -ing functions either adjectivally (e.g. "The <u>rocking</u> chair is red) or adverbially (e.g. "The man ran <u>swinging</u> his arms wildly."), or as a noun (e.g. "<u>Running</u> is fun."). Dana and Mantey write concerning the use of the participle in Greek stating that

> There are few languages which have equalled the Greek in the abundance and variety of its use of the participle, and certainly none has surpassed it. ... This wealth of significance which belonged to the Greek participle at the zenith of its development lies undiminished before the student of the New Testament, and becomes a valuable asset in interpretation when adequately comprehended.[427]

Thus the Greek language has been called a participle loving language. The participle is called a 'verbal adjective' because it is formed from a verb, yet may be used as an adjective and often modifies other words. Brooks and Winbery state

> The participle is a verbal adjective. As such it has some of the characteristics of an adjective. Like a verb the participle has tense and voice (but not mood or person); it may be modified by an adverb, and it may have a direct object (but not a subject). Like an adjective it may be declined according to case, gender, and number. Most important is the fact that the participle can be used in the very same ways in which an adjective can be used.[428]

The Greek participle can be used in one of three major categories of use. These categories are:

a. Adjective. Burton notes that "The Adjective Participle limits its subject directly and exclusively. It attributes the action which it denotes to the subject as a quality or characteristic, or assigns the subject to the class marked by that action."[429] And when used as an adjective, the participle can either be attributive or predicatively.

---

[426] Brooks and Winbery, *Syntax of the new Testament Greek*, 141.
[427] Dana and Mantey, *A Manual Grammar of the Greek New Testament*, 220.
[428] Brooks and Winbery, *Syntax of the new Testament Greek*, 143.
[429] E. Burton, *Syntax of the Moods and Tenses In New Testament Greek*, 164.

b. **Adverbial (verbal use).** Burton writes that "The Adverbial Participle logically modifies some other verb of the sentence in which it stands, being equivalent to an adverbial phrase or clause denoting time, condition, concession, cause, purpose, means, manner, or attendant circumstance."[430]

c. **Substantival.** Burton writes, "The Substantive Participle is employed as itself the name of an action. It thus performs a function which is more commonly discharged by the Infinitive."[431]

The participle, like the infinitive, is a verbal substantive. It is declined as an ordinary adjective with variations for gender, number and case, and like a verb it takes on the distinctions of voice and tense. The characteristics of the participle can be represented as by the table below:

Participle as an Adjective	*Participle as a Verb*[432]
It qualifies a noun	It takes an object
It is used as a noun	It has voice
It is used as an object	It has tense
	It is qualified by adverbs

The time aspect in the tenses of the participle are generally the same time as those of the indicative; but they are present, past, or future relatively to the time of the verb with which they are connected. Only four of the Greek tenses have participles: present, aorist, future and perfect. The meaning of the tense in participles is explained by Wenham. He says:

> Generally speaking, the Present Participle denotes action taking place at the same time as the action of the main verb. ... The Aorist Participle is however sometimes used to describe *attendant circumstances*, i.e. an action taking place at the same time as the action of the main verb, notably in the common expression: ἀποκριθεὶς εἶπεν he answered and said. The distinction between Aorist and Perfect is the same in the case of participles as in the case of the Indicative. the Aorist speaks simply of an event in the past, the Perfect of an event in the past the results of which are still felt in the present.[433]

1. Attributively

A participle can be used adjectivally to modify a noun or pronoun or to assert something about it. This it does by "attaching a verbal idea to it."[434] And like an adjective, the participle when used adjectivally to modify a noun or pronoun, the attributive

---

[430] Ibid., 169.
[431] Ibid., 175.
[432] Wenham writes that "As a verb a participle has tense and voice and may have an object." [Wenham, *Elements of New Testament Greek*, 148.]
[433] ibid., 152-53.
[434] Brooks and Winbery, *Syntax of the new Testament Greek*, 143.

participle "agrees with the noun it modifies in case gender and number"[435] This use of the participle may be with or without an article.[436] Burton explains:

> An Attributive Participle when used to limit a noun which has the article, stands in the so-called attributive position, i.e. between the article and the noun, or after an article following the noun; but when the participle is limited by an adverbial phrase, this phrase may stand between the article and the noun, and the participle without the article follow the noun. It thus results that all the following orders are possible:
>
> (1) article, participle, modifier of the participle, noun;
>
> (2) art., mod., part., noun;
>
> (3) art., mod., noun, part.;
>
> (4) art., part., noun, mod.;
>
> (5) art., noun, art., mod., part.;
>
> (6) art., noun, art., part., mod.[437]

Matthew 3:7: Ἰδὼν δὲ πολλοὺς τῶν Φαρισαίων καὶ Σαδδουκαίων ἐρχομένους ἐπὶ τὸ βάπτισμα αὐτοῦ, εἶπεν αὐτοῖς, Γεννήματα ἐχιδνῶν, τίς ὑπέδειξεν ὑμῖν φυγεῖν ἀπὸ τῆς μελλούσης ὀργῆς; – "and seeing many of the Pharisees and Sadducees coming to his baptism he said to them generations of vipers, who has warned you to flee from the wrath about to come?"

Mathew 16:16: ἀποκριθεὶς δὲ Σίμων Πέτρος εἶπεν Σὺ εἶ ὁ Χριστὸς ὁ υἱὸς τοῦ θεοῦ τοῦ ζῶντος – "and Simon Peter answering said You are the Christ the Son of the living God."

John 7:38: ὁ πιστεύων εἰς ἐμέ καθὼς εἶπεν ἡ γραφή ποταμοὶ ἐκ τῆς κοιλίας αὐτοῦ ῥεύσουσιν ὕδατος ζῶντος – "the one who believes in me just as the Scripture says out of his belly shall flow rivers of living water."

2. Substantively

A participle can be used as a substantive to take the place of a noun. And as a substantive the participle may function in the same way a noun functions. "Just as the adjective may be coupled with the article and used for a substantive, so can the participle."[438] Thus this use is to be determined by the context. Brooks and Winbery explain,

> The participle, like an adjective, may be used in place of a noun or other substantive. The participle itself then functions as a noun. Its case, gender, and number are determined by its use in the sentence. ... It may be used with or without an article. It always stands in the attributive position.[439]

---

[435] Ibid.

[436] Vaughan and Gideon say that "If the article occurs with this construction, it may precede both the participle and the substantive, but it must precede both the participle. Only on rare occasions will the article be omitted entirely." [Vaughan and Gideon, *A Greek grammar of the New Testament*, 155.]

[437] E. Burton, *Syntax of the Moods and Tenses In New Testament Greek*, 166-67.

[438] Hewett, *New Testament Greek*, 149.

[439] Brooks and Winbery, *Syntax of the new Testament Greek*, 144.

The distinction between the substantival use and the adjectival use is that in the adjectival use the participle modifies a noun and as such agrees with the noun supplied in gender, case and number, while as a substantive, the participle replaces a noun and thus it does not accompany another substantive or agree with any noun in gender, case and number.

Matthew 2:20: λέγων, Ἐγερθεὶς παράλαβε τὸ παιδίον καὶ τὴν μητέρα αὐτοῦ, καὶ πορεύου εἰς γῆν Ἰσραήλ. τεθνήκασι γὰρ <u>οἱ ζητοῦντες</u> τὴν ψυχὴν τοῦ παιδίου. – "saying rise take the child and his mother and go to the land of Israel for they are dead <u>those who seek</u> the soul of the child."

Matthew 16:28: ἀμὴν λέγω ὑμῖν εἰσίν τινες <u>τῶν ὧδε ἑστηκότων</u>, οἵτινες οὐ μὴ γεύσωνται θανάτου ἕως ἂν ἴδωσιν τὸν υἱὸν τοῦ ἀνθρώπου ἐρχόμενον ἐν τῇ βασιλείᾳ αὐτοῦ – "amen I say to you there are certain of <u>those who stand here</u> who shall never taste death until they see the Son of man coming in his kingdom."

Matthew 5:42: <u>Τῷ αἰτοῦντί</u> σε δίδου· καὶ <u>τὸν θέλοντα</u> ἀπὸ σοῦ δανείσασθαι μὴ ἀποστραφῇς. – "give <u>to those who ask</u> you and <u>he who desires</u> from you to borrow do not turn away."

Matthew 22:32: Ἐγώ εἰμι ὁ θεὸς Ἀβραὰμ καὶ ὁ θεὸς Ἰσαὰκ καὶ ὁ θεὸς Ἰακώβ. οὐκ ἔστιν ὁ θεὸς Θεὸς <u>νεκρῶν</u> ἀλλὰ <u>ζώντων</u> – "I am the God of Abraham and the God of Isaac and the God of Jacob. God is not God of <u>the dead</u> but of <u>the living</u>."

3. Predicatively

This is also called the periphrastic[440] use of the participle and is the use of the participle as the predicate nominative of a copulative verb. In this use, "the case will always be nominative."[441] This participle never takes an article and according to Hewett, (a) the present periphrastic tense takes the form of "the verb εἰμί and the present participle. When it occurs the author is usually emphasizing either customary or a general truth."[442] (b) the imperfect periphrastic tense takes the form "the imperfect of the verb εἰμί and the present participle"[443] (c) the future periphrastic tense which takes the form of "the future of εἰμί and the present participle."[444] (d) The perfect periphrastic taking "the present tense of εἰμί and the perfect participle are used so as to emphasize either the existing state or the continuation of the results of an action."[445] (e) the pluperfect periphrastic tense which employs the "perfect participle and the imperfect tense of εἰμί. It is like a regular pluperfect tense, simply makes past the perfect tense."[446] (f) the future perfect periphrastic tense which takes "the future tense of εἰμί and the perfect participle .... The construction declares that a completed heavenly action and its continuing results

---

[440] Wenham explains that "In Greek, tenses are sometimes formed, as in English, by using a part of the verb 'to be' together with a participle. They are called 'periphrastic tenses' because they show forth (φραζω) their meaning in a roundabout (περι) way. ... The periphrastic form of the tense (at least in the Imperfect and Future) tends to emphasise the continuity of the action." [Wenham, *Elements of New Testament Greek*, 156.]

[441] Brooks and Winbery, *Syntax of the new Testament Greek*, 145.

[442] Hewett, *New Testament Greek*, 151.

[443] Ibid.

[444] Ibid.

[445] Ibid.

[446] Ibid. 152

will come to exist on earth upon the completion of a future earthly event."[447] This may be presented as in the table below:

Tense of finite verb of εἰμί	Tense of participle	Finite Tense Equivalent
Present	Present	Present
Imperfect	Present	Imperfect
Future	Present	Future
Present	Perfect	Perfect
Imperfect	Perfect	Pluperfect

(a) Present Periphrastic (Present *of εἰμί* **+ Present Participle)**

2 Corinthians 9:12: ὅτι ἡ διακονία τῆς λειτουργίας ταύτης οὐ μόνον <u>ἐστὶν προσαναπληροῦσα</u> τὰ ὑστερήματα τῶν ἁγίων ἀλλὰ καὶ <u>περισσεύουσα</u> διὰ πολλῶν εὐχαριστιῶν τῷ θεῷ – "for the ministry of this service not only <u>is supplying</u> the things which are lacking of the saints but also <u>is abounding</u> through many thanksgivings to God."

Colossians 1:6: τοῦ παρόντος εἰς ὑμᾶς καθὼς καὶ ἐν παντὶ τῷ κόσμῳ καὶ <u>ἐστὶν καρποφορούμενον</u> καθὼς καὶ ἐν ὑμῖν ἀφ' ἧς ἡμέρας ἠκούσατε καὶ ἐπέγνωτε τὴν χάριν τοῦ θεοῦ ἐν ἀληθείᾳ· – "of which coming unto you as also in all the world and <u>is bringing forth fruit</u> as also in you from which day you heard and knew the grace of God in truth."

(b) Imperfect Periphrastic (Imperfect *of εἰμί* **+ Present Participle)**

Mark 1:22: καὶ ἐξεπλήσσοντο ἐπὶ τῇ διδαχῇ αὐτοῦ· <u>ἦν</u> γὰρ <u>διδάσκων</u> αὐτοὺς ὡς ἐξουσίαν ἔχων καὶ οὐχ ὡς οἱ γραμματεῖς – "and they were astonished by his teaching for <u>he was teaching</u> them as he who has authority and not as the scribes."

Luke 5:17: Καὶ ἐγένετο ἐν μιᾷ τῶν ἡμερῶν καὶ αὐτὸς <u>ἦν διδάσκων</u> καὶ <u>ἦσαν καθήμενοι</u> Φαρισαῖοι καὶ νομοδιδάσκαλοι οἳ <u>ἦσαν ἐληλυθότες</u> ἐκ πάσης κώμης τῆς Γαλιλαίας καὶ Ἰουδαίας καὶ Ἰερουσαλήμ· καὶ δύναμις κυρίου ἦν εἰς τὸ ἰᾶσθαι αὐτούς – "and it came to pass in one of the days also <u>he was teaching</u> and the Pharisees and the teachers of the law <u>were sitting by</u> who <u>were come out</u> of all villages of Galilee and Judea and Jerusalem: and the power of the lord was there to heal them."

Mark 10:32: <u>Ἦσαν</u> δὲ ἐν τῇ ὁδῷ <u>ἀναβαίνοντες</u> εἰς Ἱεροσόλυμα καὶ ἦν προάγων αὐτοὺς ὁ Ἰησοῦς καὶ ἐθαμβοῦντο καὶ ἀκολουθοῦντες ἐφοβοῦντο καὶ παραλαβὼν πάλιν τοὺς δώδεκα ἤρξατο αὐτοῖς λέγειν τὰ μέλλοντα αὐτῷ συμβαίνειν – "and <u>they were</u> in the way <u>going up</u> to Jerusalem and Jesus was going before them and they following were amazed and he took again the twelve he began to teach them the things about to happen to him."

---

[447] Ibid.

(c) Future Periphrastic (Future *of εἰμί* + Present Participle)

Luke 22:69: ἀπὸ τοῦ νῦν <u>ἔσται</u> ὁ υἱὸς τοῦ ἀνθρώπου <u>καθήμενος</u> ἐκ δεξιῶν τῆς δυνάμεως τοῦ θεοῦ – "from now the Son of Man <u>shall be sitting</u> at the right hand of the power of God."

Mark 13:25: καὶ οἱ ἀστέρες τοῦ οὐρανοῦ <u>ἔσονται ἐκπίπτοντες</u>, καὶ αἱ δυνάμεις αἱ ἐν τοῖς οὐρανοῖς σαλευθήσονται – "and the stars of heaven <u>shall fall out</u> and the powers which are in heaven shall be shaken."

Luke 1:20: καὶ ἰδού, <u>ἔσῃ σιωπῶν</u> καὶ μὴ δυνάμενος λαλῆσαι ἄχρι ἧς ἡμέρας γένηται ταῦτα ἀνθ ὧν οὐκ ἐπίστευσας τοῖς λόγοις μου οἵτινες πληρωθήσονται εἰς τὸν καιρὸν αὐτῶν – "and behold <u>you shall be dumb</u> and not able to speak until of which days these thing shall be because that you believed not my words which shall be fulfilled in their season."

(d) Perfect Periphrastic (Present *of εἰμί* + Perfect Participle)

John 6:31: οἱ πατέρες ἡμῶν τὸ μάννα ἔφαγον ἐν τῇ ἐρήμῳ καθώς <u>ἐστιν γεγραμμένον</u> Ἄρτον ἐκ τοῦ οὐρανοῦ ἔδωκεν αὐτοῖς φαγεῖν – "our fathers ate manna in the desert just as <u>it is written</u> he gave them bread out of heaven to eat."

John 20:30: Πολλὰ μὲν οὖν καὶ ἄλλα σημεῖα ἐποίησεν ὁ Ἰησοῦς ἐνώπιον τῶν μαθητῶν αὐτοῦ ἃ οὐκ <u>ἔστιν γεγραμμένα</u> ἐν τῷ βιβλίῳ τούτῳ· – "then many things indeed and other signs Jesus did before his disciples that <u>are not written</u> in this Bible."

John 3:28: αὐτοὶ ὑμεῖς μοι μαρτυρεῖτε ὅτι εἶπον Οὐκ εἰμὶ ἐγὼ ὁ Χριστός ἀλλ' ὅτι <u>Ἀπεσταλμένος εἰμὶ</u> ἔμπροσθεν ἐκείνου – "you yourselves testify of me that I said I am not the Christ but that <u>I am sent</u> before him."

(e) Pluperfect Periphrastic (Imperfect *of εἰμί* + Perfect participle)

John 3:24: οὔπω γὰρ <u>ἦν βεβλημένος</u> εἰς τὴν φυλακὴν ὁ Ἰωάννης – "for John <u>was</u> not yet <u>cast</u> into prison."

Matthew 26:43: καὶ ἐλθὼν εὑρίσκει αὐτοὺς πάλιν καθεύδοντας <u>ἦσαν</u> γὰρ αὐτῶν οἱ ὀφθαλμοὶ <u>βεβαρημένοι</u> – and coming he finds them again sleeping for their eyes <u>were heavy</u>."

Luke 2:26: καὶ <u>ἦν αὐτῷ κεχρηματισμένον</u> ὑπὸ τοῦ πνεύματος τοῦ ἁγίου μὴ ἰδεῖν θάνατον πρὶν ἢ ἴδῃ τὸν Χριστὸν κυρίου – "and <u>it was revealed</u> to him by the Holy Spirit not to behold death before he may behold the lord's Christ."

4. Adverbially

Participles can also be used in the same way that an adverb is, to modify a verb. There are different classifications and uses of adverbial participles (also referred to as 'Circumstantial participles'[448]). Boyer explaining writes,

> These participles never have the article; they stand in gender – number – case agreement with some noun or other substantive in the sentence, yet not as a "modifier" but as a connecting point for some element in some subordinating relation to the

---

[448] Brooks and Winbery explain that it "is often referred to as the circumstantial participle because it describes the circumstances under which the action of the main verb takes place. The adverbial or circumstantial participle always stands in the predicate position." [Brooks and Winbery, *Syntax of the new Testament Greek*, 145-46.]

verb of the sentence. Whereas the adjectval participle is the equivalent of a relative clause, the verbal participle is the equivalent of an adverbial clause or is involved as an integral part of the principal "verb phrase."[449]

From this it is seen that the adverbial participle in its use, surrounds the action of the verb or as Hewett points out "although the adverbial aspect of the participle is being highlighted, the adjectval is not lost. It is simply not being emphasized."[450] This means that though it is used as an adverb, it agrees with either the subject or object of the main verb or any other substantive in the sentence in gender, case, and number as highlighted by Boyer above, but it does not relate to the substantive it agrees with as a modifier, but rather, it relates to the main verb emphasizing either relationships of time, place, manner or degree and thus gives additional information that is grammatically connected to the main verb in such a way that it "occurs in a predicate construction and expresses a thought that is grammatically unessential to the rest of the sentence, "The circumstantial participle may be removed and the sentence will not bleed. (Robertson, p. 1124) The reader will simply not gain certain information by its omission."[451] Listed below are some of the most common uses found in the New Testament.

1. Temporal Participle

This is perhaps the most frequent use of the adverbial participle. ... It indicates the time at which the action of the main verb takes place. The participle itself, just like the subjunctive, optative, imperative, and infinitive, is timeless. its time is relative to that of the main verb.[452]

This use is normally translated with English words 'while' or 'after' and is used to show 'when' something happened. The Present participle[453] in this usage relays the action of the participle as simultaneous time to the time of action of the main verb. The Aorist participle[454] relays action that is antecedent to the time of action of the main

---

[449] James L. Boyer, *The Classification of Participles: A statistical study*, Grace Theological Journal 5.2 (1984) 163-179.

[450] Hewett, *New Testament Greek*, 156.

[451] Ibid.

[452] Brooks and Winbery, *Syntax of the new Testament Greek*, 146.

[453] Burton explains the use of the present participle thus, "The action of the verb and that of the participle may be of the same extent (Mark 16:20), but are not necessarily so. Oftener the action of the verb falls within the period covered by the participle (Acts 10:44). Even a subsequent action is occasionally expressed by a Present Participle, which in this case stands after the verb. ... The Present Participle not infrequently denotes the same action which is expressed by the verb of the clause in which it stands. ... The verb and the participle of identical action, though denoting the same action, usually describe it from a different point of view. The relation between the different points of view varies greatly. It may be the relation of fact to method, as in Acts 9:22; 15:24, 29; of outward form to inner significance or quality, as in Luke 22:65; or of act to purpose or result, as in Matt. 16:1; John 6:6. [E. Burton, *Syntax of the Moods and Tenses In New Testament Greek*, 55.]

[454] Burton states, "The assumption that the Aorist Participle properly denotes past time, from the point of view either of the speaker or of the principal verb, leads to constant misinterpretation of the form. The action denoted by the Aorist Participle may be past, present, or future with reference to the speaker, and antecedent to, coincident with, or subsequent to, the action of the principal verb. ... The distinction of the Aorist Participle is not that it expresses a different time-relation from that expressed by the Present or Perfect, but that it conceives of the action denoted by it, not as in progress (Present), nor as an existing result (Perfect), but as a simple fact. [E. Burton, *Syntax of the Moods and Tenses In New Testament Greek*, 59-60.]

verb, the future participle action that is subsequent and the perfect participle action that is perfective and has come to a state of being.[455] Vaughan and Gideon note,

Antecedent action relative to the principal verb may be expressed by the aorist or perfect participle. More often than not, the aorist participle will be used for this. *Contemporaneous action* relative to the main verb is ordinarily expressed by the present participle; but the aorist participle when used with the main verb in the aorist, often expresses contemporaneous action. *Subsequent action* relative to the main verb may be expressed by the future or present participle – more often by the future.[456]

Matthew 4:2: καὶ <u>νηστεύσας</u> ἡμέρας τεσσαράκοντα καὶ νύκτας τεσσαράκοντα, ὕστερον ἐπείνασε. – "and <u>when he had fasted</u> forty days and forty nights afterwards he hungered."

Matthew 21:23: Καὶ ἐλθόντι αὐτῷ εἰς τὸ ἱερὸν προσῆλθον αὐτῷ <u>διδάσκοντι</u> οἱ ἀρχιερεῖς καὶ οἱ πρεσβύτεροι τοῦ λαοῦ λέγοντες Ἐν ποίᾳ ἐξουσίᾳ ταῦτα ποιεῖς καὶ τίς σοι ἔδωκεν τὴν ἐξουσίαν ταύτην – "and when he came into the temple, the chief priests and the elders of the people came to him <u>while he was teaching</u> saying by what authority are you doing these things and who gave to you this authority?"

John 6:64: ἀλλ' εἰσὶν ἐξ ὑμῶν τινες οἳ οὐ πιστεύουσιν ᾔδει γὰρ ἐξ ἀρχῆς ὁ Ἰησοῦς τίνες εἰσὶν οἱ μὴ πιστεύοντες καὶ τίς ἐστιν <u>ὁ παραδώσων</u> αὐτόν – "but there were certain out of you who are not believing for Jesus knew from the beginning certain there are who are not believing and who it is <u>that will betray</u> him."

John 15:25: ἀλλ' ἵνα πληρωθῇ ὁ λόγος <u>ὁ γεγραμμένος</u> ἐν τῷ νόμῳ αὐτῶν ὅτι Ἐμίσησάν με δωρεάν – "but in order that it may be fulfilled the word <u>that has been written</u> in their law "they hated me without cause."

2. The Telic (Purpose/Final) Participle

This use of the participle indicates the purpose of the action of the finite verb answering the questions 'Why?' and is normally translated with the English 'infinitive' or 'with the purpose of' or 'in order to'. This use may employ both the present or future participle with future adverbial participles belonging here.[457]

Luke 10:25: Καὶ ἰδού, νομικός τις ἀνέστη <u>ἐκπειράζων</u> αὐτὸν Καὶ λέγων, Διδάσκαλε τί ποιήσας ζωὴν αἰώνιον κληρονομήσω – "and behold a certain lawyer stood up <u>tempting</u> him and saying, "teacher what must I do to inherit eternal life?""

Acts 24:11: δυναμένου σου γνῶναι ὅτι οὐ πλείους εἰσίν μοι ἡμέραι ἢ δεκαδύο, ἀφ' ἧς ἀνέβην <u>προσκυνήσων</u> ἐν Ἰερουσαλήμ – "you being able to know that

---

[455] Burton states, "The Perfect Participle is used of completed action. Like the Perfect Indicative it may have reference to the past action and the resulting state or only to the resulting state. The time of the resulting state is usually that of the principal verb. ... The Perfect Participle is occasionally used as a Pluperfect to denote a state existing antecedent to the time of the principal verb. The action of which it is the result is, of course, still earlier. [E. Burton, *Syntax of the Moods and Tenses In New Testament Greek*, 71-72.]

[456] Vaughan and Gideon, *A Greek grammar of the New Testament*, 157.

[457] Hewett observes that "Infrequently the participle expresses intention for which an action occurs. When this is so, the present or future participle will be encountered." [Hewett, *New Testament Greek*, 158.] Vaughan and Gideon further assert that "This is the principal use of the future participle" [Vaughan and Gideon, *A Greek grammar of the New Testament*, 157.]

there are to me not more than twelve days since I went up <u>in order to worship</u> in Jerusalem."

3. The Causal Participle

The causal participle indicates the Cause or Reason for the action of the main verb. It answers the question "Why?" but differs from the telic in that it gives reason for the occurrence of the action of the main verb and thus translated by 'because' (or 'since') while the telic gives the purpose or to what end the action of the main verb takes place.. Burton notes that,

> ὡς prefixed to a Participle of Cause implies that the action denoted by the participle is supposed; asserted, or professed by some one, usually the subject of the principal verb, to be the cause of the action of the principal verb. The speaker does not say whether the supposed or alleged cause actually exists.[458]

Mark 5:33: ἡ δὲ γυνὴ φοβηθεῖσα καὶ τρέμουσα <u>εἰδυῖα</u> ὃ γέγονεν ἐπ' αὐτῇ ἦλθεν καὶ προσέπεσεν αὐτῷ καὶ εἶπεν αὐτῷ πᾶσαν τὴν ἀλήθειαν – "and the woman feared and trembled <u>because she knew</u> that which had happened upon her she went and fell before him and said to him all the truth."

John 4:6: ἦν δὲ ἐκεῖ πηγὴ τοῦ Ἰακώβ ὁ οὖν Ἰησοῦς <u>κεκοπιακὼς</u> ἐκ τῆς ὁδοιπορίας ἐκαθέζετο οὕτως ἐπὶ τῇ πηγῇ· ὥρα ἦν ὡσεὶ ἕκτη – "and there was there a well of Jacob therefore Jesus <u>because he was wearied</u> from his journey sat thus upon the well the hour was about the sixth."

4. The Conditional Participle

The participle can be used as the protasis of a conditional sentence. In this use, the "participle implies a condition on which the fulfillment of the idea indicated by the main verb depends"[459]

Luke 15:4: Τίς ἄνθρωπος ἐξ ὑμῶν ἔχων ἑκατὸν πρόβατα καὶ <u>ἀπολέσας</u> ἓν ἐξ αὐτῶν οὐ καταλείπει τὰ ἐννενήκονταεννέα ἐν τῇ ἐρήμῳ καὶ πορεύεται ἐπὶ τὸ ἀπολωλὸς ἕως εὕρῃ αὐτό – "what man of you having a hundred sheep and <u>if</u> one out of them <u>is lost</u> will he not leave the ninety nine in the desert and go after the lost one until he may find it?"

Hebrews 2:3: πῶς ἡμεῖς ἐκφευξόμεθα τηλικαύτης <u>ἀμελήσαντες</u> σωτηρίας ἥτις ἀρχὴν λαβοῦσα λαλεῖσθαι διὰ τοῦ κυρίου ὑπὸ τῶν ἀκουσάντων εἰς ἡμᾶς ἐβεβαιώθη – "how shall we escape <u>if we neglect</u> so great a salvation which first received spoken through the Lord was confirmed to us by those who heard it."

5. Participle of Concession

This use of the participle indicates that the action of the main verb is true in spite of the state or action of the participle and is usually translated with the word 'although' in the English. This means that under normal circumstances, the action of the participle hinders or opposes or does not correspond with the action of the main verb but in this case it does not. Brooks and Winbery explain,

---

[458] E. Burton, *Syntax of the Moods and Tenses In New Testament Greek*, 170.
[459] Wallace, *Greek Grammar Beyond the Basics*, 632.

This use of the participle indicates the unfavorable circumstances despite which the action of the main verb takes place. The participle and the words connected with it constitute the protasis of a concessive sentence. Some word such as "although" will be used in the translation. The participle may be used with or without a concessive particle such as καίπερ, καί, γε, and καίτοι.[460]

Romans 1:21: διότι <u>γνόντες</u> τὸν θεὸν οὐχ ὡς θεὸν ἐδόξασαν ἢ εὐχαρίστησαν ἀλλ' ἐματαιώθησαν ἐν τοῖς διαλογισμοῖς αὐτῶν καὶ ἐσκοτίσθη ἡ ἀσύνετος αὐτῶν καρδία – "because <u>although they knew God</u>, they did not glorify Him as God nor were they thankful but they became vain in their reasoning and their foolish hearts were darkened."

1 Peter 1:8: ὃν <u>οὐκ εἰδότες</u> ἀγαπᾶτε εἰς ὃν ἄρτι <u>μὴ ὁρῶντες</u> πιστεύοντες δὲ ἀγαλλιᾶσθε χαρᾷ ἀνεκλαλήτῳ καὶ δεδοξασμένῃ – "whom <u>although you have not seen</u>, you love to whom <u>although now you do not see</u> him yet believing you are exceedingly joyful with joy unspeakable and full of glory."

1. Instrumental Participle (Participle of Means)

This use presents the participle as the instrument or means by which the action of the main verb is achieved thus it shows "How" the action of the main verb takes place and can be translated with 'by' or 'by means of'.

Matthew 27:4 – λέγων, Ἥμαρτον <u>παραδοὺς</u> αἷμα ἀθῷον οἱ δὲ εἶπον, Τί πρὸς ἡμᾶς σὺ ὄψει – "saying I have sinned <u>by betraying</u> innocent blood and they said what is it to us you see."

Luke 15:13: καὶ μετ' οὐ πολλὰς ἡμέρας συναγαγὼν ἅπαντα ὁ νεώτερος υἱὸς ἀπεδήμησεν εἰς χώραν μακράν καὶ ἐκεῖ διεσκόρπισεν τὴν οὐσίαν αὐτοῦ <u>ζῶν ἀσώτως</u> – "and after not many days the younger son gathering together everything went to a far country and there he wasted his being <u>by riotous living</u>."

2. The Modal Participle (Participle of Manner)

This use of the participle expresses the manner in which the action of the main verb takes place. It is very similar to the instrument for like the instrumental participle, it answers the question how, but "The manner of an action is frequently expressed by ὡς with the participle."[461]

Mark 5:33: ἡ δὲ γυνὴ <u>φοβηθεῖσα</u> καὶ <u>τρέμουσα</u> εἰδυῖα ὃ γέγονεν ἐπ' αὐτῇ ἦλθεν καὶ προσέπεσεν αὐτῷ καὶ εἶπεν αὐτῷ πᾶσαν τὴν ἀλήθειαν – "and the woman <u>feared</u> and <u>trembled</u> because she knew that which had happened upon her she went and fell before him and said to him all the truth."

Matthew 19:22: ἀκούσας δὲ ὁ νεανίσκος τὸν λόγον ἀπῆλθεν <u>λυπούμενος</u>· ἦν γὰρ ἔχων κτήματα πολλά – "but when the young man heard the word he went away <u>sorrowful</u> for he was having much riches."

---

[460] Brooks and Winbery, *Syntax of the new Testament Greek*, 147-48.
[461] E. Burton, *Syntax of the Moods and Tenses In New Testament Greek*, 172.

Mark 1:22: καὶ ἐξεπλήσσοντο ἐπὶ τῇ διδαχῇ αὐτοῦ· ἦν γὰρ διδάσκων αὐτοὺς <u>ὡς ἐξουσίαν ἔχων</u> καὶ οὐχ ὡς οἱ γραμματεῖς – "and they were astonished by his teaching for he was teaching them <u>as he who has authority</u> and not as the scribes."

3. The Complementary Participle

This is the use of the participle with verbs that do not express a complete thought. When the participle is used to complete the thought of the action expressed by the main verb, it is said to be a complementary participle. Vaughan and Gideon note that the participle

> forms so close a connection with the principal verb that the meaning of the verb is incomplete without the participle. It is used with verbs of cognition or perceiving (e.g., δῖδα, κατανοέω, γινώσκω, etc), emotion (χαίρω, ὀργίζομαι etc), beginning, continuing, ceasing, and other similar words. It will agree in case, gender, and number with a noun or pronoun in the clause of which it is part.[462]

Ephesians 1:16: οὐ παύομαι <u>εὐχαριστῶν</u> ὑπὲρ ὑμῶν, μνείαν ὑμῶν ποιούμενος ἐπὶ τῶν προσευχῶν μου – "I do not cease <u>giving thanks</u> for you making mention of you in my prayers."

Matthew 6:16: Ὅταν δὲ νηστεύητε, μὴ γίνεσθε ὥσπερ οἱ ὑποκριταὶ σκυθρωποί. ἀφανίζουσι γὰρ τὰ πρόσωπα αὐτῶν, ὅπως φανῶσι τοῖς ἀνθρώποις <u>νηστεύοντες</u>. ἀμὴν λέγω ὑμῖν ὅτι ἀπέχουσι τὸν μισθὸν αὐτῶν. – "but when you fast do not become as the hypocrites of a sad countenance for they disfigure their faces so as they may show to men <u>they are fasting</u> amen I say to you they are having their reward."

4. Participle of Attendant Circumstances

When the participle is used to give further information on the event or circumstance expressed by the action of the main verb, it is said to be a participle of attendant circumstances. Thus this use shows "an action which accompanies the action of the main verb."[463] Hewett describes it that

> It stands in a logical relationship to the main verb of the sentence, but does not quite express one of the adverbial notions. It may precede or follow the main verb and may be present or aorist tense. This participle is not like the genitive absolute ..., grammatically independent; it is merely adding an additional bit of information to the main construction.[464]

This use has no English parallel and is normally translated into English as a finite verb connected to the main verb using the conjunction (and), and having the same mood and tense as the main verb. brooks and Winbery explain,

> The participle indicates something else that happened, an additional fact or thought, an incidental fact. There is no certain parallel in English, and it is difficult to translate literally. The best procedure is to translate the participle as though it were a finite verb and to connect it to the main verb by supplying the word "and."[465]

---

[462] Vaughan and Gideon, *A Greek grammar of the New Testament*, 160.
[463] Brooks and Winbery, *Syntax of the new Testament Greek*, 150.
[464] Hewett, *New Testament Greek*, 158.
[465] Brooks and Winbery, *Syntax of the new Testament Greek*, 151.

Acts 13:11: καὶ νῦν ἰδού, χεὶρ τοῦ κυρίου ἐπὶ σέ καὶ ἔσῃ τυφλὸς <u>μὴ βλέπων</u> τὸν ἥλιον ἄχρι καιροῦ παραχρῆμά δὲ ἐπέπεσεν ἐπ' αὐτὸν ἀχλὺς καὶ σκότος καὶ περιάγων ἐζήτει χειραγωγούς – "and now behold the hand of the lord is upon you and you shall be blind <u>and shall not see</u> the sun until a season and immediately there fell upon him mist and darkness and going about he sought someone to lead him by the hand."

Mark 16:20: ἐκεῖνοι δὲ <u>ἐξελθόντες</u> ἐκήρυξαν πανταχοῦ τοῦ κυρίου συνεργοῦντος καὶ τὸν λόγον βεβαιοῦντος διὰ τῶν ἐπακολουθούντων σημείων Ἀμήν – "and these <u>went out</u> <u>and</u> preached everywhere the lord working together and confirming the word by signs following Amen."

Romans 12:9: Ἡ ἀγάπη ἀνυπόκριτος ἀποστυγοῦντες τὸ πονηρόν <u>κολλώμενοι</u> τῷ ἀγαθῷ – "let love be without dissimulation abhor the evil things <u>and cleave</u> to the good things."

5. Imperatival Participle

This is the use of the participle as a command, a feature which Brooks and Winbery say "is not found in classical Greek and is rare in Koine. The participle is used independently like a finite verb in the imperative mood."[466]

Romans 12:9: Ἡ ἀγάπη ἀνυπόκριτος <u>ἀποστυγοῦντες</u> τὸ πονηρόν κολλώμενοι τῷ ἀγαθῷ – "let love be without dissimulation <u>abhor</u> the evil things and cleave to the good things."

Matthew 28:19: <u>πορευθέντες</u> οὖν μαθητεύσατε πάντα τὰ ἔθνη βαπτίζοντες αὐτοὺς εἰς τὸ ὄνομα τοῦ πατρὸς καὶ τοῦ υἱοῦ καὶ τοῦ ἁγίου πνεύματος – "therefore <u>Go</u> and make disciples of all the nations baptizing them in the name of the Father and of the Son and of the Holy Spirit."

1 Peter 3:1: Ὁμοίως αἱ γυναῖκες <u>ὑποτασσόμεναι</u> τοῖς ἰδίοις ἀνδράσιν ἵνα καὶ εἴ τινες ἀπειθοῦσιν τῷ λόγῳ διὰ τῆς τῶν γυναικῶν ἀναστροφῆς ἄνευ λόγου κερδηθήσωνται – "likewise let the women <u>be under subjection</u> to their own husbands in order that even if any unbelieving by the word, they may be won by the conversation of the women without the word."

---

[466] Ibid., 152.

CHAPTER VII

CONCLUSION

The study of syntax is simply a study of the way in which words are put together to form phrases and sentences. In this study, before one can make sense of the use of the order and interrelationships that exist among words and thus drawing out the meaning and message in a sentence, there is a need to understand each part of the sentence as it relates to its context and thus the study of syntax is important. In the study of the syntax of a Biblical passage, the student engages in the study of all of the parts of speech: nouns, pronouns, adjectives, verbs, adverbs, prepositions, conjunctions, and interjections and how they relate to one another in the formation of the sentence. Thus there is necessity of examining the sentence structure, and how each individual word relates to one another syntactically. It is only after one has done this then can they proceed on to study the grammatical structure of the different phrases, clauses, and sentences, and understand their role in the communication process of the written word.

Where does one proceed from here? Greek syntax helps to shed light and to give insight into the Greek new Testament. With this material, the student has basics to set him on the way to studying his Greek New Testament and as such, with the assistance of the study helps available, the student should begin applying these lessons in reading and understand the Greek New Testament. Remember the knowledge and understanding of the Greek develops gradually as the student gives himself wholly to the studying of the Greek New Testament.

INDEX OF WORDS AND PHRASES

Ablative of Agency, 52
Ablative of Cause, 54
Ablative of Comparison, 53
Ablative of Exchange, 56
Ablative of Opposition, 55
Ablative of Purpose, 55
Ablative of Rank, 55
Ablative of Separation, 51
Ablative of Source, 52
abstract noun, 79, 89
Accusative, 26, 33, 68, 72-75, 143
Accusative Absolute, 73
Accusative of Cause, 74
Accusative of Comparison, 75
Accusative of Direct Object, 68
Accusative of Possession, 74
Accusative of Purpose, 73
Accusative of Relationship, 75
Accusative of Result, 74
Accusative with Oaths, 72
active, 28, 34, 58, 64, 93, 118, 119, 121, 122, 126, 143
Active Voice, 28, 118
Adjectival Genitive, 39
adjective, 25, 30, 39-41, 43, 54, 60, 82, 87-91, 150-152
adverb, 25, 41, 70, 90, 98, 150, 155, 156
Adverbial Accusative, 70-72
Adverbial Genitive, 41-44
Adverbially, 90, 155
Anaphoric Article, 79
Anarthrous Noun, 85
antecedent, 51, 90, 91, 108, 146, 156, 157
aorist, 28-30, 93, 95, 96, 101, 104, 105, 107-112, 114-117, 126-128, 130, 132, 133, 139, 143, 144, 151, 157, 160
Article with Abstract Nouns, 79
Article with Proper Names, 80
Articular Noun, 84
assertions, 100, 123
Attributive Adjective, 87
Attributively, 88, 151
autographs, 17, 18, 19
Bracket, 81
case, 15, 26, 27, 31, 33-41, 43, 45-53, 57, 58, 61, 64, 65, 67, 68, 76-78, 82, 84, 87, 90-92, 95, 111, 118, 123, 127, 139, 140, 143, 148, 150-153, 155, 156, 158, 160
Causative Active, 119
certainty, 112, 123, 126, 133, 138
Classification, 50, 129, 144, 156
Cognate Accusative, 69
Concession, 129, 158
Condition, 125, 129, 139, 140, 141
condition of reality, 139
Conditional Sentences, 138
Dative, 26, 33, 57-61
Dative of Advantage, 58, 59
Dative of Direct Object, 61
Dative of Indirect Object, 58
Dative of Possession, 59
Dative of Reference, 60
Dative of Respect, 60
Dative of Root Idea, 61
Declarative Indicative, 123
declensions, 26
Demonstrative pronouns, 91
deponent middle, 120
direct middle, 120
direct object, 15, 24, 25, 27, 33, 39, 45, 49, 58, 61, 68-70, 72, 92, 120, 148-150
Direct Object, 25, 49, 149
Disadvantage, 58, 59
Double Accusative, 69
emphatic pronoun, 91
exegesis, 13, 20
finite verb, 23, 24, 33, 34, 37, 47, 94, 147, 148, 154, 157, 160, 161
First Class, 139
Fourth Class, 141
future, 28-30, 93-96, 98, 100, 105-107, 111, 122-124, 126, 129, 132-134, 137, 139, 141, 143, 144, 151, 153, 156, 157
future denial, 107
Generic Class, 80
Genitive, 26, 33, 38-41, 45-50
Genitive Absolute, 47
Genitive of Advantage, 48
Genitive of Apposition, 46
Genitive of Association, 48
Genitive of Attendant Circumstances, 49
genitive of definition, 46
Genitive of Oaths, 49

Genitive of Root idea, 49
Gnomic, 99, 107, 111, 115
Grammar, 13, 14, 20, 23, 25, 27, 30, 33, 35-39, 41-48, 50-54, 57, 58, 60-73, 77-81, 88-93, 96-98, 100-112, 114, 115, 117-128, 130,-134, 136-141, 145, 147-150, 158
Granville Sharp Rule, 82
Helvetic Consensus Formula, 19
hierarchy, 35
Holy Spirit, 3, 17, 18, 21, 53, 70, 73, 106, 118, 122, 145, 149, 155, 161
Identification, 78
imperative, 28, 93, 106, 108, 126-129, 131, 132, 136, 147, 156, 161
Imperative Mood, 28, 126
imperfect, 28, 30, 93, 95, 101-105, 108, 110, 117, 139, 153
impersonal means, 53, 64
impersonal pronouns, 91
indefinite pronoun, 91
Independent Nominative, 37
indicative, 28-30, 93-96, 102, 105-109, 111, 123-126, 129, 132, 133, 137, 139-141, 143, 151
Indicative Mood, 28, 123
indirect object, 15, 25, 27, 33, 57, 58, 60, 92
infallible, 15, 17
infinitive, 20, 25, 31, 72, 95, 108, 124, 143-149, 151, 156, 157
Infinitive, 130, 143, 144, 146-149, 151
inflection, 26, 27
Inspiration, 17, 18
Instrumental of Agency, 67
Instrumental of Association, 67
Instrumental of Cause, 65
Instrumental of Manner, 65
Instrumental of Measure, 66
Interpretation, 16, 20
Interrogative Indicative, 124
Interrogative pronouns, 91
intransitive verb, 24, 33, 119, 144
kind, 27, 29, 30, 39, 41-43, 50, 80, 93-96, 112, 115, 122, 126, 129, 144
King James Version, ii, 14, 20, 136
limits, 39, 42, 43, 60, 62, 63, 68-70, 150
Linear, 29, 94, 95
linking verb, 24, 27, 34, 35, 60, 118
Locative of Place, 61
Locative of Sphere, 63
Locative of Time, 62

main verb, 15, 24, 73, 74, 105, 108, 144-146, 149, 151, 155-160
middle, 28, 67, 93, 118-121, 126, 131, 143
Middle Voice, 28, 119
Monadic Article, 78
Mood, 24, 28, 29, 93, 130
Nestle/Aland[26/27]/UBS[3/4], 13
New Testament, 3, 13-15, 17, 19, 20, 28-31, 33, 34, 36, 39-48, 50-58, 60-73, 77-83, 87-128, 130-141, 143, 144, 146-153, 156-160, 163
Nominative, 26, 33-36
nominative absolute, 37, 38
Nominative of Appellation, 36
Nominative of Apposition, 35
noun, 20, 23-27, 30, 31, 33-36, 39-49, 51, 52, 54, 60, 68, 77, 79, 81-85, 87-91, 93, 143, 144, 147-153, 155, 160
Number, 24, 27, 33, 93
Objective Genitive, 45
optative, 28, 29, 93, 108, 125, 131, 136-139, 141, 156
parenthetic nominative, 38
participle, 20, 25, 30, 38, 47, 82, 95, 105, 108, 117, 144, 150-161
Participle, 150-152, 154-161
Partitive Ablative, 56
passive, 28, 34, 52, 58, 64, 67, 71, 93, 117, 118, 121, 122, 131, 143
Passive Voice, 28, 121
perfect, 3, 14, 15, 28, 30, 75, 89, 95, 98, 101, 110, 112-117, 144, 151, 153, 157
Perfective, 29, 94, 95, 101
periphrastic tense, 153
Person, 24, 27, 93
personal interest, 27, 57-59
personal pronoun, 90, 91, 92
plenary inspiration, 17
pluperfect, 28, 30, 93, 95, 103, 116, 117, 139, 153
possessive pronouns, 91
Potential Indicative, 124, 125
predicate, 23, 24, 27, 33, 34, 36, 69, 70, 76, 78, 87-89, 148, 153, 155, 156
Predicate Accusative, 76
Predicate Nominative, 34, 35, 135
Predicative Adjective, 87
Predicatively, 88, 153
preposition, 25, 39-43, 48, 49, 55, 56, 64, 67, 74-76, 118, 143

INDEX OF WORDS AND PHRASES

present, 14, 15, 19-21, 23, 28-30, 41, 47, 52, 76, 88, 89, 93-105, 107, 108, 111-117, 122, 123, 126, 127, 130-132, 139, 141, 143, 144, 150, 151, 153, 156, 157, 160
Preservation, 14, 18
price, 44, 73, 115, 120, 145
prohibitive future, 106
pronoun, 25, 27, 30, 34, 35, 40, 47, 83, 84, 90, 91, 92, 120, 143, 151, 160
Punctiliar, 29, 94, 95
reflexive pronouns, 92
relative pronoun, 91
Scripture, ii, 13, 16, 17, 18, 20, 21, 84, 113, 152
Second Class, 140
sentence, 3, 15, 16, 23-28, 31, 33, 36-38, 46, 47, 64, 73, 78, 81, 87-89, 91-93, 130, 137, 138, 140, 141, 144, 147, 151, 152, 155, 156, 158-160, 163
Simple Active, 118
subject, 15, 17, 23-28, 33-38, 44, 45, 47, 58, 64, 72, 77, 78, 84, 90, 92, 93, 118-122, 131, 143, 144, 147, 148, 150, 156, 158
Subject Nominative, 34
subjective genitive, 44, 45, 52
subjunctive, 28, 29, 73, 93, 108, 124, 126, 128-134, 136-139, 141, 144, 156
Subjunctive Mood, 28, 93, 130
Substantival Infinitive, 147
Substantivally, 89
substantive, 23-25, 33, 35-37, 39-41, 43, 45-49, 51-54, 58, 60, 68, 73, 74, 76, 78, 79, 82, 89, 91, 93, 149-153, 155, 156
Syntax, 13, 14, 15, 33, 34, 36, 39-46, 48, 50, 52-58, 61-63, 65, 66, 68, 70-73, 77-81, 88, 90-101, 103-110, 112, 113, 115, 116, 118, 120, 121, 125, 127, 128, 132, 134, 138, 143, 147-153, 155-160
Tense, 24, 28-30, 93, 94, 96, 109, 112, 154
tenses, 15, 26, 28, 93-95, 97, 108, 115, 122, 126, 130, 139, 144, 151, 153
Textual Criticism, 13, 14
Textus Receptus, ii, 14, 20
The Aorist Tense, 107
The Future Tense, 105
The Imperfect Tense, 101
The Optative Mood, 136
The Present Tense, 93, 96
Third Class, 141
time, 14, 19, 28-30, 42, 47, 62, 63, 66, 70, 71, 78, 91, 93-105, 107-109, 111, 113-117, 122, 125-127, 131, 133, 134, 137, 139, 141, 144, 146, 147, 151, 156, 157
transitive verb, 24, 25, 33, 58, 68
transmission, 19, 20
Verb, 24, 93, 94, 96, 149, 151
verbal adjective, 30, 52, 53, 88, 150
Verbal Infinitive, 144
verbal inspiration, 17
verbal plenary inspiration, 17, 19
verbal plenary preservation, 18, 19
vocative, 27
Voice, 24, 28, 93, 118
Westminster Confession of Faith, 19

BIBLIOGRAPHY

Boyer, James L. *A Classification of Imperatives: A statistical study*. Grace Theological Journal 8.1 (1987) 35-54.

_____. *Second Class Conditions in New Testament Greek*. Grace Theological Journal 3.1 (1982) 81-88.

_____. *The Classification of Infinitives a statistical study*. Grace Theological Journal 6.1 (1985) 3-27.

_____. *The Classifications of Optatives: A Statistical Study*. Grace Theological Journal 9.1 (1988) 129-140.

_____. *The Classification of Participles: A statistical study*. Grace Theological Journal 5.2 (1984) 163-179.

_____. *Third (and Fourth) Class Conditions*. Grace Theological Journal 3.2 (1982) 163-75.

Brooks James A. and Carlton L. Winbery. *Syntax of New Testament Greek*. Lanham Madison: University Press of America, 1979.

Burton, Ernest DeWitt. *Syntax of the Moods and Tenses in New Testament Greek*. Edinburgh: T. & T. Clark, 1908.

_____. *Syntax of the Moods and Tenses in New Testament Greek*. Illinois: The University of Chicago Press, 1923.

Chamberlain, William Douglas. *An Exegetical Grammar of the Greek New Testament*. Grand Rapids: Baker Books, 1941.

Dana H. E. and Mantey. *A Manual Grammar of the Greek New Testament*. New York: Macmillan, 1950.

Duff, Jeremy. *The Elements of New Testament Greek*. Cambridge: Cambridge University Press, 2005.

Green, Samuel S. *A Brief Introduction to New Testament Greek with vocabularies and exercises*. London: The Religious Tract Society, 1911.

Goodwin, William W. *A Greek Grammar*. Boston: Ginn and Company, 1892.

Goodwin, William Watson. *Syntax of the Moods and Tenses of the Greek Verb*. New York: Ginn and Company, 1897.

Hewett, James Allen. *New Testament Greek a beginning and intermediate grammar*. Peabody Massachusetts: Hendrickson Publishers, 1986.

Lockyer, Herbert. *All the Doctrines of the Bible*. Grand Rapids: Zondervan, 1964.

Machen, J. Gresham. *New Testament Greek for Beginners*. Tennessee: The Trinity Foundation, 2000ed.

McKay, K. *A New Syntax of the Verb in New Testament Greek*. New York: Peter Lang, 1994.

Moulton J. H. and Nigel Turner. *Grammar of New Testament Greek, in four volumes*. Edinburgh: T. & T. Clark, 1908.

Nunn, H. P. V. *A Short Syntax of New Testament Greek*. London: Cambridge University Press, 1913.

Robertson, A. T. *A Grammar of the Greek New Testament in the light of Historical Research*. Nashville: Broadman press. 1923.

Rutherford, W. Gunion. *First Greek Grammar Syntax*. London: Macmillian and Company, 1912.

Sharp, Granville. *Remarks on the use of the Definite Article in the Greek Text of the New Testament containing many new proofs of the Divinity of Christ*. obtained from URL: http://www.net-magic.net/users/bmj/sharp.html.

Smyth, Herbert. *Greek Grammar for Colleges*. New York: American Book Company, 1920. digital book obtained at URL: http://www.textkit.com.

Tense, Aspect and Modality I. Obtained from http://www.hfntnu.no/englesk/staff/johannesson/111gram/lect11.htm

BIBLIOGRAPHY

Vaughan Curtis and Virtus E Gideon. *A Greek Grammar of the New Testament*. Nashville Tennessee: Broadman Press, 1979.

Wallace, Daniel B. *Greek Grammar Beyond the Basics: An Exegetical Syntax of the New Testament*. Grand Rapids Michigan: Zondervan Publishing House, 1996.

_____. *The Basics of New Testament Syntax: an Intermediate Greek Grammar*. Grand Rapids: Zondervan Publishers, 2000.

Wenham, J. W. *Elements of New Testament Greek*. Edinburgh: Cambridge University Press, 1965.

Zodhiates, Spiros. *The Complete Word Study New Testament*. Chattanooga Tennessee: AMG Publishers, 1992.

ABOUT THE AUTHOR

Rev. Nelson Noel Were is an ordained minister with the Holy Trinity Church in Africa and teaches both at the Faith College of the Bible and Bomet Bible Institute in Kenya. He earned His Bachelor of Theology, Masters of Divinity and Masters of Theology at the Far Eastern Bible College in 2003, 2005, and 2006 repsectively. He is married to Christine Kendagor with whom they are blessed with two children Charmaine and Nathan.

www.ingramcontent.com/pod-product-compliance
Lightning Source LLC
Chambersburg PA
CBHW081408160426
43193CB00013B/2131